Long overlooked in history books, Adela Sloss-Vento was a Mexican American feminist activist who fought for gender equality, civil rights, and progressive ideals. Cynthia E. Orozco presents a timely critical investigation into Sloss-Vento, a Latinx activist who shaped Texas, US, and women's history.

—Karla Strand, *Ms.* magazine

Cynthia E. Orozco has marshalled in-depth materials that convincingly spell out how Adela Sloss-Vento took on the powerful and proved herself to be a committed, smart, and tough servant of her people. Through her actions and her innumerable writings, Sloss-Vento proclaimed the urgent necessity "to build a better America." This essential and timely book reinforces her significance to that cause and to Mexican American history.

—Teresa Palomo Acosta, *Southwestern Historical Quarterly*

Writing a biography provided Orozco the opportunity to zoom in on the power of Sloss-Vento as a public and organic intellectual who shaped the Mexican American civil rights movement in the early twentieth century. Orozco's book is a forerunner to what is taking shape in Mexican American and Latina/o history, and readers should bookmark this volume.

—Tiffany Jasmin González, *Western Historical Quarterly*

Cynthia E. Orozco presents a compelling argument that Adela Sloss-Vento deserves a place of honor in American history, especially Texas history, as a passionately persistent activist and archivist of the Mexican American civil rights and Chicano movements. . . . This extensive narrative showcases a woman who fearlessly and indefatigably pursued her goal to foster awareness and effect change, even when her endeavors were either ignored or indiscernible.

—Ruthie Jones, *Lone Star Literary Life*

Agent of Change

ADELA SLOSS-VENTO, MEXICAN AMERICAN CIVIL RIGHTS ACTIVIST AND TEXAS FEMINIST

CYNTHIA E. OROZCO

University of Texas Press
AUSTIN

Printed in the United States of America
First edition, 2020
First paperback printing, 2022

Requests for permission to reproduce material from this work should be sent to:
Permissions
University of Texas Press
P.O. Box 7819
Austin, TX 78713-7819
utpress.utexas.edu/rp-form

♾ The paper used in this book meets the minimum requirements of
ANSI/NISO Z39.48-1992 (R1997) (Permanence of Paper).

Library of Congress Cataloging-in-Publication Data

Names: Orozco, Cynthia, author.
Title: Agent of change : Adela Sloss-Vento, Mexican American civil rights activist and Texas feminist / Cynthia Orozco.
Description: First edition. | Austin : University of Texas Press, 2020. | Includes bibliographical references and index.
Identifiers: LCCN 2019020691 | ISBN 978-1-4773-1987-1 (pbk.) | ISBN 978-1-4773-1988-8 (library e-book) | ISBN 978-1-4773-1989-5 (e-book)
Subjects: LCSH: Sloss-Vento, Adela. | Women political activists—Texas—Biography. | Mexican American women authors—Biography. | Mexican Americans—Civil rights—Texas—History—20th century. | Women civil rights workers—Texas—Biography.
Classification: LCC F391.4.S56 O76 2020 | DDC 323.092 [B]—dc23
LC record available at https://lccn.loc.gov/2019020691

doi:10.7560/319864

CONTENTS

ILLUSTRATIONS

ACKNOWLEDGMENTS

I thank Professor Michael A. Olivas for inviting me to prepare a chapter for his book on Alonso S. Perales, the principal founder of the League of United Latin American Citizens (LULAC), the oldest Latinx civil rights organization in the United States. While working in the Perales archive at the University of Houston, I saw several manuscripts written by Adela Sloss-Vento. Professor Mario T. García spurred my interest in Sloss-Vento as a public intellectual when he invited me to prepare a paper for an Organization of American Historians conference.

This gave me the impetus to research other archives at the University of Texas in Austin. Likewise, it gave me cause to look at my own papers, which included letters she wrote me. Arnoldo Vento, Adela's son, readily agreed to collaborate on a book. He allowed me to use his mother's archive at his home in Austin. His wife, Bea, assisted in the project and was a gracious host at their home. After several years of collaboration, we decided to produce two books. This book would not have been possible without their help.

I thank Vicki L. Ruiz, Gabriela González, and Teresa Palomo Acosta for their comments and insights. I also thank Christian Kelleher, then at the Nettie Lee Benson Latin American Collection at the University of Texas in Austin, and Lisa Cruces at the M. D. Anderson Library at the University of Houston, as well as librarians at the Jernigan Library at Texas A&M University in Kingsville, Dolph Briscoe Center for American History at the University of Texas in Austin, Bancroft Library at the University of California in Berkeley, Chicano Studies Research Center at UCLA, and Ruidoso, New Mexico, public library.

The work-study students Lorena Aguilar and Niosha Vigil at Eastern New Mexico University in Ruidoso assisted. Halen Anderson helped prepare the manuscript. Sister Irma, a professional Spanish-language translator and Spanish teacher, assisted with translations. I thank the editors at the University of Texas Press.

Special thanks go to my husband, Leo Martínez; my sister Sylvia, who shared her home in Austin; my sister Meta, who shared her home in Houston; and our dog, Lucky.

Agent of Change

INTRODUCTION

This book focuses on one of the most important Latinas in the twentieth century. It is a biography of Adela Sloss-Vento of the Lower Rio Grande Valley in South Texas near the US-Mexico border in the twentieth century. I introduce her as a major activist in the Mexican American civil rights movement and a minor activist in the Chicano movement. I also identify her as a public intellectual and a path-breaking woman activist in the male-dominated Mexican American civil rights world and white-male-dominated electoral politics in Texas.

Adela Sloss was born in 1901. Her activist career spanned from 1927 to 1990, over two major eras in Chicano history: the Mexican American civil rights movement and the Chicano movement. Only an extraordinary woman—and a feminist—could achieve so much in civil rights, public opinion, and politics through civic engagement and writing. And she did so mostly as a wife, mother, and woman employed as a jail matron. She was a movement woman even though she claimed she contributed only "a grain of sand for our cause."[1]

This project is unique since it involves my personal relationship with Adela Sloss-Vento, which began in 1978, when I was a twenty-year-old sophomore at the University of Texas in Austin. I was conducting research on the League of United Latin American Citizens (LULAC), the oldest Latino civil rights organization in the United States. It was founded in 1929. Arnoldo Carlos Vento, a professor of Spanish, directed the Mexican American Studies Center at the University of Texas in Austin, where I was a work-study student. Raised by a feminist, Vento took me seriously and connected me with his mother, who began her activism while in her mid-twenties and collaborated with LULAC's founders. In 1977 she had just published a book on the Mexican American civil rights leader Alonso S. Perales, the principal LULAC founder.

Sloss-Vento proved to be of valuable research assistance for me as a young Chicana undergraduate historian writing a senior honors thesis. When I met her I had already written a thirty-page research paper on LULAC. She gave me access to some of her papers in her home in Edinburg, Texas. Hers proved to be the most important archive about the Harlingen Convention of 1927. At that convention, Mexican American male leaders came together to form the genesis of LULAC. The convention did not permit women, so Sloss-Vento could not attend; my thesis focuses on a men-only event.[2]

Sloss-Vento and I corresponded over several years. She saw potential in me as both a young woman historian and someone who could help give Perales scholarly and public recognition. In 1978 she ended a letter to me with this invocation: "May God will that more Cynthia Orozcos and Adela Sloss de Ventos surge in the future who honor the memory of Alonso S. Perales."[3] She was not interested in public recognition for herself.

Sloss-Vento helped me with historical research, identifying contacts and thereby suggesting her support of young Chicana professionals in the late 1970s. She contacted Marta Pérez Perales, the wife of Alonso S. Perales, so that I could visit his archive housed in their San Antonio home. Using the Sloss-Vento and Perales archives, in 1980 I completed my thesis about conflict between Mexicans Americans and Mexicans at Harlingen, Texas.[4] I was the only person to access the Perales archive before it was acquired by the University of Houston.

I thought Sloss-Vento might be a key to history though she did not encourage me to see her role in Mexican American civil rights activism. On January 25, 1980, I wrote her,

> I am trying to find more autobiographical written material on Perales, Sáenz, Canales and if you have any, on yourself. I would like it to be known that a woman (and at the time, a young woman) was also involved with LULAC. Although they say women did not join LULAC or were involved in it until the Ladies Council, your participation attests to the falsity of this belief. There are many misconceptions about the League; I hope someday I will be able to clear some of them up.[5]

She ignored my request for information about herself but sent me a few newspaper clippings, some of which she wrote. At the time I did not consider Sloss-Vento worthy of more attention. There was no professional training in women's history at the University of Texas when I was an undergraduate in the late 1970s, so I did not know what questions to ask.

Sloss-Vento and I lost contact in fall 1980 when I moved to California to attend graduate school in history at the University of California at Los Angeles. At UCLA I was trained in women's history and finally asked Sloss-Vento if I might interview her, but she declined. As she was advancing in age, her social contacts were fewer. I returned to Texas in 1987 to conduct dissertation research, again on the topic of LULAC. In 1988 I was hired as a research associate for *The New Handbook of Texas*, an encyclopedia of Texas history for which I wrote eighty articles on Tejana and Tejano history, many of them related to civil rights and politics. Since Sloss-Vento was still alive, she was not eligible to appear in the handbook, so I conducted an interview about her with her son, Arnoldo.[6]

When Adela Sloss-Vento died in 1998, Arnoldo Vento invited me to speak about her at a LULAC tribute in McAllen, Texas.[7] I spoke of her as a leader, journalist, writer, historian, archivist, and activist. I said her book was the only biography of Perales and that her archive held the best collection on the Harlingen Convention.[8] The *Latina Historical Encyclopedia* published my brief biography of Sloss-Vento in 2006, and I discuss her in my 2009 book on the origins of LULAC, *No Mexicans, Women, or Dogs Allowed*.[9]

My interest in Sloss-Vento was reignited after a conference on Perales was announced. In 2011 the University of Houston and the Recovering the US Hispanic Literary Heritage Project obtained his archives, and the project and the scholar and lawyer Michael A. Olivas organized an event in 2012. Historians, attorneys, critical race theory scholars, and literary scholars were invited to prepare book chapters. Donna Kabalen de Bichara, Norma Mouton, and I took note of Adela Sloss-Vento's materials in the Perales archive. Since then Kabalen de Bichara authored an essay on Sloss-Vento based on the Perales archive.[10] In 2012 the University of Houston doctoral student Laura Patricia Garza completed her dissertation on women writers including Sloss-Vento and has since written an essay on her.[11] The historian Mario T. García, who also was a Perales conference presenter, invited me to prepare a paper on Sloss-Vento for the Organization of American Historians conference in San Francisco in 2013.[12] It was in preparation of the paper that I realized there were enough Sloss-Vento writings to assemble a small book; I approached her son, Arnoldo, and he agreed to collaborate on a modest project.

Vento told me his mother had compiled a significant archive, and he offered to share it. The totality of the Sloss-Vento archive was available to me for the first time, and it was much more substantial than I had expected. She had several hundred items including letters, opinion pieces, news clippings, and manuscripts. The project became larger than I originally conceived.

Much of this book is based on that archive. I am the only scholar who has had access to the archive and the first historian to give voice and context to Sloss-Vento's life. Painting her full portrait is only now possible.

Before looking at the archive, I was unable to see Sloss-Vento as a major civil rights figure, as she did not inform me of her numerous writings or share the bulk of her archive with me. Another reason she had not shared her papers with me I discovered while writing this book. Apparently Marta Pérez Perales was apprehensive about my visit with her in San Antonio and my use of the Perales archive. I later learned that an acquaintance had taken some papers she lent him. She relayed her discomfort to Sloss-Vento, and they agreed it was best not to allow others into their archives, as they were not sure of the researchers' sincerity or purpose.[13] My intentions were honorable, but Marta was wary—she wanted to protect her husband's legacy. She gave no one else access to the papers while she was alive.

Arnoldo Vento and I wrote our book chapters independently in our shared endeavor. He had familial ties as well as literary expertise and historical knowledge, while I was a trained historian familiar with relevant LULAC archives. For several reasons we decided to write separate books with the understanding that neither of them would have been possible without the other. We are content that his book was published in 2017, some forty years after his mother's book, and mine is also finished more than ninety years after LULAC's founding. To help promote his book I wrote an article about Sloss-Vento for the *Corpus Christi Times* in 2017 and for which Tejano Talks, a historical video project affiliated with Texas A&M University in Kingsville, prepared a short video to share on YouTube.[14]

Besides her son, I am best suited to write her biography. The only other scholar who met her was Donna Tobias of Texas A&M University in Kingsville, and no other scholar corresponded with her. As a historian of Texas, women, civil rights, and politics, I can properly situate her historical context. I also have completed a book manuscript on Alonso S. Perales.[15] The lives of Perales and Sloss-Vento, I now see, are intertwined in my own.

TERMINOLOGY

The question of identity is key to this study, and readers will benefit from understanding naming. Identities, as understood by insiders and outsiders, are important. In this study I mention how outsiders named the Mexican-origin community through racial formation and racialization, two concepts critical in understanding racial identity. Michael Omi and Howard Winant define "racial formation" as the "process by which social, economic, and political forces determine the content and importance of racial categories, and by which they are in turn shaped by racial meanings."[16]

In the 1920s, when Sloss was becoming an adult, "whites," "Mexicans," "Mexican Americans," "México Texanos," "Americans," and "La Raza" were common identities. The 1920s witnessed a new era in how Mexican-origin people were being imagined, defined, and constructed both by whites and on their own. The meaning of "Mexican" in the United States changed from the 1910s into the 1920s, with a "Mexican race" being constructed and becoming synonymous with "immigrant." After the 1920s the dominant community continued to call all of La Raza "Mexican" despite the individual's citizenship or class. During World War II the term "Latin American" began to appear to describe Mexican-descent people in the United States; by the late 1960s the term "Mexican American" appeared in US discourse to describe US citizens of Mexican descent. The term "Chicano" emerged in the late 1960s and the 1970s as youth sought to re-envision and rename the community. Sloss-Vento used all these terms with pride. When referring to Hispanic people, I typically use "Latino" to refer to men and "Latina" to refer to women. "Latinx" and the plural "Latinxs" also are used to refer to Hispanic people in the United States. "Latinx" is giving more attention to an inclusive gendered identity.

Racialization, "the extension of racial meaning to a previously racially unclassified relationship, social practice, or group," is another central concept.[17] Understanding the use of "Mexican" as a racialized imaginary in the United States is vital to this study. As "the Mexican race" and "Mexicans" were being defined in a different way, a new paradigm—"the Mexican problem"—emerged. LULAC arose in response to the supposed Mexican problem, a paradigm Euro-Americans created to racialize and subordinate La Raza. I employ the term "Mexican" in quotes to denote racialization—racist and essentialized Euro-American perceptions of La Raza. The labeling of La Raza as a homogeneous Mexican problem was synonymous with Euro-Americans' appropriation of "Americanness" for themselves. The early 1910s saw the dominant society defining "American" in a typically WASP way, that is, as white Anglo-Saxon Protestants. Mexican immigrants were also part of this racialization. In the 1920s they were referred to as "illegal aliens" and in the 1950s as "wetbacks" to mean undocumented Mexican immigrants but also pejoratively to the entire Mexican-descent community in the United States.

I give attention to how insiders in the Mexican-descent community named and defined themselves through self-identity, class formation, community formation, nationalism, and citizenship. Self-reference and identity are both historically specific, reflecting a particular time in history. Variables of citizenship, class, birthplace, residence, language use, education, and color have influenced ethnic, racial, and national identity. Social, cultural, political, and ideological differences have existed within the Mexican-origin community.[18] Gender also framed identity within the Raza community.

While acknowledging the multiplicity and impermanence of identities, I use specific terms in specific ways. I reject the labeling of an entire community as "Mexican" or "Mexican American." I use "Mexican-origin" and "Mexican-descent" to denote a "common" group distinct from Euro-Americans. "Euro-American" will also be used and is synonymous with "white" and "American." "Mexican" will designate those born in Mexico, whose life experiences were largely there, and who were citizens there. "Mexican" in quotes will designate the racialized imaginary.

"La Raza" was another popular self-referent in the 1920s. Its use here is not my attempt at pan-Latino or pan-American nationalism. Nor is it a term of biological determinism. Rather, it reflects usage by the people being studied and by Sloss-Vento, who identified a community based on race, nationality, and transnationalism across the US-Mexican border. The term "La Raza" first appeared in the United States in the 1850s but was popularized with the publication in 1925 in Mexico of José Vasconcelos's *La Raza Cósmica*, a book about that nation's racial mixture.

Frances Jerome Woods has explained the use of "La Raza" in San Antonio in the 1940s as

> a generic denomination by which he includes all Mexicans regardless of class differences or place of birth. This ethnic consciousness becomes intensified in those who live in a predominately Anglo or non-Latin society that regards Mexicans as culturally different, and for the most part, socially inferior. Sociologically, therefore, recognizable physical or cultural characteristics do not per se indicate membership in an ethnic group. It is rather the identification of self with the group or the "we-feeling" that is significant.[19]

The term fostered group solidarity. "La Raza" was a self-referent used by Mexican Americans and Mexicans. In her 1948 dissertation Woods states, "Pride in La Raza, which has persisted over generations, is at the basis of ethnic activities sponsored by Mexican leaders."[20] Common culture based on language, religion, and customs, real or imagined, unified La Raza and was reinforced by immigration from Mexico.[21] Woods also notes that La Raza was typically idealized.[22] The historian Elliot Young argues that there was an "artificial unity" around the term that was used to constitute a community and nation, whether imagined or real.[23] "La Raza" was commonly used from the 1920s onward, although a person's citizenship could be distinguished simultaneously. Sloss-Vento referred to "La Raza" but also made distinctions between Mexicans and Mexican Americans.

The term "Mexican American" was barely emerging in the 1920s and would not become common until the 1960s. Still, its emergence represented a shift from a Spanish to an English cultural milieu and by Mexican Americans in Texas from a regional to a national identity.[24] Activists like Sloss-Vento used it to signify US citizenship. "Latin American" is another important term in this study. Due to the US Good Neighbor policy of the 1930s, the group reference "Latin American" became popular in the 1940s and remained so through the 1950s. It meant the same as "Hispanic" or "Latino" today, specific to the United States. It was used to refer to US citizens or all of La Raza, usually to mean persons of Mexican descent. By the late 1960s "Chicana" and "Chicano" came to refer to Mexican American people in the United States as reflective of the Chicano movement. "Chicano" was a folk term that was popularized and radicalized by youth in the 1960s. "Latina" and "Latino" arose in the 1980s and have been used to encompass all Hispanic peoples in the United States. "Latinx," a new term, is also used here to refer to the same populace and emphasizes gender neutrality. "Tejano" refers to men of Mexican American descent in Texas while "Tejana" is specific to women.

One last term related to identity requires clarification. On occasion I refer to "borderlanders," people living in or near the US-Mexico borderlands; in Spanish they are known as *fronterizos* and *fronterizas*. Sloss-Vento lived most of her life in those borderlands in South Texas, mostly in Hidalgo County, one of the poorest counties in the nation and latter-day home to Gloria E. Anzaldúa, a scholar, poet, and lesbian feminist. Sloss-Vento called herself "a native of the border" and considered herself an expert on border life.[25] The region was colonized by Euro-American agribusiness interests and often controlled by their political puppets. Living there, Sloss-Vento was an early critic of the "isms" such as racism and classism, of which Anzaldúa would later write, that marginalized Mexican Americans and Mexicans alike.[26] Woven throughout Sloss-Vento's writings is a critique of class inequality. Born working-class and committed to working-class interests like Anzaldúa, many of Sloss-Vento's critiques focused on the 1942–1964 Bracero Program, low wages, the Rio Grande Valley's exploitative agribusiness, and poverty.

As a fronteriza Sloss-Vento was influenced by developments in Mexico. During the 1910–1929 Mexican Revolution, women participated as soldiers, nurses, and intellectuals. Women were becoming more important to the nation even if they could not vote in Mexico until 1958. Reading Mexican newspapers, living next door to Mexico, and traveling into Mexico,

Sloss-Vento was aware of emerging opportunities for women. She believed in Mexico's modern gendered nationalism. Still, Sloss-Vento was formed in the United States and by modern gender notions emanating from the Progressive Era and women's suffrage.

Other terms requiring definition are "gender," "feminist," and "homosociality." Karen Offen defines "gender" as "the differential social construction of the behavior of the sexes [genders] based on their physiological differences." Offen defines "feminist" as an "ideology and a movement for sociopolitical change based on a critical analysis of male privilege and women's subordination within any given society."[27] The feminist scholar Jean Lipman-Bluman defines "homosociality" as "relating to social interactions between members of the same gender"; she introduced the term in 1976, when it was common to recognize only two genders.[28] More recent gender studies have distinguished between "hierarchical homosociality" and "horizontal homosociality," suggesting both positive and negative aspects of homosociality.

Two other concepts are central to this study: "modern gendered selfhood" and "third-space feminism." Sloss-Vento was a movement woman characteristically thinking about the community while typically acting as an individual. Only as an individual in an era that permitted some degree of modern gendered selfhood could she be active.[29] In her book *Out on Assignment*, the historian Alice Fahs uses the concept to discuss the emergence and acceptance of women journalists in the 1920s. The idea of women as free agents became particularly possible after women's suffrage in 1920, and a new cultural ideal for US women emerged in the post–World War I era. Women were seen as individuals distinct and separate from their families, and Sloss-Vento used this perception of women to insert herself into the male domains of civil rights, public opinion, and politics during the Mexican American civil rights movement and the Chicano movement. She graduated from high school in 1926 in her mid-twenties ready to act as an individual rather than primarily as a family member. Most of her selfhood she enacted through writing opinion pieces and letters that were published in newspapers, which was available to her as a woman writing from home. Fahs notes that newspapers were "a richly articulated public world at the turn of the twentieth century."[30] Thus Sloss-Vento performed modern gendered selfhood as a public intellectual to enter the public arena, a space reserved for men, especially in the Mexican-descent community.

Modern gendered selfhood as well as Sloss-Vento's creative use of "third spaces" allowed for her self-insertion into civil rights, civic engagement, and politics. The historian Emma Pérez has described ways that Mexican-descent women have invented spaces and praxis to subvert patriarchy and colonialism.[31] She notes, "Women's politics may have been subordinated under a nationalist paradigm, but women as agents have always constructed their own spaces interstitially, within nationalism, that often miss women's subtle interventions." Pérez argues this "intervention as third space feminism—in nationalism."[32] Before the modern US feminist movement of the late 1960s and the Chicana feminist movement of the 1970s, Sloss-Vento found creative ways to participate in the male-defined Mexican American civil rights movement and the white-male-controlled Democratic politics in Texas.

ORGANIZATION OF THIS BOOK

This introduction to Adela Sloss-Vento as a civil rights leader, public intellectual, and feminist is followed by part I (Across Time) and then part II (Personas). Part I extends the discussion of Sloss-Vento within the eras in which she lived. Chapter 1 sets the historical context during an era of Jim Crow and Juan Crow, patriarchy, and homosocial civil rights organizing especially prominent among Tejanos. I focus on the status of Mexican-descent people in Texas from 1920 to 1970, the era in which she was most active. I examine public recognition of Sloss-Vento during her lifetime and begin to explain why she is unknown as a public intellectual.

Part I also focuses on Sloss-Vento in two major social movements. Two chapters address the Mexican American civil rights movement in Texas from 1920 to 1963 and one chapter on the Chicano movement from 1963 to 1978. These three chapters are organized chronologically and touch on her principal political and civic issues in each decade.

Chapter 2 focuses on Sloss-Vento's civil rights activism and public intellectual work during the Mexican American civil rights movement from 1927 to 1950. The Mexican American civil rights movement in Texas, a decades-long liberal effort to improve the political, economic, and social status of the Mexican-origin community, arose in the 1920s. In the chapter I focus on her work in South Texas and in international issues such as Russian communism, European fascism, and pan-Americanism in the 1930s and 1940s. I examine her relation to Alonso S. Perales, the activist and principal founder of LULAC. She had a lifelong comradeship with Perales, but more importantly she began to honor Perales in her writings in the 1930s. I address her relation to male-only LULAC chapters from 1929 to 1970 and women-only Ladies LULAC chapters that existed from the early 1930s to 1970. Why she failed to join a homosocial (gender-segregated) chapter is a central question of this book.

In chapter 3 I spotlight Sloss-Vento's role in the Mexican American civil rights movement from 1950 to 1963 in Texas. She critiqued the Bracero Program of 1942–1964, an international labor arrangement between the United States and Mexico; wrote protest letters to US and Mexican presidents; condemned an academic study published by the University of Texas; and criticized the Texas Good Neighbor Commission. Mexican immigration was one of her major topics. I show her brazen attitude as she willingly protested to US presidents, Texas governors, University of Texas academics, male civil rights leaders, and local rural racists.

In chapter 4 I discuss Sloss-Vento in the Chicano movement. In Texas that movement lasted from 1963 to 1978 and was a continuation of the longer social movement that began in 1920. The Chicano movement was a new endeavor to improve the political, economic, and social status of Mexican-origin people that was spurred by youth, ethnic nationalism, and radicalism. While it was a civil rights movement, it was also a movement for political self-determination and cultural revival. Since Sloss-Vento was an elder in this era, she did not participate in much activism in person but continued her activism until her last letter in 1990. She supported and advocated for multiple tenets of the Chicano movement, its new leaders and members, and its tactics and ideology. She upheld Chicano cultural nationalism and welcomed Chicana feminism.

In part II I take a thematic approach to the various personas that Sloss-Vento enacted. I address Sloss-Vento as a feminist in the gendered Mexican American civil rights movement, as a public intellectual, and as a Democrat in the United States as well as a democrat toward Mexico.

In chapter 5 I treat Sloss-Vento as a gendered activist among men in the Mexican American civil rights movement. I examine gender in LULAC within its homosocial chapters. I again posit why Sloss-Vento did not join Ladies LULAC. I discuss the homosocial nature of other major Mexican American civil rights organizations in Texas and the United States as a dominant exclusionary tactic to the detriment of women. I explain the critical role attorneys played in the leadership of these associations and in maintaining male privilege.

I identify how Sloss-Vento negotiated and transcended Mexican American gender rules and gender borders. She established unique relations with three Mexican American male civil rights leaders—the activists Perales, J. Luz Sáenz, and J. T. Canales, all LULAC founders—despite predominant homosociality in Texas before 1970. I analyze the unique epistolary relations she maintained with these men over decades; I ask whether the men subordinated, mentored, or influenced her as a fellow activist. I base this discussion on letters between Sloss-Vento and male activists I found in four archives. The correspondence suggests that Sloss-Vento was a civil rights movement insider but also a gendered outsider. Finally, I ask why Sloss-Vento did not challenge these men on the issue of gendered segregation of LULAC and why the men did not do more to promote her.

In chapter 6 I investigate Sloss-Vento as a public intellectual. I first interrogate various definitions of "public," "intellectual," and "public intellectual" and consider the concept of an "organic public intellectual." I then introduce structural and ideological constraints on public intellectuals and examine constraints on Sloss-Vento, considering race, class, and gender. I show how gendered ambivalence by Sloss-Vento led her to constrain herself as a public intellectual so she did not promote herself. Finally, I explain why she has eluded notice as an intellectual. In this chapter I contribute to the topic of our Latina intellectual heritage.

Chapter 7 focuses on Sloss-Vento as a Democrat. She was an exceptional Democrat in an era that discouraged Mexican American women from participating in electoral politics in Texas as political thinkers, party activists, and candidates. She acted as a leader rather than an ordinary volunteer and party worker. I show her accessing government officials at local, county, regional, state, national, and international levels. Especially notable are her letters to US presidents to whom she typically offered unsolicited advice.

Sloss-Vento is shown to be a party loyalist but also an independent Democrat committed to Mexican American political empowerment, first during the Mexican American civil rights movement and then the Chicano movement. Thus, as a questioning Democrat she used third-space practices to advance her political cause. The chapter highlights her as a woman seeking to democratize the white male political establishment in Texas with her own inclusion before the ideology of feminism permitted women to do so after 1970. Sloss-Vento was a transnational political actor in the borderlands in attempting to influence politics in Mexico. She wrote several Mexican presidents and other governmental and labor officials. As a fronteriza she made it clear that she was a Mexican American and a democrat toward Mexico, acknowledging Mexico's sovereignty.

Sloss-Vento was a formidable agent of change. Ironically, she subverted US women's domesticity to perform her politics. Until now she has mostly been undercover.

PART I

ACROSS TIME

CHAPTER 1

CIVIL RIGHTS LEADER, PUBLIC INTELLECTUAL, AND FEMINIST

In 1977 Adela Sloss-Vento of the Lower Rio Grande Valley in South Texas inserted herself into history when she wrote *Alonso S. Perales: His Struggle for the Rights of Mexican Americans*.[1] Perales was the principal founder of the League of United Latin American Citizens (LULAC), founded in 1929, the oldest and most significant Latinx civil rights organization.[2] He was the author of *En defensa de mi raza* (1937) and *Are We Good Neighbors?* (1948), two important civil right books documenting racial wrongs against people of Mexican descent.[3] Perales and Sloss-Vento were friends and activists who corresponded between 1927 and 1960.[4] In her writing about Perales she recognized his significance long before Chicano historians did. Her book introduced him to historians including this author as a young, undergraduate historian in the making in the late 1970s. Part of Sloss-Vento's life project was to promote recognition of him through "monuments, museums and libraries," places where history is preserved and heroes honored.[5] Sloss-Vento's larger life project was to fight what she called "the persecutions and stupidities of ignorant Anglos of Texas, who have had greed and hatred towards the people of Mexican descent."[6]

Sloss-Vento wrote her book when she was seventy-five years old and determined as ever to promote Perales's legacy. She penned numerous opinion pieces and letters published in newspapers from the 1930s into the 1970s, making her the most prolific Mexican American civil rights woman writer and public intellectual in the United States. She was among the first Mexican American activist women in the area of civil rights, but there were earlier activists, even in the 1910s, like Jovita Idar of Laredo. Idar belonged to an activist family that organized the first Mexican American civil rights congress in Texas, in 1911, to fight lynching and racial segregation.[7] And even before Idar in Texas, Sara Estela Ramírez and other women wrote for *La mujer moderna* and the anarchist and syndicalist press in the early 1900s and 1910s connected with the transnational Partido Liberal Mexicano.

Career-wise Sloss-Vento was not a journalist, teacher, professor, historian, archivist, or lawyer. She worked as a secretary and a county jail matron, which were lower-middle-class jobs for women in the colonized Mexican American community in the mid-twentieth century. She wrote throughout her life as both a single woman and a married woman with two children. She first wrote while in her twenties. Her published works took diverse forms—a book, pamphlets, a chapbook of poetry, opinion pieces, and letters to the editor. She also wrote manuscripts that went unpublished or whose whereabouts are unknown. She did so in a rural setting and without a college education.

Sloss-Vento was exceptional across the United States in leaving more published civil rights writings before 1970 than any other Mexican American woman. The LULAC member and feminist Alice Dickerson Montemayor of Laredo, Texas, wrote a few essays in the monthly magazine *LULAC News* in the 1930s. The activist María L. Hernández of San Antonio published *México y los poderes que dirigen la gente* (Mexico and the powers that direct the people) and testified at a US Commission on Civil Rights hearing in San Antonio in 1968. The labor activist, communist, and intellectual Emma Tenayuca, also of San Antonio, co-wrote the 1940 pamphlet *The Mexican Question*, an insightful analysis of Mexican Americans' colonization. Tenayuca obtained a college degree in the 1940s in California and became a teacher. Around 1930 Jovita González of Rio Grande City completed a master's thesis in history at the University of Texas. González, a scholar, lived in San Antonio, Del Rio, and Corpus Christi and wrote several books, articles, and academic essays. She sought to reach the public by co-writing children's textbooks in the 1940s with her husband, Edmundo Mireles, but she did not have many writings published in newspapers.[8]

Other Mexican or Latina civil rights advocates were active in the Southwest. The Californians Josefina Fierro de Bright and Luisa Moreno were associated with the Congreso de Habla Española (Spanish-Speaking Congress), a pan-Latinx civil rights and pro-labor association especially strong in California in the late 1930s and 1940s.[9] Isabel González, the executive secretary of the Committee to Organize the Mexican People in Colorado, wrote *Step-Children of a Nation: The Status of Mexican-Americans*, which was published in 1947, but no other published work.[10] In New Mexico civil rights activism was taken up in the northern part of the state, where there was less racism against Hispanos; however, there were no Hispanas writing civil rights essays before World War II.

Until recently most scholars have not known of Sloss-Vento despite her self-published 1977 book. However, in 1979 Martha Cotera, a Chicana librarian and historian who began writing in the 1970s, contacted Sloss-Vento about her papers.[11] She responded but remained mute about her archive and discussed only Perales with Cotera. The Rio Writers' book *One Hundred Women of the Rio Grande Valley*, published in 1983, should have included Sloss-Vento but missed her.[12] José Ángel Gutiérrez, Michelle Meléndez, and Sonia Noyola's book *Chicanas in Charge* on trail-blazing political Tejanas also missed her.[13] Sloss-Vento had even mailed a copy of her book to Gutiérrez, a leader of the Texas Chicano movement, but he ignored her.[14] Likewise, Francisco Arturo Rosales did not include her in his works on the Mexican American civil rights movement, nor did Matt Meier and Margo Gutiérrez in their encyclopedia of the movement.[15] Why is she unknown, forgotten, and ignored even after writing a book? Or has she been silenced, as suggested by the literary scholar Laura Garza?[16]

Who was Adela Sloss-Vento? Why did she write a book about Perales? Who was she to write a book about him when there was no book about Perales to consult, when there was no Perales archive in any library, and when she was not a trained historian? What was her political and intellectual life project? What were her political agenda and ideology, and how did they change over time? Her life spanned two major social movements, the Mexican American civil rights movement beginning in the 1920s and the Chicano movement that arose in the 1960s. How did her politics manifest themselves in these two social movements? To answer these questions, one must assess her activism and writings. I begin with the status of Mexican Americans and Mexicans in Texas from 1920 to 1980, when Sloss-Vento was most active.

TEXAS MEXICANS AND MEXICAN AMERICANS

Texas has historically been at the crossroads of Native American homelands, Spanish borderlands, Mexican borderlands, and the American South. Its "ownership" has been contested. In the area now called South Texas, tribes like the Coahuiltecan and Apache claimed expanses of the lands as their own. After 1536 the Spanish claimed Texas as part of New Spain. In the 1770s José Escandón settled what is now South Texas, particularly around Laredo and the Lower Rio Grande Valley. After 1821 the area became part of Mexico and after the 1846–1848 US-Mexican War, it again remained a contested space. From 1848 to 1920 Mexican Americans experienced land dispossession, racial violence, and political and economic marginalization. And in the 1910s

South Texas experienced the rise of lynching and a new era of racial violence not seen before.

Economic and political developments in the 1920s brought changes especially to San Antonio, Corpus Christi, Laredo, and the Rio Grande Valley. The Valley's ranching economy declined in the post–World War I era, and new patterns of landownership and agribusiness transformed the regional economy before World War II. After 1945 the Valley continued to urbanize, with new jobs in fruit and vegetable produce, government, the service sector, and education. Valley agribusiness was particularly thriving from the 1920s to the 1970s based on exploited Mexican American and Mexican labor. In the 1970s the economy and education expanded significantly, creating more opportunities.

The Valley consists of four counties—Hidalgo, Cameron, Starr, and Willacy. In 1930 the Valley had 176,000 residents; 320,484 in 1950; 537,811 in 1980; and 700,000 by 1990.[17] In 1940 only the towns of McAllen and Harlingen had more than 10,000 persons; Harlingen had 13,000; McAllen, 11,000; and Brownsville, 2,200 residents.[18] Smaller communities include San Juan, Pharr, Alamo, Mercedes, La Feria, and Edcouch-Elsa. San Juan had fewer than 2,000 residents around 1930.[19]

By the 1960s the Valley was urbanizing, with Brownsville, Harlingen, McAllen, and Edinburg its centers. Sloss-Vento's hometown of San Juan had fewer than 10,000 residents by 1970. In the 1940s she moved to Edinburg, where she and her husband worked at the jail. The Valley had an ethnic mixture in which people of Mexican descent were predominant. Euro-Texans established dominance there in the 1910s through racial violence including lynching.[20] Estimates of those lynched and murdered range widely, from three hundred to five thousand Mexican-descent people. Although the numbers vary, many of the victims are known to have been killed by Texas Rangers in state-condoned violence.[21] Lynchings also occurred in 1923 and 1926.[22] People of Mexican descent believed that the KKK was responsible for a murder of a Mexican in Harlingen in the 1920s.[23]

Everett Ross Clinchy Jr. notes, "By the 1920s the Latin group was clearly relegated to a position comparable almost to that of the Negro population of the state," referring to Euro-Texan dominance and Mexican-descent subordination.[24] Although racial violence declined in the 1920s, new patterns of race segregation emerged in public schools, public facilities, churches, and privately owned businesses. Racial discrimination against people of Mexican descent was common until the 1970s. "No Mexicans Allowed," "No Dogs, Negroes, and Mexicans Allowed," and "Whites Only" became typical signs at restaurants, hotels, motels, theaters, and even cemeteries.

FIGURE 1.1. "No Dogs, Negroes, Mexicans" sign, Lonestar Restaurants Association, Dallas, Texas, 1942. Adela Sloss-Vento was refused service in a Harlingen, Texas, restaurant, and her husband and son were denied service in George West in South Texas. Courtesy of Dr. Gilberto Hinojosa.

The racial segregation that was common through the 1950s had largely disappeared by 1970. My mother, Aurora E. Orozco, perhaps best describes the situation in the 1930s in her hometown of Mercedes in Hidalgo County, a few miles from Sloss-Vento's hometown of San Juan:

> The Anglo community didn't have anything to do with Mexicans except in things related to business, at drugstores, in doctor's offices, in lawyers' offices. The other contact with Mexicans was hiring them to work as maids, cooks, drivers, and other kinds of jobs. Their barrios were nice. Some of their houses were made of brick and wood, and their lawns were kept clean. They had paved streets, electric lights, and running water. Some had cars. The town was divided by the railroad tracks. Most of the Mexicans lived on the north side; the Anglos lived on the south side, away from the warehouses of fruits and vegetables.[25]

Such was still the case in 1951, when a Texas legislator reported,

> Spanish-speaking people live in their own part of town and have their own businesses. . . . They are excluded from swimming pools and barber shops. The exclusion from pools is because it is not possible to tell the clean ones from the dirty, so we just [keep] them all out. We just can't have all those dirty, possibly diseased people swimming with our wives and children. . . . Mexicans are excluded from barber shops because of the fact that 80 percent of them have lice in their hair or scalp diseases.[26]

This racialized discourse was common.

The Valley population was composed of both US citizens and Mexican immigrants. Mexican immigration surged there in the 1920s and again in the 1970s. The US Border Patrol was established in 1924 to further separate citizens of Mexico and the United States. A tightening of the US-Mexico border fostered an awareness of US citizenship and gave impetus to a Mexican American identity that LULAC, Perales, and Sloss-Vento adopted. Also, after the late 1920s, Mexicans were not allowed to vote in Texas. Still, it was common for Mexican Americans to include Mexican immigrants in their communities and refer to "La Raza" as a cultural and political family not divided by citizenship. The term "La Raza" was especially popular in the 1920s and 1930s, but its use seems to have declined by the 1940s and 1950s. The term was resurrected in the 1970s. In that decade La Raza Unida Party was founded; although its members were Mexican Americans and could only register US citizens to vote, they still concerned themselves with Mexicans in Texas.

The new economy of the 1920s privileged agribusiness controlled by a planter elite of Euro-American men. In 1930 half of Mexican-descent adults in Texas worked in agriculture, mostly as farm laborers. As for women in 1930, about 17,000 Mexican-descent women were domestic workers, and 5,415 were farm laborers.[27] Mexican-descent women worked in laundries, garment and cigar industries, and pecan shelling and packing sheds. There were few factories in the Valley, and in the 1940s and 1950s agribusiness expanded with the US-Mexico labor agreement called the Bracero Program, which from 1942 to 1964 permitted Mexican manual laborers to work in the United States. By 1950 Mexican Americans made up only 49 percent of the farm labor force in the Valley.[28] McAllen gained some manufacturing jobs in the 1950s and 1960s.[29] By the 1960s it was common to see Mexican American men working as salespersons and proprietors and Mexican American women as clerks. Still, most of La Raza, including women, belonged to the working class. Farmworker, packing-shed employee, and domestic worker were common jobs for Mexican-descent women.

Severe freezes in 1949, 1951, 1961, 1983, and 1989 caused agribusiness to decline in the Valley, but farm labor remained an important occupation in the Valley through the 1970s.[30] The new planter elite exploited labor to make the Valley one of the most productive farming regions in the United States. Race relations were somewhat similar to those in the US South after 1865, at least in terms of exploitative wages and substandard housing that made the Valley more a colony than a US region. The federal minimum wage law passed in the 1930s exempted farm labor. Indeed, the President's Commission on Migratory Labor in Texas in 1950 found that Valley growers paid half the wages of other parts of Texas.[31] Rebecca Flores, a Texas Farm Workers Union activist in the 1970s, reports that as late as 1973 workers had short-handle hoes and no portable toilets, unemployment benefits, or minimum wage but plenty of pesticides.[32] Sloss-Vento refers to farmworker labor as "slave labor."[33]

Valley labor exploitation, intertwined with racism and sexism, led to poverty among Mexican Americans as well as braceros. The labor exploitation was intimately connected to the availability of Mexican immigrant workers. Many immigrants arrived in the 1920s and 1970s; among them, braceros and braceras arrived in large numbers in the 1940s and 1950s. Mexican American workers from the Valley were unable to compete for jobs when agribusinesses paid braceros and undocumented workers less than legal minimum wages in the 1940s and 1950s. Consequently, poverty, high dropout rates in the schools, and migration out of Texas resulted in a Tejano—Texas Mexican American—diaspora in the US Midwest and Northwest.[34]

Unionization was underdeveloped in Texas and the Valley. Mexican Americans did not begin to significantly enter skilled labor until World War II. Most unionization among Mexican American women occurred in the laundry, garment, cigar, and pecan industries, but unions were not prominent in the Valley. More than three hundred fruit and vegetable packing plants existed in the Valley around 1950. By 1950 the American Federation of Labor had formed the Citrus Cannery Workers and Food Processing Union,[35] but unions were mostly absent from the Rio Grande Valley, and serious efforts to unionize farmworkers did not occur there until the 1960s and 1970s.

Valley agribusiness, especially citrus and cotton in the 1940s through the mid-1960s, exploited Mexican braceros and braceras. A typical workday for most was ten to twelve hours long, and the prevailing wage was twenty-five cents an hour, versus forty cents for US citizens. Workers' water came from ditches and canals, and communicable diseases were common. Social scientists in 1951 saw "poor housing, a lack of sanitary facilities, improper and inadequate food, and few or no medical services."[36] Valley agribusiness used immigrants to create its "colonial empire."[37]

Economically, few Mexican Americans in the Valley belonged to the upper class. Exceptions were the family of J. T. Canales of Brownsville and prominent families including the Longorias, Guerras, De la Vinas, Velas, Cavazoses, Cárdenases, Hinojosas, Ballis, and Yturrias.[38] A small middle class existed in the nineteenth century and expanded after World War I when Mexican immigrants sought out businesses where Spanish was spoken or required services that some white-owned business owners refused them. World War II gave another boost to the middle class when veterans were able to attend college and access growing employment opportunities. Postsecondary education in the 1970s also helped expand the middle class.

Before 1970 there were few independent Mexican American middle-class women. Most teachers came from Mexico in the early twentieth century, and some taught in private Mexican schools in Texas. Mexican American teachers were few. Ester González Salinas of Matamoros taught students in San Diego and Kingsville.[39] Brownsville hired its first Mexican American woman public schoolteacher in 1925 and the second in 1940.[40] Adela's son, Arnoldo, recalled having only two Mexican American teachers in his public schooling in the Valley in the 1940s and 1950s.[41] The town of La Feria in Hidalgo County had Mexican American teachers' aides only in the 1970s.[42] Some women worked as clerks and secretaries. As a secretary in San Juan in the 1930s and a jail matron in Edinburg, Sloss-Vento belonged to the lower middle class. In 1950 women accounted for about 26 percent of the workforce in Texas and 30 percent of the US workforce,[43] so Sloss-Vento was part of the minority of employed women.

There were few Tejana journalists between 1920 and 1970. Partido Liberal Mexicano women were active writers in the early 1900s. Jovita Idar wrote for the family-owned *La Crónica* in the 1910s and for *La Evolución* in Laredo in 1916 that continued for a few years. Other writers included Beatriz Blanco of San Antonio's *La Prensa* and Consuelo Aldape de Vega Hidalgo of Brownsville's *El Puerto de Brownsville*. Most women writers appeared on the society pages, conforming to prescribed gender rules.[44] Few Tejanas owned, ran, or edited newspapers. María Luisa Garza of *La Época* of San Antonio was an exception in the 1920s.[45] Dora Mirabal owned *El Progreso* of Corpus Christi in the 1930s, and Margarita Muñoz Simón owned *El Demócrata* of Austin in the 1940s.

Mexican Americans were affected by political subordination. The poll tax took root in Texas in 1902 and lasted until 1965, when it was terminated by the federal voting rights law. Before 1930 Mexican Americans were emerging from decades of "boss rule" in which Euro-Texan Democrats controlled the Mexican American vote especially by buying their poll taxes and offering petty favors in exchange for their vote. In some counties Mexicans could vote until the late 1920s because it helped bosses win. Even Cameron County, with Brownsville as its seat, ended boss rule in 1920; the John Closner–A. Yancey Baker machine of Hidalgo County, with McAllen as its seat, ended in 1930 when Republican Euro-American newcomers challenged it and Baker died.[46] Mexican American voters in Valley counties were few in the 1920s but slowly became the majority by the late 1940s. The number of

Mexican Americans who were paying their poll taxes independent of any boss was increasing. Mexican American women joined voters after the 19th Amendment to the US Constitution was adopted in 1920, but their numbers grew slowly. The poll tax, poverty, lack of education, and machismo disenfranchised many. Independent paying of the poll tax by Mexican Americans became a primary tool of political empowerment.

In some parts of Texas, Mexican American and even Mexican voters were needed, so color and citizenship were ignored. After 1905 the state legislature let county Democratic committees determine primaries' racial inclusion.[47] The white primary was instituted across the state in 1923. Perhaps sensing Republican ascendance and feeling the pressure of the National Association for the Advancement of Colored People (NAACP), the Texas Democratic Party began to slowly end white primaries in the 1930s. *Smith v. Allwright*, a lawsuit filed by African Americans in El Paso in 1944, challenged Texas's white primary as a violation of the 15th Amendment.[48] Mexican Americans benefited from the *Smith* decision in favor of the plaintiffs. Still, in the late 1940s four Texas counties outside of the Valley prevented African Americans or Mexican Americans from entering polling places.[49]

Mexican American men who were active in civic and political life had more privileges than Mexican American women. Men were expected to join civic and voluntary associations, and many in the middle class were encouraged to join political clubs, express political opinions, and run and hold office. Civic leaders like Alonso S. Perales accessed and lobbied the predominantly male state legislature. Many traveled nationally and even internationally without fear of sexual assault, though not of racial assault. Married men often had little worry over responsibilities to their wives, elders, or children.[50] Some middle-class men were leaders, thinkers, and office holders and as such were invited to speak at civic events.

Even so, Texas has had few Mexican American elected officials, male or female. Texans have not elected a Mexican American governor. Before 1950 there were only three Tejanos in the state legislature: J. T. Canales (1910s), Augustine F. Celaya (1933–1949), and John Charles Hoyo (1941–1946).[51] Henry B. González of San Antonio became a state legislator in 1956. In 1969 there were eleven Mexican American men in the Texas House and one in the Texas Senate.[52] Even in the Valley most political officeholders were Euro-Texan men until the 1970s. The first Tejano in Congress was González, in 1961; two Tejanas were elected to Congress in 2018.

From 1920 to 1970 heterosexuality, homosociality, and domesticity were prescribed norms for Mexican-descent women. Women were expected to socialize with women and men with men. In the Mexican-descent community, that became the hegemonic pattern in civic and political participation. Mexican-descent women were expected to organize with women from 1920 to 1970. Domesticity was another prescribed norm. Ozzie Simmons has observed of Mexican American women in the 1950s, "The primary emphasis in the feminine role is on domesticity, with all the restrictions this implies." He adds, "The male expectation that the female will focus her attention on the household, the children, and the church, is still the rule, although there are exceptions."[53]

Women earned the vote in the 1920s but were still expected to take a back seat to male voters and male politicians. The historian Angela Boswell notes, "When entering the political arena, Texas women had to face possible stereotypes that women did not belong in this public male domain. Social mores held that women were weaker, intellectually inferior, and more morally pure."[54] Texas has Southern mores. Euro-Texan women organized in electoral politics in the 1920s and began to win public offices. They were elected to the Texas legislature after 1920, and Miriam "Ma" Ferguson became governor in the 1920s. But Euro-Texan women were admitted slowly to the state legislature. There were few white women in the legislature between 1930 and 1960, and in some years such as 1924 and 1938 there were none. Texas women won the right to serve on juries only in the 1950s. The Texas Women's Political Caucus was founded in 1972 when two women joined the Texas legislature. In 1990 Ann Richards became the second woman to win a Texas gubernatorial race, after Ferguson. No woman has served as Texas governor since Richards.[55]

There were no women of color in the Texas state legislature before the 1960s.[56] Euro-Texan women state legislators were elected fifty-seven times before the African American Barbara Jordan of Houston was elected to the 60th legislature in 1966. She followed the last African American man to be elected at the state level, in 1883.[57] While Euro-American women saw greater electoral participation after the 1920s, participation was more limited in the Mexican-descent community until the 1970s.

Mexican American women were slow to enter politics. Jovita Idar participated in the Democratic Party in the 1920s.[58] Adela Jaime was active in San Antonio in the 1930s. Mexican American Democratic women organized in the Valley through the Latin American Democratic Women, a group connected to the 1930s campaign to elect Manuel Bravo as Zapata County judge.[59]

Ladies LULAC and the American G.I. Forum women's auxiliaries played important roles in promoting Mexican American male electoral candidates. Ladies LULAC was organized in 1933.[60] LULAC offered these separate councils for women, institutionalizing the homosocial political tradition until the early 1970s. Women supported voter registration, individuals' payment of their own poll taxes, and nonpartisan campaigns to get out the vote. Women's auxiliaries in the American G.I. Forum, a Mexican American veterans and civil rights organization founded in 1948, helped male candidates get elected. In the 1950s Ladies LULAC and the forum women's auxiliaries in San Antonio helped elect Henry B. González to the Texas legislature.[61] Olga Peña Ramos played a key role in helping get her husband, Albert Peña, elected to office in San Antonio in the 1950s; Mamie López worked as a Southside community activist at that time.[62] In the early 1960s women of LULAC and the forum in El Paso helped get Raymond Telles elected as mayor.

On the state level there was no major Mexican American women's civic or political organization. Before World War I there were more than fifty chapters of the Partido Liberal Mexicano across Texas; the radical organizations were organized by women or included them.[63] The Cruz Azul, a mutual aid society and social service organization that included immigrants, fit this category in the 1920s but died by 1940.[64] LULAC was the most important statewide Mexican American organization after 1929. In the late 1940s the American G.I. Forum gave men a dominant voice as women formed separate clubs in the forum, once again allowing for a separate political voice.[65] So, from the early 1930s to the 1970s, homosocial political organization was the norm in Texas in the Mexican-descent community; homosociality may have had a different meaning or response in the gay, lesbian, questioning world at that time.

Tejanas gained elected offices mostly after 1970. The first Tejana to win a public office was Norma Zúñiga Benavides, who joined the Laredo school board in 1959. In 1969 Anita Martínez was elected to the Dallas City Council; the first Tejana city council member in San Antonio was elected in 1981.[66] Because of racism, sexism, and classism, Tejanas did not run for state office until 1964, when Virginia Múzquiz of Crystal City in South Texas ran for the legislature. Alma Canales of La Raza Unida Party, an alternative to the Democrats and Republicans, ran for state office in 1972. Sloss-Vento could visit with no Mexican American woman legislator before Irma Rangel of Kingsville was elected in 1976, followed by Lena Guerrero of Austin in 1984.[67] Two Tejanas were elected to national office in 2018. The native Tejana Susana Martínez became governor of New Mexico in the mid-2010s. Moreover, Valley women of any race have been slower to become electoral candidates.[68] At the congressional level to date, South Texas has not elected a woman to any of its three seats.[69]

Euro-Texan women's clubs excluded Tejanas. Texas had an active General Federation of Women's Clubs.[70] As early as 1892 there were 495 women's clubs, with more than 100,000 members, but they would not mix with "dirty Mexicans."[71] Even the Pan American Round Table, an organization established to promote better US–Latin American relations, hardly included Tejanas. The McAllen chapter in the early 1940s had thirty-six active and auxiliary members but no Tejanas; only four Tejanas were honorary members. The chapter in San Antonio in 1943 had forty-five Euro-Texan members and only four Mexican-descent women, one of them Marta Pérez Perales, Alonso's wife.[72] Marta was college-educated, but even her education did not allow for much inclusion.

Education was yet another tool to segregate and exclude. Segregated schools also impeded Mexican-descent communities' progress, as did the lack of enforcement of compulsory school attendance. Segregated, inferior Mexican schools existed from the 1890s through the 1950s. A 1948 Texas Good Neighbor Commission report noted that of 799 school districts in Texas, 139 had "some degree of segregation."[73] Although Mexican-descent people paid taxes, they were in fact funding white schools. Segregated schools continued after the 1954 US Supreme Court *Brown* decision, which officially mandated desegregation of schools. By 1956 cities around the state—San Antonio, Corpus Christi, Austin, San Marcos, El Paso, and Amarillo—had desegregated the schools largely as the result of efforts by LULAC and the NAACP.[74] With exceptions like Adela Sloss-Vento, most Mexican-descent women did not graduate from Texas high schools until the 1950s.

In 1930 there were about 250 Mexican-descent college students at the University of Texas in Austin and fewer than 30 Raza college students in all of San Antonio. In 1946 only 1.6 percent of all Texas college students, 114, were of Mexican descent.[75] Their numbers increased in the 1950s and 1960s. Protests and financial aid opened the opportunity wider in the late 1960s and the 1970s. Women of Mexican descent began attending college in significant numbers only in the 1970s. Until then, college graduates like Ester Pérez Carbajal and Rachel Garza were rare.[76] Pérez Carbajal of San Antonio earned a master's degree from the University of Chicago in the 1910s; Rachel Garza obtained a bachelor's degree from the University of Texas in 1923 and became its first Mexican American woman graduate. At the graduate level, Jovita González earned her master's degree from the University of Texas in 1929, and Elena Farías of the Valley graduated with a master's degree in sociology from the University of Texas in 1932.[77] Tenayuca obtained a master's degree in California after she left San Antonio in the early 1940s.

Tejanas were expected to attend college near their hometowns if at all. Traveling away from *la familia* (the family) was discouraged. Heterosexuality, marriage, children, and domesticity were expected of Mexican American women; these were gendered expectations that Sloss-Vento experienced before 1970. Because European Americans in the Texas legislature controlled decisions about higher education, Valley colleges were few and underdeveloped. There was a Valley Business School in the 1920s. Pan American University, now the University of Texas at Edinburg, was founded in 1927.[78] Texas Southmost College was established in Brownsville in 1926 but expanded in 1948. A community college was founded in McAllen decades later.

PUBLIC RECOGNITION OF ADELA SLOSS-VENTO

While the name Adela Sloss-Vento is new to most, she received some recognition during her life. Prominent male leaders acknowledged and praised her. Eduardo Idar, Jovita Idar's brother and a LULAC founder, was among those who praised her activism. Perhaps because they were Methodists, the Idars tended to include women in the civic realm.[79] In a 1928 letter to Perales he writes, "We are inviting a lady from the Valley of name, Miss Sloss which is doing very wonderful work defending our people."[80] A 1929 newspaper headline describes Sloss as "A Young Woman Who Defends the Community."[81] The article states that Sloss condemned sheriff's deputies for entering a Mexican immigrant family's home in San Juan in the Valley, and the Mexican consul then protested the sheriff's acts. The article also mentions that three months earlier she worked on a political campaign. By 1931 the major Spanish daily newspaper of Texas, *La Prensa* in San Antonio, calls Sloss "a well-known resident of the Rio Grande Valley in Texas."[82]

Besides these early endorsements, Sloss-Vento was recognized a few other times. She was honored in the 1950s but did not attend the public event. In typical Sloss-Vento style, she did not seek praise. In the 1960s, after Perales died, Luis Alvarado organized the first statewide LULAC Founders and Pioneers Awards Banquet in San Antonio, where she was honored. Alvarado was married to the daughter of J. Luz Sáenz, yet another LULAC founder and close friend of Sloss-Vento.[83]

In 1968 one hundred LULAC founders and pioneers of the league's formative years were honored. "Mrs. Adela Vento" of the Valley was awarded one of three pioneer awards along with Fortino Treviño of Alice, Texas, and Candelario Barrientos, city unspecified. Sloss was the only woman nominated and honored, but again she did not attend.[84] While she was not a LULAC founder or member, she was a "LULACer" in spirit. Perhaps she did not attend because she was too humble, or perhaps her duties as wife, mother, or jail matron did not permit her to attend.

Sloss-Vento was also recognized in the 1970s. In 1977 Marta Perales acknowledged her in "Carta para el libro de Mrs. Adela Sloss Vento," published in Sloss-Vento's book, *Alonso S. Perales*. In it Marta Perales offers this tribute: "Mrs. Vento has been a collaborator since she was young. She's a brave woman and decided very early on to get to work. She too recognized that our community pleaded to bring forth justice. She did not hesitate to join the leaders so as to contribute to the monumental tasks at hand."[85] She calls Sloss-Vento a "collaborator" who joined the (male) leaders, but Sloss-Vento was also a leader.

Arnoldo Vento is likely responsible for the appearance of his mother's inclusion in a mural in the Midwest in the 1980s. The artists and educators Martha Ramírez-Oropeza and Patricia Quijano Ferrer included her image in the mural *Latina/Mestiza Woman via Tlazolteotl*.[86] Sloss-Vento received no other recognition before she died. In 1999 LULAC Council 4591 of McAllen, a women's council, organized a scholarship fund-raiser tribute initiated by Arnoldo Vento.[87] I was proud to attend and speak of her legacy.

BRIEF BIOGRAPHY OF SLOSS-VENTO

Who was Adela Sloss-Vento? Her only son, Arnoldo Vento, has described her as having an "impeccable character and willingness to help others."[88] She was born to Ancelma Garza Zamora and David Sloss on September 27, 1901.[89] Her father was of German and Mexican descent and served as a city commissioner in Brownsville, the county seat of Cameron County.[90] His father was David H. Sloss, a Confederate colonel who settled in Minatitlán in the state of Veracruz, Mexico, after the US Civil War.[91] As fronterizos, the Sloss family spoke Spanish and identified with Mexican culture. Adela Sloss did not identify as a German American. She called herself a Mexican American and a member of La Raza. She considered Texas German Americans to be prejudiced. Her son said the name Sloss made some people ask, "Why is this German lady fighting for Mexicans?"[92] Her parents divorced, and her mother was left with four children and struggled financially. When her mother married Marcos González, two more children, Aurora and María, were added to the family.[93]

Arnoldo Vento credits the women of the Sloss family as his mother's role models. Her mother was a midwife and *curandera* (folk healer) with a reputation as a "self-made woman who openly confronted men and difficult or dangerous situations."[94] Adela's father also married again, and he and his second wife had a son they named Jesse. Jesse became a stenographer, secretary, bookkeeper, interpreter, Brownsville city secretary, city manager, and city commissioner. He attended Valley Business College in the 1920s, then Brownsville Junior College, and served in the US Navy during World

War II. Jesse was the Brownsville city secretary from 1946 to 1975.[95] He was a member of LULAC in 1940.[96] While Adela was capable of all these positions as well, her generation and gender barred her from these higher-level jobs.

Adela Sloss was raised in the Rio Grande Valley along the Texas-Mexico border, where Spanish was the common language.[97] By the late 1940s Hidalgo County, where she lived, and Bexar County, with San Antonio as its center, together comprised 25 percent of the entire Mexican-descent population in Texas.[98] She walked from San Juan to Pharr to attend school.[99] When the Valley experienced a boom in the 1920s, her stepfather worked on a farm in 1920, and Adela worked as a dry goods store clerk.[100] At some point she built and ran a small restaurant.[101] Because she had to work, she was twenty-six years old when she graduated from the Pharr–San Juan Independent School District in 1927.[102] Among the twenty-one graduates were two Mexican American women in this small, racially integrated class. Sloss could not attend college in the 1920s because of its costs. Even so, she declared her passion to be a writer.[103]

After graduation Sloss contacted civil rights leaders. Sloss was old enough to understand the significance of the emerging Mexican American civil rights movement in South Texas. The attorney Alonso S. Perales and the teacher J. Luz Sáenz were activists who held rallies advocating for the racial and political empowerment of La Raza. In July 1927 Perales posted a notice in *El Fronterizo* newspaper of Rio Grande City that he was beginning his work as a lawyer in the Valley.[104] In August 1927 the two men helped organize the Harlingen Convention, a South Texas conference at which Mexican American male activists decided to establish a civil rights organization composed only of US citizens as a group similar to the NAACP.[105] Women were not invited, and reports did not mention any women there. However, Adela Sloss read about the event and saved newspaper clippings about it. Her archive documents the event better than any other, even those of Perales and Sáenz. So, as early as 1927 she took an interest in civil rights, history, and archives. She began her lifelong work documenting events. She kept newspaper clippings, biographies, and pamphlets written by Mexican American leaders; records of events she attended; copies of letters she sent and received; copies of her published writings, which include opinion pieces and letters to newspaper editors; and her own manuscripts.

Sloss maintained active correspondence with several Mexican American civil rights activists, in particular Perales, Sáenz, and the attorney J. T. Canales, three of the major LULAC founders. In 1927 Sloss began to correspond with Perales after she read one of his articles in *El Fronterizo*. She met him, his wife, Marta, and Sáenz. Her book on Perales includes brief autobiographical notes about their initial meeting such as this one: "It was in 1927 when I became an enthusiastic collaborator on behalf of the cause of the Mexican American."[106] So began a long, active relationship with Perales and his family and lifelong civil rights activism by Sloss, even though she called herself a "collaborator" and not a "leader."

Across the decades from 1927 to 1990, Sloss-Vento worked on numerous issues: red light districts, municipal corruption, racial segregation, racially segregated schools, women's roles in the home, equality for Latino soldiers, inferior wages for agricultural workers, forced migration of Tejano farmworkers, exploitation of undocumented workers, treatment of incarcerated Mexican immigrant women, and the Bracero Program. She worked with an active and engaged citizenry. She promoted electoral participation and women's participation in politics. She supported major ideological developments like Good Neighbor policies and pan-Americanism during World War II; both were attempts to improve US relations with Mexico and Latin America. She condemned fascism and communism, which she saw as threats to democracy especially during World War II. Democracy and Christian values were her moral foundations.

Besides addressing these issues, Sloss-Vento was active in partisan politics. She was a Democrat who supported the Democratic platform and Mexican American and Euro-American candidates at the local, county, state, and national levels. She openly supported Presidents Franklin Delano Roosevelt, John F. Kennedy, Lyndon B. Johnson, and Jimmy Carter. She wrote to President Harry S. Truman, a Democrat, and President Dwight D. Eisenhower, a Republican. And she supported women politicians including Governor Ann Richards of Texas. As a fronteriza her politics transcended the US-Mexico border, and she sought to have an impact on Mexico's policies.

Sloss-Vento's activism paralleled two social movements in the United States—the Mexican American civil rights movement and the Chicano movement. The Mexican American civil rights movement began around 1920 in San Antonio and spread to South Texas in the late 1920s. Much of its activism was propelled by LULAC and after World War II by the American G.I. Forum as well. The Mexican American civil rights movement varied across the Southwest, Midwest, and Northwest but was especially strong in Texas. Sloss-Vento was part of the movement as neither a LULAC member nor a Ladies LULAC member.

As the Mexican American civil rights movement waned by the early 1960s, it was replaced by the Chicano movement. The Chicano movement was inspired by the African American civil rights movement, anti–Vietnam War efforts, and youth rebellion. In Texas it started with the rise of an electoral rebellion in Crystal City in South Texas in 1963 when Mexican American men were voted into the city council previously controlled by whites. Sloss-Vento supported the Chicano movement by advancing its ideology and tactics. She advocated for La Raza Unida Party, which was tied to Crystal City politics. She rallied behind youth and student movements and the teaching of Chicano history and Spanish in high schools.[107] She praised Chicano movement leaders like the United Farm Workers leader César Chávez and the Texas Farm Workers Union leader Antonio Orendain in the Valley. She condoned strikes and walkouts, too.

Beyond her civil rights activism, civic engagement, and partisan political participation, Sloss-Vento focused much of her activism on writing as a public intellectual. Her activism and political ideology are revealed in opinion pieces and letters to the editors in newspapers like *La Prensa* of San Antonio, the only Texas statewide Spanish-language newspaper from 1912 to the early 1960s, with wide distribution in Mexico and elsewhere in Latin America as well. *La Prensa* covered international as well as state news from a more Mexicanist than Mexican American stance, as it was owned and run by the Mexican-immigrant Lozano family. Conchita Hassell Winner has called *La Prensa* the "voice of the elite exiled conservative intellectuals."[108] Sloss-Vento considered *La Prensa* "our right arm in forming and in organizing the Mexican-Americans toward solutions of our many problems."[109] *La Prensa* referred to Sloss-Vento as a "norteamericana."[110]

Sloss-Vento was not a paid journalist or columnist. In contrast, Perales had a weekly or biweekly column in *La Prensa* called "Architects of Our Own Destiny" for two decades.[111] Perales was also a columnist for a Catholic newspaper in the 1950s. Sloss-Vento was not asked to write a column, nor did she seek this more ongoing fame. She is the only known Tejana who wrote civil rights essays, opinions in newspapers, and letters to politicians across seven decades—the 1930s through the 1990s. A perusal of *LULAC News*, the official LULAC monthly publication, from 1931 to 1965 reveals that no other Mexican American woman did so.[112]

Sloss-Vento's family background helps explain patterns in her writing. In the early 1930s she worked in the mayor's office in San Juan and then for the Edinburg tax collector. She was thirty-four years old in 1935 when she married Pedro C. Vento of Relampago and Mercedes, near San Juan. They had two children; Irma Dora was born in 1938, and Arnoldo was born in 1939. Pedro had graduated from Mercedes High in 1928 and attended Texas A&M College from 1928 to 1931. He worked at a Mercedes grocery store from 1931 to 1936. He then became a guard at the Edinburg sheriff's department, where he worked until 1939. After farming for a few years in Mercedes, he returned briefly to his job at the sheriff's department in Edinburg, from June 1942 to January 1943. The family moved to Corpus Christi, where he worked in 1943–1944 as a guard at the naval air station.[113] From 1944 until his retirement in the 1980s Pedro worked in law enforcement, much of the time as the chief jailer and warden at the Hidalgo County jail.[114] He commuted from San Juan to Edinburg until 1952, when the family moved to Edinburg. He completed his career in law enforcement as a US marshal and traveled to Mexico to work with Mexican officials.

In 1949 Sloss-Vento began her employment as a matron at the jail where her husband worked in Edinburg, where they had moved. If she was not already busy, she certainly was when she worked at the jail. The Bracero Program brought many Mexicans into the Valley, including women. She was hired as the warden of women, a position created because many immigrant women were being detained. The Hidalgo County jail had about seven hundred inmates during the so-called Wetback Lift, an operation in the early 1950s to return unauthorized immigrants to Mexico.[115]

Sloss-Vento took the job to pay for her children's college education, not to make ends meet or for self-fulfillment. In several letters she wrote that she was not happy with her job but sacrificed for her children. Years later she wrote to her brother describing her employment as "sixteen years at a job that was not of my choosing. The hours were so long I thought I was buried alive and that injured my health."[116] In 1953 she was certified as a deputy sheriff in Hidalgo County, and she became a notary public, a service that allowed her to help less educated and non-English-speaking people.[117] By 1956 their daughter, Irma Dora, entered college, and Arnoldo Carlos followed.[118] Sloss-Vento took advantage of living in Edinburg, where Pan American University was established in the 1950s; she took a few English classes at night to improve her writing.[119] She retired in 1965. But her work paid off. By 1966 Irma was studying English literature and working on her doctorate at the University of Missouri and as an assistant editor at a Catholic press in New York.[120] Arnoldo became a professor of Spanish and Chicano studies at the University of Texas in Austin.

Sloss-Vento was churchgoing, but most of her activism was secular. While gender norms encouraged church work for women, that is not where she placed most of her time and energy. Her archive includes only a few references to church activities. She attended church in San Juan, Alamo, and later in Edinburg when the family moved there. She drove the children to a Catholic school in Alamo, a nearby town.[121] As a good Christian mother she later sent them to Sacred Heart School in Edinburg.[122] In the late 1940s she became active in her Catholic church. Her church work was apparently the only organizational activity she undertook with women. She volunteered at St. Joseph's Church Council in Alamo.[123] In May 1948 she was elected to the diocesan board of the National Council of Catholic Women at a meeting in Corpus Christi. In 1953 she wrote a letter to the Bishops Committee for the Spanish-Speaking about the need to solve problems created by braceros.[124] Her archives include little about her church activism or her work with women in any organization. Sloss-Vento's concern for the church and its parishioners is expressed, however, in a letter written about the San Juan church honoring the Virgin. In 1972 she wrote to Archbishop Francis J. Furey about impending renovation of the church after a plane crashed into it.[125]

The moral base of Sloss-Vento's activism was Christianity, and her political foundation was democracy. Often when pointing to racism and labor exploitation she referred to Christianity. She writes, "It is not enough to say I am a Christian or to go to Church, if we don't practice the principles of Christianity."[126] In 1943, after denouncing racial segregation in Texas towns, she argues in an opinion piece, "If we boast of practicing Christianity, we must practice one of God's principle [*sic*] Commandments, 'Love thy Neighbor as Thyself.'"[127] Responding to racist letters published in the *Valley Morning Star* of Harlingen in 1947, Sloss-Vento writes, "The letter of Mrs. L. J. Ring of San Juan . . . reveals a lack of Christianity and the lack of democratic principles."[128] In the same opinion piece she reacts to Mrs. Grace Ann Miller's letter by writing that the worst disease was "discrimination and lack of Christianity."[129]

Likewise, her anticommunist stance was related to religion, as she explains in another opinion piece: "Communism is a theory aimed against capitalism, as well as a theory opposed to religion."[130] She further asserts that democracy involves civic engagement: "For a workable democracy, it is not enough, that the government of a nation, practice democracy, it is the duty of every community, of every citizens [*sic*], of every neighbor, to see that injustice, selfishness and race discrimination is not being practiced among our fellow-men."[131]

Sloss-Vento's typewriter was her weapon. Her archive contains manuscripts ranging from three to seven pages. Using the technology of her day, she typed some one hundred characters a minute. Most of her work was created before mimeograph and copy machines existed, and she never owned these machines. She rarely used carbon copies, though at times she kept multiple copies or typed out copies for herself. In advancing her causes she did not access the radio, which became available in the 1930s, or television, which was in use by the 1950s.

Sloss-Vento was a grassroots archivist without training in library science or professional archival practices. Some of her writings have been lost because she mailed them to others. In 1947 she wrote to George Esqueda of Harlingen, "I am enclosing some of my latest letters in reference to our problem. I had to make copies of some as I left only one clipping for my scrap book."[132] Perhaps when she was older and less active she paid more attention to her archive. This typed note was clipped to twelve envelopes: "Letters that were lost over the years that I keep the envelopes [for] as a memento of that grand fight of our great defender Lic. [attorney] Alonso S. Perales. Empty envelopes—Letters that are lost but [envelopes] that are proof of the extensive correspondence of Sra. Adela Sloss de Vento with our defenders Lic. Perales and Lic. Jose T. Canales, though more with Lic. Alonso S. Perales."[133] Sometimes she mailed off copies and did not keep any for herself. In 1947 she wrote to Perales, "I did not send you a copy of the newspaper because I had to send it to Mr. Héctor Pérez Martínez, Secretary of State of Mexico."[134]

Sloss-Vento's roles as archivist and activist were often at odds because she sometimes sent her only copy. As an activist she wanted to share, inform, and enlighten. She wanted to document Texas racism and struggles against it; she understood the significance of evidence through written documentation. In 1945 she told a Texas senator, "I have a scrap book with many clippings of incidents of said discrimination."[135] And in 1969 she told the president of a school board, "My scrap books are full of proof of the noble and hard struggle of the great and immortal Alonso S. Perales."[136] Thinking like an archivist and historian she kept proof.

Typescripts for Sloss-Vento's book on Perales reveal her awareness of her role as archivist: "I kept in my Album of correspondence and records of Atty. J. T. Canales his books. . . . I also keep clippings of newspapers. . . . I also keep his book."[137] When Perales died in 1960 she wrote to his wife, Marta, and asked her to tell Luis Alvarado, Sáenz's son-in-law, to return her scrapbooks. She explains, "I am going to buy a chest to lock everything with a key."[138]

In January 1961 Alvarado sent Sloss-Vento a letter with this postscript: "I plan to reproduce some of the material in the Scrap Books sometime this week—then I will send them to you immediately."[139] She kept papers and scrapbooks in the chest, away from light and heat. Fortunately, she did not permanently paste or glue her materials to scrapbooks. In some cases, she would use blank envelopes and type out descriptions of documents or newspaper articles. Today her papers are not in scrapbooks, but they were never put in file folders or in acid-free materials, either, practices used by professional archivists.

Sloss-Vento was a documentarian. Her son has described her early work in recording events: "I recall she would make recordings very early with a 'wire' recorder before celluloid tape was introduced as its replacement."[140]

She owned a microphone and recorded a few speeches, but no tapes survived; perhaps she threw them out when they deteriorated. Only one of the recordings has survived—from the 1952 Latin American Convention in Mission, Texas, in response to the "wetback pamphlet."[141] She also gave Perales a tape recorder for his personal use.

From the 1920s to her death in 1998, Sloss-Vento did not seek assistance from any libraries, archives, or repositories; perhaps she was unaware of their roles or thought they were controlled by Euro-Texans. Distinctive Chicano archive repositories did not exist before World War II. The University of Texas established its Chicano archive program only in the 1970s, and no LULAC archive existed until 1980. So even when Sloss-Vento was writing a book on Perales in the 1970s, she could visit no Perales, Sáenz, Canales, or LULAC archive in any library.

Before 1970 Sloss-Vento was the most important Mexican American woman civil rights activist and public intellectual in Texas. Recognized a few times during her lifetime, she is relatively unknown. A Mexican American woman born to working-class parents, she was well educated by 1927, when she began her journey as a civil rights leader, public intellectual, Democrat, feminist, and fronteriza.

CHAPTER 2

THE MEXICAN AMERICAN CIVIL RIGHTS MOVEMENT, 1920–1950

The Mexican American civil rights movement in Texas emerged after World War I and waned by 1963. This movement's objectives were to uplift the Mexican American and Mexican community in the United States and to combat the racism and poverty that resulted from their colonization after the US-Mexican War. The movement had decades of antecedents in resistance through violent banditry, mutual aid societies, and labor unions. The Mexican American civil rights movement was led by Mexican Americans and a few Mexicans, by the middle class, and by men. Most of the men were influenced by ideological currents of the 1910s and World War I; many were veterans.

The historian Mario T. García has conceptualized the years 1930–1965 as the "Mexican American generation" and "Mexican American era." In my book *No Mexicans, Women, or Dogs Allowed* I emphasize the Mexican American civil rights movement associated with the era and shift the beginning of the era to 1920. Still, García explains the goals of the Mexican American movement's leaders.

> [The leadership was] uncompromising in its demands for first-class citizenship and pursued these goals through a variety of tactics, including direct action. Furthermore, World War II rather than dividing links the struggles of the 1930s with those of the 1940s. Both the Great Depression and World War II can be seen together as forming the twin central historical experiences for a political generation committed to actively struggling for civil rights and first-class citizenship for Mexican Americans. World War II, with its stress on the preservation of democracy, intensifies this movement but does not give birth to it. The Mexican-American campaign for civil rights and a new identity envelops the entire period from the 1930s into the 1950s.[1]

I chronicle Sloss-Vento's activism in the Mexican American civil rights movement here by highlighting her political and intellectual agenda across the first decades of this movement, the 1920s through the 1940s. She was in her twenties when Mexican American men started to form civil rights organizations in the Valley in the 1920s. Women were not invited or encouraged to do so. Yet, over the course of several decades Sloss-Vento inserted herself into the movement as a writer and activist. As the literary scholar Donna Kabalen de Bichara has noted, "Sloss-Vento's act of writing can be seen as an attempt to contest the limits imposed on the speech act of women at the beginning of the twentieth century."[2] She was involved in a broad spectrum of issues and problems that both persisted and changed. Nonetheless, she had a fundamental concern for Mexican American civil rights, immigrant rights, and labor rights, and she believed that women had the right to advocate for these.

ARCHIVING THE CAUSE IN THE 1920S

When Sloss graduated from high school in 1927 she began to familiarize herself with Mexican American civil rights activism and archive items related to the cause. Right out of school and proficient in typing and shorthand, she started writing.[3] Her former teacher published her poem "The Butterfly" in the local newspaper; it was her first published work.[4] In March 1927 she received a note from a fellow high school senior who called her "brilliant" and a "foreigner"; the student said she deserved "much credit for finishing high school in a country not your own."[5] Another student also wondered how she could finish a "foreign school."[6] Euro-Texans saw her as Mexican and not Mexican American or American, so she experienced prejudice firsthand. While not able to pursue college in the 1920s, Sloss acknowledged her own intellectual curiosity. Years later, she sometimes wrote of herself in the third person: "She read every book she could get hold of, and *La Prensa*, the great daily of San Antonio, was her favorite newspaper, both to read and to write for."[7]

Within a year of graduating, Sloss was reading about Alonso S. Perales's and J. Luz Sáenz's efforts in Spanish-language newspapers as they informed Mexican-descent people of their civil rights. She read about the upcoming Harlingen Convention.[8] The conference was a meeting of Mexican-descent male activists from mutual aid societies and civil rights organizations; the Order Sons of America (OSA) of San Antonio, a civil rights group, was the largest association represented there. Though not stated publicly, women were not invited; this homosocial principle was the norm. The meeting attendees would determine which organization would take the lead in the

FIGURE 2.1. Adela Sloss's graduating class, Pharr–San Juan High School, Texas, 1927; Sloss, second row, far right. Courtesy of Dr. Arnoldo Carlos Vento.

collective effort and decide a more important question—whether Mexican immigrant men would be allowed to join the civil rights association being formed there.

After the Harlingen Convention Sloss read about the new organization founded there—the League of American Citizens of Latin Descent (LAC), also called the Mexican American Citizens League. The new association excluded Mexican immigrants. It spread throughout the Valley and Laredo. In 1929 this group would join forces with the OSA, which had chapters in San Antonio, Corpus Christi, Somerset, and Pearsall, as well as with the Order Knights of America (OKA) of San Antonio to form the League of United Latin American Citizens (LULAC). Sloss would thereafter cite the origins of LULAC as August 14, 1927, and not February 17, 1929; the 1927 date was stamped and imprinted in her mind as the beginning of both the Mexican American civil rights movement and LULAC. Though the civil rights movement's and LULAC's true origins date back to the OSA in 1921, she was unfamiliar with those earlier efforts since she was younger and the founding of the OSA was in San Antonio, not the Valley.

Perhaps one of Sloss's first political and intellectual acts was to serve as an unauthorized archivist for the emerging LULAC organization by collecting newspaper clippings and pamphlets. The earliest document in her collection is "Border Aliens to Be Taught U.S. Ways" from the *San Antonio Light* in 1924 about Perales and Saenz's tour across South Texas to educate and organize fellow Mexican Americans. A 1927 article in *El Fronterizo* of Rio Grande City reports on the two men's efforts to organize a civil rights meeting. Other articles came from *La Prensa* of San Antonio, *La Avispa* of Del Rio, and the *Brownsville Herald*.

VALE 5 Centavos En la calle o en los expendios

EL COMERCIO

(THE COMMERCE)

Call Us When in need of any Spanish Job Printing

Bienvenidos los Delegados A la Asamblea en HARLINGEN

SUGESTIONES

ALERTA

"PRO-RAZA"

"EL COMERCIO"

PROGRAMA

Enfermita

Lamentable Tragedia en Laredo

Por el Anexa Cafe

EN CAMA

Apreciable paciente

Gira de Propaganda

Compre Ud. "El Comercio" Vale 5 centavos

EL PROPOSITO

FIGURE 2.2. *El Comercio* newspaper (Harlingen) announcing the Harlingen Convention, where Mexican American male activists excluded Mexican American women. The convention decided to exclude Mexican immigrants from their organization, Latin American Citizens, in 1927. Collected by Adela Sloss-Vento for her archive. Courtesy of Dr. Arnoldo Carlos Vento.

Also in Sloss's collection is a flyer from LAC, the organization founded at the Harlingen meeting, dated November 1927.[9] It is a call by Amado Vera Jr. and Tristán Longoria of La Grulla in the Valley to "Ciudadanos Americanos de Origen Mexicano" (American citizens of Mexican origin). Among her papers is the clipping "Nuevo Concilio de la Liga de Ciudadanos de Origén Latino" (New Council of the Latin Citizens League).[10] Sloss kept academic pamphlets such as Oliver Douglas Weeks's "The League of United Latin-American Citizens: A Texas-Mexican Civic Organization," an ethnographic and historical report of 1921–1929 Mexican American South Texas civil rights efforts, especially those led by the OSA of San Antonio. She kept Perales's 1930 pamphlet "El México Americano y la Política del Sur de Texas" (The Mexican American and the politics of South Texas). Both pamphlets are considered rare documents today.

FIGURE 2.3. LULAC constitutional convention, Corpus Christi, May 19, 1929. Left to right from bottom: (row 1) J. T. Canales (1), Ben Garza (9); (row 4) M. C. Gonzales (4); (row 5) J. Luz Sáenz (5). Alonso S. Perales was unable to attend because he was on a US diplomatic mission in Latin America. Courtesy of the University of Texas at Austin, General Libraries, Benson Latin American Collection.

Sloss initiated her personal and professional relations with Perales and Sáenz in 1927. She wrote to Perales, and he responded with a courteous letter congratulating her for graduating from high school and "upon your firm determination to continue to improve your mind."[11] Since she was a woman he did not invite her to join LAC. By December 1928 Perales sent her a New Year's card, saying "I trust you have kept up the good work in behalf of our race." What kind of good work she was conducting is unknown. Perales notes that "leaders" (read: men) would be meeting in Corpus Christi to consolidate the various civil rights organizations.[12]

In February 1929 representatives of LAC, OSA, and OKA met in Corpus Christi and founded LULAC. Female family members attended the founding convention in February 1929 and the constitutional convention in May 1929 in Corpus Christi but were not invited to act outside of their familial roles. LULAC was the first permanent civil rights organization dedicated to the empowerment of La Raza, but it followed decades of resistance and empowerment by mutual aid societies, anarcho-syndicalist groups, and unions. Its constitution specifically referred to male members. Though supportive of its efforts, Sloss could not join LULAC.

SLOSS-VENTO'S ACTIVISM IN THE 1930S

The 1930s were defined by the economic woes of the Great Depression, with more than 400,000 workers unemployed across Texas joining millions in the United States. Racist, sexist, and homophobic practices continued unabated. In this decade Sloss increased her activism, targeting problems in her hometown of San Juan—municipal corruption, prostitution, and gambling.[13] She participated in school desegregation efforts in Del Rio in South Texas, a case LULAC litigated. She began a long career of promoting LULAC founder Perales. When LULAC permitted women to join homosocial councils called Ladies LULAC in 1933, she did not join though she still promoted them. It was in this decade that Sloss began to write as a public intellectual; in doing so she overstepped traditional gender lines. In 1930 she was twenty-nine years old.

There is no evidence that Sloss concerned herself with the deportation of people of Mexican descent to Mexico or repatriation that occurred during the Depression. About a half-million Mexicans and Mexican Americans were deported from the United States to Mexico as scapegoats of economic woes. The Mexican-descent population of Texas dropped from 266,046 in 1930 to 159,266 in 1940, with 132,639 sent to Mexico from Texas.[14] Many people were deported from Bexar County (San Antonio) and Karnes County

(Kenedy).[15] Deportations were even more common from California and the Midwest than from Texas.

San Juan's Red Light District

Municipal corruption in Sloss's hometown of San Juan was one of her first known struggles. In the early 1930s she worked as the mayor's secretary, a job that gave her insight into city government and politics. Sloss contended that the town had "shooting, bootlegging, gambling places, prostitute dances."[16] Mexican-descent people complained to the mayor about the red light district's noise, violence, and poor men wasting wages needed by families. Sloss noted that Mexican immigrants were reluctant to complain for fear of deportation, and moreover, the Euro-Texan mayor turned a deaf ear to those who did.[17] Indeed, deportations were the norm there after 1924, when the United States created the Border Patrol. The Valley had many Mexican immigrants. As a bilingual Mexican American, Sloss complained. Years later she recalled him saying, "No, we can't stop the dances and vices—that is what the Mexican people like."[18] As a Christian woman, Sloss saw prostitutes as victims of poverty who were exploited by men.

Arnoldo Vento describes how his mother "single-handedly took on the corruption in San Juan and won her first political victory."[19] But a document suggests that she joined the Good Government League, a new group in the Valley created to reform boss politics and eliminate the red light district. In 1931 Sloss wrote letters to newspapers, made speeches, and cooperated with the Good Government League to close the district on the Mexican side of town and expose corruption by the administration of A. Y. Baker, the county political boss.[20] In a manuscript dated 1931 she asserts, "There still remains to act against some of the leaders who run the vice centers and who since Bakers Regime are experts in getting by with the law, for some are men who boast of having political pull, men who control votes or who have been in charge of paying poll taxes."[21]

Decades later Sloss-Vento reminisced about the civic successes in San Juan: "I joined a new Administration and with their aid I was able to clean my town of prostitution, gambling places and other vices."[22] This would be one of the few times that Sloss credited herself for her activism. In February 1969 she wrote about the effort in the *McAllen Monitor* but did not reveal the town, her name, referred to a "girl," and used the third person. She notes, "So said girl, without being a writer, wrote long articles to newspapers denouncing the harm of the vices in her community. Without being a public speaker, she made fiery speeches in both English and Spanish at political meetings. . . . She talked to many people in the county and finally the old administration came to an end." She adds, "The dance hall was closed, gambling ended, and prostitutes were ordered to leave."[23] In 1970 she wrote that her first job was cleaning up vice in San Juan.[24] And in 1977 she recalls, "At that time the author joined a political party only on the condition that it would rid the town of its red light district and without being a writer wrote the newspapers and exposed complaints and suffering."[25]

Sloss's work was appreciated by some city officials, but she was harassed by others. In 1934 City Clerk H. L. McCombs wrote her a letter of recommendation, referring to her as a "respectable citizen of the City of San Juan and of the United States" and "well educated, and a desirable citizen."[26] This was great praise in an era when Mexican Americans were not typically treated as US citizens. But she was also taunted for her activism. In one reminiscence she notes, again in third person, "For that effort, she received insults and threats from those who were responsible for said community corruption."[27]

Sloss also received accolades for her work in speaking up about abuses by the San Juan sheriff. On February 20, 1931, *La Prensa* published "Una señorita que defiende a la colonia," an article about Sloss reporting a break-in of a Mexican immigrant's family home and saying she hoped for justice "not just for North Americans of Mexican descent but also for Mexican citizens, residents of the United States."[28] She showed her pro-Raza sentiment, arguing on behalf of Mexican citizens. Sloss could no longer tolerate San Juan corruption and quit her job in the mayor's office during the Depression.[29] However, shortly afterward, she found employment with the Edinburg tax collector's office.[30]

School Desegregation in Del Rio

Despite the prescribed heterosexual, patriarchal ideology that assigned women's place as the home, Sloss began to transcend gender boundaries through civic engagement. She helped LULAC raise funds in its cause against segregated schools in Del Rio. On June 14, 1931, she and Zacarías Gonzalez organized La Gran Kermesse, a benefit in San Juan to fund the Comité Pro Defensa Escolar Del Río (Del Rio School Defense Committee) for the school desegregation case brought by LULAC.[31] *Salvatierra v. Del Rio Independent School District* was the first class-action lawsuit in Texas against a district with separate Mexican schools.[32] Perales, J. T. Canales, and M. C. Gonzales, all LULAC founders and lawyers, argued that "Mexicans" were legally white and thus did not merit segregation; the judge disagreed.[33] The US Census listed persons of Mexican descent as "Mexican," not "white," in 1930 though they were described as "white" in the 1920 census. LULAC noted the racialization of persons of Mexican descent of the 1930 Census. In the late 1930s LULAC worked to change the classification so that "Mexicans" became "white" again in the 1940 Census; it was an attempt to initiate legal strategies against racial segregation, prevent disenfranchisement of the Mexican American vote, and allow for school inclusion.

Promoting Perales and LULAC

Besides acting on problems in San Juan and Del Rio, Sloss began recognizing Perales, LULAC, and women in LULAC as heroes. To understand Sloss, it is useful to become familiar with Perales. Along with Canales and Sáenz, from 1920 to 1965 he was one of the most accomplished Tejanos and one of the most accomplished Mexican Americans in the United States. He was born poor and orphaned early in life yet became an activist, civil rights leader, lawyer, US diplomat, author, columnist, orator, teacher, publisher, translator, and the major LULAC founder. He was either the second or third Tejano to become a lawyer in Texas by 1925. He was ethical, caring, intelligent, and pro-active, and he avoided self-aggrandizement.[34]

It would be appropriate to compare him to Martin Luther King Jr.; he was among the most important civil rights activists in the United States in the twentieth century. He and Canales conceptualized LULAC, and unlike other Mexican American and Latino civil rights and labor rights organizations, the league expanded to become a national organization that has persisted into the twenty-first century. US Senator Dennis Chávez of New Mexico was also an exceptional leader and LULAC member; he advocated for establishing the Federal Employment Practices Commission, which LULAC also supported. The Alianza de Habla Española was founded in Arizona in the 1890s and engaged in important civil rights work in the 1950s, but it did not survive. The Congreso de Pueblos de Habla Española (Spanish-Speaking People's Congress) was another notable civil rights and left-leaning organization; it was founded in California but did not survive anticommunism in the 1950s.

Sloss saw Perales's genius early on, while others were unaware of his stature and accomplishments. Her early accolades in various publications cemented their lifelong friendship.[35] In May 1931 in "Nuestra gratitud y estimación hacia el autor de la Liga de Ciudadanos Unidos Latino-Americanos" (Our gratitude and esteem to the founder of the League of United Latin American Citizens) she writes, "He is the citizen whom so many communities admire and esteem so much that Latin Americans must exclaim that he is the Mexican American who stands above all."[36] In a letter to the editor of *La Prensa* she writes, "Attorney Perales is a valiant and sincere guide for the Mexican Americans who reside in the state of Texas." She lauds his work as a "constant struggle for which he imparts justice to those residents who deserve justice."[37]

The first of LULAC's aims and purposes as laid out in its constitution was "to develop within the members of our race the best, purest, and most perfect type of a true and loyal citizen of the United States of America."[38] While superpatriotic, the second aim immediately referred to discriminations, plural: "to eradicate from our body politic all intents and tendencies to establish discriminations among our fellow citizens on account of race, religion, or social position as being contrary to the true spirit of Democracy, our Constitution, and Laws." The league's major effort in the 1930s was on desegregating Mexican schools and ending discriminatory school practices.

Sloss praised LULAC as early as January 1931. She wrote "L. Unidos de Ciudadanos" (League of United Citizens), which was published in *El Paladín*, a LULAC newspaper in Corpus Christi.[39] She later penned "Importancia de la Liga de Ciudadanos Unidos Latinoamericanos" (LULAC's significance) for *LULAC News*, the league's monthly news magazine founded in 1931. The December 1932 article begins, "The founding of the League of United Latin American Citizens constitutes one of the most transcendental phases in the intellectual betterment of the Americans of Latin origin element."[40] She notes that no Latino had served as governor or any minor statewide office and laments the lack of solidarity and failure to exercise the vote. The league's constitution advocated for exercising the vote, and Sloss indicates in the article that she saw LULAC as a potential political tool. She points to LULAC's cultural work such as that in Mission in the Valley and praises Perales, Sáenz, and Canales.

LULAC grew tremendously during the Depression although the colonized Mexican American middle class suffered. Indeed, racism continued in new forms in this decade: Mexican Americans and Mexicans were denied employment, as were women. Middle-class Mexican Americans paid membership fees to LULAC, and by 1940 more than 120 councils existed in Texas, New Mexico, and Washington, DC. Still, other LULAC councils struggled to stay alive, and some had already gone dormant. In 1932 Canales wrote to the LULAC leader M. C. Gonzales that the McAllen, Penitas, and La Grulla councils, all in the Valley, probably could not be reorganized because "the people haven't got any money."[41]

Ladies LULAC

Besides praising Perales, Sloss congratulated women in LULAC. As noted, when LULAC was founded in 1929, only men were allowed. Perales did not favor women in LULAC and suggested that civic-minded Mexican American women participate in the Spanish-speaking Parents and Teachers Association (PTA) instead.[42] But the Spanish-speaking PTA dealt only with school issues, and few chapters existed. Women began to insert themselves into LULAC circles and events as early as 1929. Finally, in 1933 LULAC, in its leaders' own language, "permitted" women to join LULAC in separate, segregated "ladies" councils. Joe V. Alamia and J. M. Canales of the Edinburg LULAC introduced the resolution for women's inclusion. Whether they were familiar with Sloss's activism is unknown.[43] The two men considered women capable and key to racial uplift.

Homosociality had long been a practice in most Mexican-descent mutual aid societies, though Sloss did not write about this second-class inclusion. Perhaps homosociality seemed natural and not socially constructed at the time; moreover, as an individual Sloss found ways to include herself, and Perales and other male leaders continued to encourage her activism. Perhaps symbolic of her own political florescence was the poem "The Butterfly," which she wrote in the late 1920s but contributed to *LULAC News* in 1932.[44] The butterfly had emerged from its cocoon as a mature adult.

Sloss may have helped form LULAC councils. In January 1931 *El Paladín* of Corpus Christi reported that she was helping form a LULAC council in the Valley.[45] It is unclear if this was a ladies auxiliary she helped found. It was not typical for women to organize men's councils, so either the report was incorrect or Sloss overstepped gender boundaries. Several auxiliaries existed between 1929 and 1931 before Ladies LULAC that were separate and unequal. Another report, in the April 1933 *LULAC News*, indicates that Sloss joined a Ladies LULAC council in Alice that Sáenz organized.[46] Sáenz's role in organizing the council suggests his pro-feminist approach as LULAC special organizer. But Sloss did not live in Alice, which is outside the Valley, and the article was likely incorrect in stating she was a member. Eighteen married women and five single women joined the Alice council including a listed Adela Sloss. Perhaps she was an honorary member. *La Prensa* reported the organization as a ladies auxiliary; however, it had a council number, and ladies auxiliaries did not have chapter numbers.[47]

Although Ladies LULAC councils were common after 1933, Sloss did not join any Ladies LULAC or male LULAC councils. In the 1930s Valley ladies councils included one in Donna, Harlingen, Mission, and McAllen. Women in San Juan did not have a ladies council, and Sloss did not organize one in that town. By 1940, with the Depression lifting, there were ten ladies councils in Texas and New Mexico; by 1945 twenty-five ladies councils existed in these two states.[48]

Ladies LULAC could have given Sloss-Vento a leadership base, but she rejected that mode of operation. By eschewing Ladies LULAC she shunned potential statewide and national leadership positions. The league established the statewide position of ladies organizer general in 1934, and that year Estefana Valadez of Mission in the Valley assumed the honor. Alice Dickerson Montemayor of Laredo became LULAC national vice president in the late 1930s. Until then the position of vice president had been held only by men. After Montemayor, the office became gendered as a position for women until the 1970s.

Despite its name, Ladies LULAC chapters were civic and political organizations, not social clubs. "Ladies" was perhaps "Southern" in tone but in Spanish translated to "señoras," suggesting married or older women. Ladies councils worked independent of one another in towns and cities and met separately from local men's councils. They promoted women's involvement in civic affairs, fought for school integration, and advocated that voters pay their own poll taxes to curb political patronage. In Goliad women helped desegregate the "Mexican" school in the 1930s, and El Paso women helped elect the city's first Mexican American mayor, Raymond Telles, in 1960. Ladies councils often took up social service causes such as buying eyeglasses, clothes, shoes, and food for the poor and initiated Junior LULAC chapters for children that were not segregated by gender.[49] It was Montemayor, a critic of sexism and homosociality in LULAC, who made sure that the Junior LULAC chapters were not homosocial.

Perhaps Sloss did not join LULAC or Ladies LULAC because women experienced sexism in LULAC. The annual Texas state and national conventions were male-dominated, as was the leadership. The sixth annual LULAC men's convention program in 1934 shows that Elodia G. Uveda addressed the audience and other women recited poetry and sang.[50] LULAC women were subordinated in mixed-gender conventions and meetings; Sloss would have been subordinated too. Not until the 1970s would gender segregation become a serious political issue for LULAC women; mixed-gender councils emerged as well as openly feminist councils in the 1970s.

Another reason Sloss may not have joined LULAC was personal or family-related. Perhaps she was too busy with San Juan municipal politics in the early 1930s. In 1935 she married Pedro Vento; she had three miscarriages in succession. It was a difficult time. Finally, their daughter,

Irma Dora, arrived in 1938 and Arnoldo Carlos in 1939. Her life in the 1940s would be defined in part by marriage and motherhood. In "La mujer americana y el marido latino-americano" (The American woman and the Latin American husband), which she probably wrote in the 1950s, she criticizes Euro-American women ("americanas") who use love or flattery to gain their Latino husbands' approval to work or study. She recommends that the husbands tell their wives, "If you want to study or work you must first attend to your obligations at home [and] keep it in order." She adds, "The woman who neglects her obligations to her husband in the end enslaves him and even prevents her own liberty." She mentions preparing meals and washing clothes as a wife's responsibilities.[51] In her view, a woman could study or work for advancement or self-fulfillment upon attending to household chores and marital obligations first. Perhaps she resented white women's perceived freedom. Or did she think Euro-American women had found another kind of privilege over Latinos? What is clear is that Sloss-Vento, like the majority of US women, did not question women's labor in the home and women's obligations to the family.

Why Sloss-Vento failed to join LULAC is an important question because she spent significant time promoting the league, praising its early leadership, and collaborating with its founders and because LULAC's issues were her own. Was she simply choosing not to participate in the organization? Perhaps she was avoiding engagement in too many organizations. Maybe she did not have time to belong to one and had to place family and employment before civil rights activism. Did she believe her intellect was above that of other Ladies LULAC members? Maybe she was simply focused on her individual intellectual contribution. She was a leader at the level of Perales, Sáenz, and Canales, in the upper echelon of intellectual, activist men in her generational cohort. So perhaps she chose not to insert herself into the assumed role of a woman's place, subject to LULAC men, as Montemayor experienced.

It was Montemayor of the Laredo Ladies LULAC, not Adela Sloss-Vento, who would be the major feminist voice in LULAC before 1970. In the 1938 essay "Son muy hombre" (They are so male), Montemayor informed LULAC members of sexism in the organization. *LULAC News* editors, all men, published Montemayor's protest.[52] Montemayor reported on a sexist incident and pattern. National LULAC President Ramón Longoria of Harlingen ignored correspondence from the El Paso Ladies LULAC, so the council disbanded. Perales, Sáenz, Canales, and Carlos Castañeda, a historian, educator, and LULAC ally, were all silent on the issue, as was Sloss-Vento if she knew about it. There is no archival evidence that Montemayor and Sloss-Vento knew one another.

Had Sloss-Vento commented on the El Paso issue, LULAC's homosociality, or sexism, perhaps the men would have ostracized her. If she knew about the situation, perhaps she considered how far she might have gotten in convincing male leaders to her side and whether they would have continued their friendships. Mexican American men were not advocating for women's inclusion in civic engagement and politics in the 1920–1970 era during the Mexican American civil rights and Chicano movements.

Since Sloss-Vento did not join LULAC she had no conflict with men about gender in LULAC. Montemayor wrote about sexist men and in a 1980s interview said that Laredo LULAC men "hated" her.[53] Montemayor joined the Laredo Ladies LULAC and had numerous conflicts with men in local chapters and national LULAC, which was defined at the time as Texas, New Mexico, and Washington, DC.[54] In contrast, Perales, Canales, and Sáenz admired Sloss-Vento, and none regularly corresponded with Montemayor. Sloss-Vento preceded Montemayor with a feminist essay in *LULAC News* in 1934,[55] but Montemayor stressed sexism more, especially within LULAC.

I met both Sloss-Vento and Montemayor, and in my conversations with each woman, Montemayor emphasized fighting sexism, while Sloss-Vento stressed fighting racism. Laredo had a majority of Mexican-descent people and different racial dynamics than the Valley. Sloss-Vento had close professional and personal ties with Perales, Sáenz, and Canales, and they treated her with respect. Moreover, she was sheltered from sexism in LULAC. She did not have the same experiences as women in Ladies LULAC.

Nevertheless, Sloss's beliefs in the 1930s stood in contrast to the prescribed gender ideology expressed in LULAC circles until the 1970s. This ideology was advanced by the LULAC member J. Reynolds Flores in "How to Educate Our Girls," published in *LULAC News* in the 1930s: "The foundation of society rests on the homes. The success of our homes rests on the wives. Therefore, first of all, teach our girls how to be successful wives." To achieve that end, he said parents should "train them to do small things well, and to delight in helping others, and instill constantly into their minds the necessity for sacrifices for others' pleasure as a mean[s] of our development."[56] This was the mindset of the pre-1970 era but one Sloss never fit, even though she married in 1935, had two children, and accepted wifely and motherly duties. "Wife" and "mother" did not define her identity, nor did domesticity.

Sloss praised women in LULAC and in civic engagement generally, who by acting in public challenged domesticity. She called them "women fighters." The Del Rio newspaper *La Avispa* published her essay "Barco de LULAC" (LULAC ship) in May 1933.[57] In it she lists the league's successes with its chapters in Texas towns and cities: Corpus Christi, San Antonio,

Brownsville, McAllen, Mission, La Grulla, Encino, Alice, Robstown, Edinburg, Falfurrias, Floresville, Sugarland, Laredo, San Diego, Crystal City, Uvalde, Del Rio, Eagle Pass, Rio Grande, Penitas, Roma, Hebbronville, Kingsville, Sarita, Marfa, San Angelo, Ozona, Sonora, Seguin, Dilley, Harlingen, Mercedes, Donna, Benavides, Cotulla, Hondo, Lockhart, and Gonzales. Then she focuses on Ladies LULAC chapters. She proclaims that members in Alice were "WOMEN FIGHTERS" (emphasis hers), "unselfish women who want to provide an example of volunteerism and energy."[58] Her son has commented that her use of "capital letters signals a stroke of pride for women's activism."[59] She acknowledged gendered LULAC and impressive civic engagement by women. Yet, she did not criticize gendered councils, and she ignored women's initial exclusion from LULAC and the organization's failure to address sexism.

Condemning Women's "Slavery" in the Home

Still, Sloss wrote about sexism in the 1930s. At age thirty-three and not yet married, in 1934 she wrote "Por qué en muchos hogares latinos no existe verdadera felicidad" (Why there is no true happiness in many Latino homes) for *LULAC News*.[60] It is her most poignant essay on sexism among heterosexual couples and a stinging critique of women's subordination in the home. She refers to "Spanish" customs that lent themselves to a "perpetual chain of suffering." She asserts that since childhood Latinas are imprisoned and that "the Latino man has all the privileges and rights." She idealizes romance but also says romance and marriage eventually result in the domestic oppression of women. Too many husbands become terrible husbands over time and engage in double standards. Should a woman want to go out, a husband would respond, "That can't be, darling daughter, women were made to keep house, wash clothes, iron clothes, and take care of the kids, etc." She was against being a martyr, warning women, "Live the life of a martyr by obeying these beautiful sentiments, creating the law of Latino life." Sloss describes a stereotypical binary in the manner in which Latino men treat their wives versus how Anglo men treat theirs. In Anglo homes, she argues, the wife "is the husband's companion and not the slave," while Latina wives live in "una prisión" (a prison). She asks why the romantic and idealized courtships could not continue instead of men converting into "esposos terribles" (terrible husbands). But in her view both groups, Anglos and Latinos, tended to have unequal relationships.

Sloss posits two types of Latino men: bad husbands and modern men. She goes on to say Latinas could be martyrs by not marrying at all, so they would not end up with bad husbands. But she offers an alternative: "The other is the ideal man, modern in today's times." This man is a true companion, taking his wife out and allowing her to have fun. Her happiness would be his, and they would have a happy home. Sloss still does not say if the happy wife was performing less gendered housework.

After 1934 Sloss did not write about machismo in the home or in the public arena. She married Pedro C. Vento in 1935, and in several letters to Sáenz she complains about her husband occasionally nagging her about her activism. Still, Pedro Vento supported her and knew he married a feminist activist. The couple's son, Arnoldo Vento, says they agreed that "between 1935 and 1952 there will be no interpersonal issues between the two." He describes his father as kind, intelligent, and compassionate, a husband who permitted a "propitious environment for Adela to continue her work."[61] Only with a supportive husband—a modern man—could Adela have done so.

SLOSS-VENTO'S LIFE AND WRITINGS IN THE 1940S

In 1940 Sloss-Vento turned thirty-nine. She was married and had two toddlers to tend. Though she felt "trapped" by motherhood in the 1940s, her son has said, she found ways to be active and write. He said she sent him and his sister to school early so she had time to write, and she took them to civil rights meetings.[62] While she continued to address racism in Texas, she also turned to national and international issues such as the rise of fascism and communism, the United States' Good Neighbor policy, and the US-Mexico Bracero Program. She advocated for true neighborliness in US-Mexico policy in Texas and opposed the Bracero Program. She lobbied the Texas legislature to make segregation illegal, and she condemned low wages paid to Mexican-descent workers.

In the 1940s Sloss-Vento had no membership in LULAC or the American G.I. Forum and almost no correspondence with their official leaders. The forum was a new Mexican American civil rights organization, founded in 1948 by the LULAC member Héctor P. García of Corpus Christi. She did not participate in the organizations' major racial desegregation lawsuit efforts. Nor did she have any connection to the Federal Employment Practices Commission, the first federal agency to address racial discrimination in employment, with which LULAC, Perales, Castañeda, and Gonzales were especially involved in coordination with Senator Chávez.[63]

Through letters and opinion pieces Sloss-Vento extended her reach beyond South Texas to the halls of Austin, beyond Texas to Washington, DC, and beyond the United States to Mexico City. As a woman, wife, mother, and

FIGURE 2.4. Adela Sloss-Vento, civil rights leader, public intellectual, and feminist, around forty-two years old, 1948. Courtesy of Dr. Arnoldo Carlos Vento.

after 1949 a worker, she had mobility issues in reaching Austin or Washington to lobby politicians. So, instead, she wrote letters to state legislators, Texas governors, and US and Mexican presidents, always with a sense of mission that she describes in her book about Perales: "It was necessary for us to write our representatives, to committees, to newspapers in an effort to end those problems which prevented the advancement of the Mexican-American people."[64]

Antifascism and Pan-Americanism

In the 1940s Sloss-Vento entered debates about the war in Europe and Asia and corresponding political ideologies and practices. She feared the rise of Hitler and fascism in Europe. Fascism posed a threat not only to Europe but to the United States and the Americas, she argued. In an opinion piece in *La Prensa* of San Antonio she writes that fascist Germany, fascist Italy, and communist Russia threatened democratic nations in the Americas. In it she compares fascism to US racism: "The ideals and future of America should come first. . . . We should forcefully rid ourselves of unjustified attitudes. We should prevent the formation of a second Europe in our continent, full of hate and evil interpretations."[65] She concludes, "We need preparedness to join hands with the Latin American people in cleansing America of German propaganda and fifth columns and spies."[66]

As a Mexican Americanist, her writings contain borderlands, nationalist (both ethnic and US), Western Hemispheric, and transnationalist perspectives. She was a native of the US-Mexico border who crossed national boundaries fluidly. She cared about the plight of Mexican immigrants. She was patriotic toward the United States, but as she was a hemispheric writer, Mexico was part of her world. And she spoke of the Américas, especially Latin America, not a singular "America." Like other key LULAC figures—Perales, Sáenz, Sánchez, and Castañeda, she had a hemispheric consciousness.[67] As a fronteriza, she cared more about La Raza in the United States and especially Texas than she cared about Mexico. However, she was not a narrow nationalist or assimilationist like those depicted in outdated stereotypes of LULAC members.

With her Latin American hemispheric and borderlander/fronteriza consciousness and through her intellectual formation influenced by *La Prensa*, she called upon Latin America to respond to fascism. She did so in "Mi súplica a todas las naciones de la América" (My plea to all the Americas), a letter published in *La Prensa*.[68] In it she cautions, "It is important to understand that Germany and her Italian and Russian allies have dangerous theories that are contrary to our democratic theories." She implores all nations in the Americas to help France and England and promote democracy.

Sloss-Vento's pan-Americanism and transnationalist perspective can also be seen in her 1940 letter to the editor in the *Brownsville Herald* "The Awakening of the Real Needs of Our Country and of America." Noting that the US government was building material preparedness for the war, she argues for "spiritual preparedness" as well. She adds, "There is no room in our hearts for misunderstandings, hatreds, or racial discrimination toward

Latin Americans. This is the type of citizen needed today to defend our Country and our Hemisphere."[69]

Sloss-Vento's good neighborliness and transnationalism extended to all of the Americas. In the same letter she addresses English-speaking readers about pan-Americanism, the Spanish language, and spiritual preparedness.[70] She contends that Spanish was needed in the United States and English in Latin America. To accomplish spiritual preparedness, she writes, "we need to master Spanish." She argues that "through the knowledge of Spanish we will find that there is much to learn from civilizations of our sister nations to the South." Then she mentions LULAC and its spiritually prepared members, who tended to speak Spanish. Ending discrimination was the "secret" to improving Latin American and US relations, she concludes.

As part of her fronteriza ethos and neighborliness, Sloss-Vento also sought to influence Mexico. Mexico was not her country but the place where her co-nationalists, Mexican immigrants, originated; she was part of what the borderlands scholar Américo Paredes has called "Greater Mexico" (Mexico outside of Mexico) and the historian Richard García has called "México de adentro" (Mexico inside the United States).[71] She traveled to Mexico with her husband on criminal justice matters for his work; she joined a friend traveling to Veracruz, traveled to Mexico City, and often went to Reynosa on the border.[72] She read Mexican newspapers and watched Mexican television after the 1950s. She understood Mexico's problems.

Like Perales and Gonzales, at times Sloss-Vento would argue that Mexican Americans were "white," as when they successfully lobbied to change the 1930 US Census classification from "Mexican" to "white." A strategy for persons of Mexican descent to gain access to schools and public accommodations was to claim membership in the Caucasian race. This strategy avoided association with African Americans and legal association with being "colored," a categorization that proved detrimental in schooling and public accommodations; their strategy avoided tackling the exclusion of other people of color. While claiming whiteness, Sloss-Vento acknowledged having Native American roots. Too often, she said, whites called Mexican Americans "Mexican" because they had Indian ancestry.[73]

While claiming whiteness, she was nonetheless a compatriot to Mexican citizens. Moreover, as LULAC members called for recognition of Mexican Americans' whiteness, they were including Mexican immigrants as members of their race, nation, and community. Sloss-Vento considered Mexican Americans white because they were born in the United States. She used *Webster's Dictionary* to look up "Mexican" and found the definition "native or citizen of Mexico."[74] Since Mexican Americans were not citizens of Mexico,

Mexicans born in the United States should not be called "Mexican" because that is a nationality and not a race. Perhaps yet another way Sloss-Vento claimed whiteness was as a person of Spanish descent.

World War II Latino Soldiers

After the United States officially entered the war in 1941, Sloss-Vento protested the US military's World War I policy of segregating Latino soldiers. LULAC founders like Sáenz experienced racial segregation in that war. His autobiographical book on the experiences of Mexican-descent soldiers, *Los méxico-americanos en la Gran Guerra y su contingente en pro de la democracia, la humanidad y la justicia* (Mexican Americans in the Great War and its contingent for democracy, humanity, and justice), was published in 1933. Sloss purchased and read it. In a 1942 letter to the editor she raises similar issues regarding World War II soldiers: "The places where Mexicans are segregated should be regarded as harmful as the fifth columns themselves."[75]

She wrote to the US secretary of state on the issue of racism in July 1940 and called for friendlier (nonracist) attitudes of Texans toward persons of Mexican descent. Knowledge of Spanish and the study of Latin America would foster cordial relations, she said.[76] In October 1940 Sloss-Vento denounced the McAllen resident Perry Clark, who favored racial segregation of soldiers and was seeking support from the US State Department.[77]

Around 1943 in a letter to the editor, "A Latin American Speaks," Sloss-Vento applauds an editorial titled "Toward Racial Harmony" in a Corpus Christi newspaper in support of Latino soldiers. She writes, "I am sure you have seen the busses leaving here for the induction centers full of our boys, Latin Americans, white race, natives or naturalized citizens of our United States. If they are good enough to go give their lives for those Anglo-Americans staying at home, why aren't they classified under their race without discrimination by these same people?"[78] In a 1944 letter to the editor she compares racist treatment of Latino soldiers to that of Hitler's victims and points out that racialization and poverty made it hard for some Latinos to qualify for induction. She says Euro-Texans passed the physical exam for induction, but many persons of Mexican descent could not due to bad lungs and other health problems caused by poverty:

> How could they expect them to be strong and healthy with wages of 75 cents and $1.00 as they were paid until recently, and with five, nine and ten children sometimes to support? For who has built and enriched this great Valley? Who has grubbed all these lands, and who still do all the hard

work in the fields and in the packingsheds? Why do Anglo-americans want to ignore the fact that while these people have been reduced to poverty and ill-health, many Anglo-americans have grown prosperous and have lead [*sic*] an easy life.[79]

A year earlier Sloss-Vento argued for the support of undocumented Mexican immigrants in the US military. She asserts that 11,000 Mexican "aliens" were serving in the war.[80] She advocates for men in Brownsville who offered to fight in the war despite their Mexican citizenship. She argues, "Not one will be a traitor or a spy, for the Mexican alien is as patriotic, loyal and courageous as any true American."[81] While casually using the derogatory "alien," as did the dominant society, she nonetheless respected Mexican immigrants and considered them part of her Raza.

Good Neighbor Policy with Mexico

Sloss-Vento advocated for genuine neighborliness between Texas and Mexico as part of the US Good Neighbor policy with Latin America adopted in 1933. Since the United States needed more trade, resources, and labor from Latin America, the program was ramped up once World War II began.

In 1943 the US government established the Good Neighbor Commission (GNC) to improve US–Latin American relations and improve domestic race relations. Initially funded by Nelson Rockefeller and federal grants, the GNC became a Texas state commission in 1945 that was entirely dependent on state funds.[82] As a permanent state agency, its initial nine male board members were appointed. Its true purpose was to respond to Mexico's blacklisting of Texas as a state authorized to receive braceros from Mexico as guest workers. Mexico blacklisted Texas in 1943 because critics complained to the US State Department, and the GNC sought, in the words of the historian John Weber, "not to protect Mexicans and Mexican Americans in Texas but rather to muffle news of discriminatory acts and help the state's economic elite secure cheap labor and new customers."[83] Sloss-Vento supported the ban. In a letter to Perales she declares, "Hopefully so and Mexico will put all these Valley counties on the blacklist and prevent the wetbacks' passing. It would be a step forward."[84] Sloss-Vento used both the derogatory "alien" and "wetback" while still advocating for them.

Sloss-Vento monitored Texas's GNC policy and efforts. She penned "Discrimination Defeats Idea of the Good Neighbor Policy," published on September 4, 1943, in the *Corpus Christi Caller*.[85] In it she criticizes the practice of segregating Mexican American soldiers, a segregated swimming pool in McAllen, housing discrimination in Kingsville, and discrimination in Corpus Christi restaurants. She says racism cut across class lines and was experienced by the Mexican American middle class, the educated few, as well as by cotton pickers all across the state.[86]

As she traveled and lived outside the Rio Grande Valley, Sloss-Vento saw racism as a Texas problem that affected all people of Mexican descent regardless of education, class, or status. In 1945 she again writes about the broad prejudice she had witnessed:

> Race discrimination against Latin Americans includes the poor, the uneducated, the highly educated as well as the well to do. Here in Texas, we have race discrimination for even Senators and Mexican Consuls have been denied the right to service in restaurants. Even in San Antonio as well as in the Valley and other parts of Texas, we have exclusive residential districts, where not even Veterans who won Congressional Medals of Honor or well to do Mexicans are allowed to buy.[87]

In 1943 Sloss-Vento wrote to Texas Governor Coke Stevenson about the state's lack of neighborliness, and the letter was published in the *Corpus Christi Caller*.[88] She congratulates the governor on efforts by local Good Neighbor councils that were investigating discrimination against Latin Americans, specifically Mexican Americans in Texas. But she adds, "A frontal attack against said discrimination is needed by all newspapers and magazines. A law must be passed in Texas and in all other States where said prejudice exists."[89] She bids the governor well on his trip to Mexico City, where he was to discuss these issues with Mexican officials. However, once there, Stevenson said people of Mexican descent in Texas wanted separate schools for their children. Sloss-Vento condemns him for this lie and instead blames "narrow-minded and selfish Anglo- and others mixtures of Germans and other descent of Texas."[90] Stevenson merely forwarded her comments to the GNC.[91]

Around 1945 Sloss-Vento outlined a potential agenda for the GNC. In "Legislative Action as Well as a Campaign against Race Discrimination against Latin Americans Is Needed" in the *Corpus Christi Caller* she argues that teaching Spanish in public schools would reduce discrimination but that ending school segregation was a better solution.[92] She recommends Spanish classes for Euro-Texans and students of Mexican descent but contends that stronger state legislative action was needed. The 1940s would bring token efforts by the GNC to promote Spanish and to establish local councils to foster interracial understanding—in other words, minimal actions to end racism. Some Spanish classes were instituted, but the GNC's authority was weak; it was an advisory group that had no power to legislate.

Sloss-Vento sought to have an impact on the GNC's board and staff composition. One year its board was composed of seven members, all men, two of whom were Latino.[93] In 1947 there were nine members and still only two of them Latinos, the wholesaler grocer Ramón Guerra and the Dallas medical doctor J. T. Saldívar.[94] That same year, with nine members, Matías de Llano of Laredo and Andrés Rivera Jr. of San Antonio served as members.[95] Sloss-Vento contends that more Latinos with will were needed: "We need a Good Neighbor Commission comprised also of Latin American members with the necessary will and power to act on the problem of racial discrimination toward Latin Americans in Texas."[96] She apparently considered the members token Mexican Americans who were not having much success. She saw the GNC as ineffective and doubted that a permanent GNC was needed because in her view, commissioners were merely socializing and exchanging souvenirs.[97]

Although she did not comment on women's absence from the board, Sloss-Vento called for the support of the GNC executive secretary, Pauline R. Kibbe. In 1947 the liberal Kibbe was fired for her book published the previous year by the University of New Mexico, *Latin Americans in Texas*, in which she exposes Texas agribusiness's exploitation of Mexican workers and Valley racism. She wrote it as a "personal document," and the white establishment said it was too personal. Indeed, even titles within the book bothered some; the first chapter is titled "What's the Matter with Texas?"; a section is titled "Problems of Latin Americans in Texas," and another chapter is "Social and Civil Inequalities."[98] Kibbe reported that Mexican American farmworkers were earning twenty and twenty-five cents an hour instead of the seventy-five cents earned by their Anglo counterparts.[99] Sloss-Vento wrote to the governor in support of Kibbe.[100] What Sloss-Vento did not know was that Kibbe was also a mole for the US State Department who reported on the civil rights activists M. C. Gonzales and George Sánchez, a University of Texas professor of education and a past national LULAC president.[101] Writing in 1954, Everett Ross Clinchy Jr. called Kibbe's book "angry," perhaps showing his own racial and gender bias.[102]

Lobbying for Laws at the Texas Statehouse

While World War II raged, racial segregation against Mexican-descent people continued in Texas and across the nation. Sloss-Vento hoped state legislation would reform the home front. Other states had begun to legislate against racism. By 1948 across the nation more than 217 civil rights laws had been passed. Many were passed after 1941 with the start of the war. After 1941 Illinois, Indiana, New Jersey, and Wisconsin passed antisegregation school laws, especially for African Americans. Antidiscrimination laws in employment were passed by New Mexico, Connecticut, Indiana, Massachusetts, New Jersey, New York, Oregon, Rhode Island, and Washington, again mostly for African Americans. New Mexico's laws benefited both African Americans and Mexican Americans. Nondiscrimination laws in public housing were passed in Connecticut, Massachusetts, Minnesota, New York, Pennsylvania, and Wisconsin.[103]

This was not the case in Texas or the South, where anti–African American and anti-Mexican sentiment was grounded in slavery and empire building. Clinchy notes about Texas in 1954, "There is no legislation forbidding segregation in education or housing. There are no laws attempting to prevent discrimination in public places. Finally, there is no legislation protecting equality of opportunity in employment."[104] Clinchy overlooked the *Delgado v. Bastrop Independent School District* decision, which made segregation of Mexican children illegal in 1948.

In 1941 the LULAC founders and attorneys Perales and Gonzales convinced the San Antonio state legislator Fagan Dickson to introduce legislation. House Bill 909 read, "All persons of the Caucasian Race within the jurisdiction of the State are entitled to the full and equal accommodations, advantages, facilities, and privileges of all public places of business or amusement."[105] LULAC had success in labeling Mexican Americans "white" in the 1940 Census and thus were to be officially considered members of the Caucasian race. The bill would continue to segregate persons of African descent. Texans of all colors wrote their legislators to keep or end segregation. The historian Thomas Guglielmo mentions the Mexican Americans Perales, Gonzales, Sánchez, and Castañeda among those who wrote letters supporting the bill's passage. Guglielmo evidently was not aware of Sloss-Vento. Perales and Gonzales appeared before a Texas Senate committee. But she was a woman and because of distance, money, work, or familial and household obligations she did not have the mobility male activists had. She had toddlers.

Sloss-Vento created her own political access by writing opinion pieces and letters.[106] She corresponded with Fagan Dickson and Speaker of the House Homer Leonard as well as Perales.[107] In a letter to Leonard that was later published she advises, "Mr. Leonard, rest assured that all that you can do in favor for its passage as law will be a great contribution in meeting the urgent needs of America."[108] She also expresses concerns to the state legislator Rogers Kelley of Edinburg: "I am writing you about what is in the heart of every citizen of the US of Latin descent and it extends to all Latin America."[109]

Kabalen de Bichara cites Sloss-Vento's condemnation of discrimination against "Latin Americans regardless of whether they are citizens of the US or citizens of Latin America" as "the obstacle that prevents the building of a United, Stronger and Safer America."[110] House Bill 909 did not pass. Guglielmo points out that white legislators met the bill with "laughs, murmurs of disapproval and a few shouts of dissent."[111]

In her book on Perales Sloss-Vento explains why House Bill 909 failed: "Due to our apathy and disunity, we were less in number writing to the Legislators for favorable passing of the Bill,"[112] while Euro-Texans sent thousands of letters against its passage.[113] If the bill had passed, Sloss-Vento surmises, "This law would have curbed the existing inequality in many of the towns in Texas where Mexicans are not allowed in restaurants, barbershops, recreational centers etc.; it would have enforced fines or even their closing. This would have also provided a state law that would have eliminated further humiliation for all people of Mexican descent."[114] Sloss-Vento admonishes Mexican American voters, "It would have been necessary for all of our people in mass to send letters in support of the aforementioned law."[115] Apathy or disunity by Mexican Americans was only one small factor—there was only one Tejano in the state legislature, no African Americans or other people of color, and too many white racists.[116]

Two years later Sloss-Vento would urge Governor Stevenson to promote racial goodwill "in the homes and in the schools" through newspapers, magazines, and a state law.[117] In 1945 activists tried to pass another antiracist bill, Senate Bill 1. Sloss-Vento joined Perales and LULAC in writing letters to Texas Senator J. Franklin Spears.[118] In April 1945 she wrote to the editor Clarence La Roche of the *Brownsville Herald* in response to his editorial against the bill; in it he suggests that through education, not legislation, mutual understanding would result. She responds with three elements needed for change: "First, God's Christianity and commandments; Second, the respect to the rights of the Constitution which are rights for all American alike. Third, the passage of just laws against the injustices of said problem."[119] She calls upon Christian values, equal application of the US Constitution, and equality through legislation. But like the earlier one, the antidiscrimination bill died, and the racist Texas regime remained. She argued for better politicians and more Mexican American politicians. In a 1953 analysis she still finds unity lacking among the Latinx electorate: "Politicians in the State legislature of Texas continue to be the recipients of thousands of Latin-American votes while we continue asleep and disunited. Politicians move from one election to another and with a patronizing pat on our back, we are left contented. That, in my opinion, is to continue voting without reason, guarantees, or rights that belong to us."[120]

FIGURE 2.5. Adela's husband, Pedro C. Vento, a modern man, with their children, Arnoldo Carlos and Irma, at their San Juan, Texas, home, circa 1944. Despite occasionally nagging, Pedro supported his wife's activism. Courtesy of Dr. Arnoldo Carlos Vento.

Racial Segregation, Racist Stereotypes

When the family moved to Corpus Christi, where Pedro worked as a security officer at the naval air station, Sloss-Vento turned her attention to racism outside of the Valley. It was still common to see "No Mexicans Allowed" signs throughout Texas and the Southwest. In "The Problem of Many Texas Towns" in *El Heraldo* of Corpus Christi she condemns "hatred against people of Mexican descent."[121] She gives details of racism in Kingsville, San Antonio, Corpus Christi, and McAllen and compares the hatred to the "same evil found in Hitlerism, hatred against others." She adds, "We must bear in mind that our Country not only stands for Liberty, but also for Justice and Equality," and she suggests paying attention to the commandment "Love Thy Neighbor as Thyself."[122] Perhaps this essay gave Perales impetus to write *Are We Good Neighbors?* In the book, published in San Antonio in 1948, Perales includes affidavits from residents of 150 Texas towns documenting racist acts between 1942 and 1948.[123] Despite the legal desegregation of Mexican schools in Texas in 1948, Texas towns would continue to segregate residents of Mexican descent into the 1950s and 1960s.[124]

The Ventos experienced racial segregation firsthand. In Corpus Christi, Arnoldo Vento recalls, they initially lived in a trailer park but were evicted with their small house trailer because an Anglo neighbor had protested.[125] When they returned to the Valley in 1943 Sloss-Vento was kept out of a restaurant that had posted a "No Mexicans Allowed" sign. In a letter to the editor in the *Brownsville Herald* she writes about her visit to Harlingen's Zimberoff Café and asks, "Why do these so-called 'Whites' (or is it Aryans) do these things to us?"[126] Likewise, in the 1950s her husband and son were refused service at a restaurant in the town of George West near Corpus Christi.[127]

Racially segregated schools remained another of her concerns. In 1948 she wrote a letter to the editor that the *McAllen Monitor* published with the title "Segregation Hurts Educational Chances for Latin-American Child, Says Reader." In it she contends, "Poverty is the principal factor in denying our children the right education. The border for many years has been a land of slavery for a large percentage of Latin Americans."[128] Here again we see her analysis in considering race and class along the border. In the letter she congratulates the *Monitor* for its editorial "The Constitution Still a Strong Refuge," which called for an end to school segregation.[129] She recommends José Elias Chapa's study of Texas in *El Todo* of Mexico City.[130]

In the 1940s Sloss-Vento responded to several local newspaper commentaries by Euro-Texan men and women that were replete with racist stereotypes. One such letter was by Perry Clark of the Valley, to which she responds, "Prejudice is a very unpopular word among cultured people." She goes on to describe the colonizing effects of racism: "Because of public humiliations that the Latin-American child has gone through in the Valley at school, at playgrounds, in public swimming pools, theatres, restaurants they have developed an inferiority complex."[131] In 1944 she responded to Mrs. Lewis in the *Valley Morning Star*.[132] Mrs. L. J. Ring in a 1947 letter says Latin Americans had lice and sore eyes, to which Sloss-Vento responds that Latin Americans were a tolerant people, but she ends with the question "Furthermore, why pick on Mexico and the Mexicans when she can't do without them?"[133] Apparently Sloss-Vento sought to respond to Ring a second time, protesting that "she attacked 75 percent of Latin Americans," but the editor did not permit it.[134] Sloss-Vento answered Grace Ann Miller's letter by inviting her to investigate Mexican laborers' wages and housing conditions: "I suggest a compromise with Mrs. Miller that she see that the

Mexican laborers get at least 60 cents an hour wage every day and that they be provided with decent houses, with at least floors and screens, and we will do the rest."[135]

Sloss-Vento had firsthand knowledge of those conditions because in 1947 she was selling clothes to Mexican workers and could see their conditions and "lend them a helping hand."[136] Indeed, she asserted that farmworkers were exploited and class privilege was wrong. She even sent her son to work in the fields so he would understand his own lower-middle-class privilege.[137]

The Bracero Program

After the Bracero Program began in 1942 and throughout the 1950s Sloss-Vento addressed the problems of exploited Mexican braceros, living wages for Mexican immigrants, and forced Tejano migration out of the Valley and out of Texas. In a mid-1940s essay she notes, "And today thousands of wetbacks are here working for starvation wages; for the Tejano worker, it is more than a land of slavery but the land where one cannot live. There are literally thousands of Tejano laborers and their families who are forcibly obligated to go north to search for their daily bread." Here we see her distinguish between "wetbacks" and Tejanos and the nature of Mexicans' problems in Mexico and Mexican Americans' problems. She continues, "We have nothing against our brothers from Mexico, but the economic problem of the Mexican workers corresponds to Mexico; in the same light, it is up to us to resolve our own problems."[138] She saw the "wetback" issue as Mexico's issue.

In an essay titled "Problems in the Lands of America" Sloss-Vento once again makes a distinction between the situation of "native" Mexican Americans and Mexicans.[139] She argues that cheap wages had long been a problem for natives. In a section of the essay called "The Economic Conditions of the Labor Class of Mexico" she addresses the Mexican Revolution and her hope for the fulfillment of the revolution's promise in contemporary times. She says 100,000 "wetbacks" were on the border, at times 2,000 were being deported daily, and even skilled and semiskilled laborers were crossing without papers outside of the official Bracero Program.

In the essay Sloss-Vento assesses the impact on native Mexican American workers: "The result is that the native Mexican American workers [*sic*] is left to keep wandering from one place to another. This group is forced to close their homes in the Valley, take their children out of school and go north or west in search of work." She adds, "How cheap wages and the wetback affects the native workers, is one of the many harmful ways that our citizens and our communities are affected through the heavy influx of cheap labor. To deprive Americans of Mexican descent of decent wages, of the right standard of living, of an education and of health, is in my opinion un-American as well as unpatriotic; for Americans of Mexican descent are also the American citizens of the future."[140] She describes the impact on school-age children as well when "boys and girls are old enough to finish high school but are still in grammar school grades."[141] Because they were older they ended up dropping out of school.

She contends that the nature or quality of immigrants changed after the Bracero Program began: "Years back we used to get a few undocumented, mostly men, by this I mean, honest men who came to earn a few dollars and who almost all went back. This did not constitute a problem for anybody." That changed when "a large percent of undesirables" arrived. She asserts, "This problem is not only costing millions of dollars to our government and its citizens, but causing crimes, burglaries, broken homes, delinquency, more poverty, more ignorance, and more ill health."[142] In her view the immigration service lacked personnel and funds and Mexico should shoulder more of the burden: "But let Mexico solve its own problems within its own borders so that we can be able to solve ours here."[143] The Bracero Program of 1942 to 1964 stimulated a surge in unauthorized Mexican immigrants, and Sloss-Vento began to more vehemently call for protection of native Mexican American workers.

In 1947 Sloss-Vento sought to influence readers in Mexico with a letter to a Mexican newspaper that it published as "The Problem of Exploitation and Racial Hatred Can Have an Immediate Solution by Not Exporting Braceros to the State of Texas."[144] The same year the *Valley Evening Monitor* published her response to an editorial of a week earlier. Her letter is titled "Cheap Labor Does Not Pay in the Long Run."[145] In it she points out that farmers paid braceros twelve dollars a week when they should have been paying sixteen dollars for forty hours weekly, at forty cents an hour; she calls for a wage increase.[146] She references an article in the *McAllen Monitor* by Clarence La Roche titled "Billion Dollar Wetback" about bracero labor's profitability to Euro-Texan agribusiness. She criticizes the United States for spending money in Mexico to fight hoof and mouth disease and says instead the United States should help Mexicans get decent wages in Mexico.[147]

The exploitation of bracero labor was a key issue for Sloss-Vento. In 1947 in the *Harlingen Star* she criticizes the US chambers of commerce and discusses the problems that the Bracero Program created for Mexico: "We should worry because the wetback cheap labor is not only a threat to the economic welfare of our lower and middle classes, but also to our influential chambers of commerce. If the wetback would work as hard for himself in his own country . . . as he works for another in this country, he would be better off economically and spiritually."[148] In her book about Perales she recalls, "Some worked for 75 cents or a dollar a day. Later they were paid 20 cents an hour. In later years some earned $3.00 a day to operate a tractor. These were starvation wages."[149]

So while she did not want unauthorized Mexicans to enter the country, she still argued for their living wage and better conditions while they were working in the United States. In "Cheap Labor Does Not Pay" she gives attention also to the laborers and their families: "We cannot afford cheap labor. It does not pay in the long run. Cheap labor ruins the health of workers, of their wives and children. It deprives the children from obtaining an education."[150] She saw workers as men even if she herself worked for wages; she offers the example of a traditional male-headed family with a wife and children. She speaks of workers who had to choose between beans, potatoes, and flour tortillas and of a worker who lacked an extra pair of work pants. She calls for a minimum wage of forty cents an hour and says the United States should help the working class "who come to help us."[151]

Sloss-Vento witnessed the effects of the Bracero Program on both Mexican and Mexican American workers. In another letter she describes the impact of cheap Mexican labor on Mexican American workers: "This group is forced to leave homes in the Valley by the hundreds every year, to harvest the crops of the Northern states where they can get better wages."[152] She reasons, "There are plenty of farm labor citizens willing to work, but not for $2. Social evolution has to have a living wage."[153]

CONCLUSION

Sloss-Vento's published writings, correspondence, and manuscripts reveal her activist legacy beginning in the late 1920s and across the 1940s. She was a brave, high school–educated woman who spoke out on issues of concern to people of Mexican descent, often focusing on immigrants, laborers, and women. Her public writings express interest in the public good, especially the empowerment of Mexican American and Mexican-descent people in Texas regardless of citizenship.

Sloss-Vento's life and work paralleled the rise of the Mexican American civil rights movement in Texas in the 1920s. Just as she graduated from high school in her twenties, she began her activism as a friend of male Mexican American leaders and as a LULAC ally after 1929.

Sloss-Vento worked as an archivist, activist, and public intellectual. She maintained activist records beginning in the 1920s with newspaper clippings related to the Harlingen Convention of 1927. She sought to uplift South Texas Mexican Americans through LULAC and gave special attention to women's civic engagement. She advocated for Perales's legacy in the early 1930s, before historians or anyone else recognized his work. In the 1930s she sought to affect civic and educational practices in San Juan and Del Rio. The latter part of the 1930s she dedicated to her husband and children.

By the 1940s, Sloss-Vento began to more clearly draw distinctions between Mexicans and Mexican Americans due to the Bracero Program. Unable to stop the repercussions of the Bracero Program, she made distinctions between Mexico's interests and Mexican American interests. Yet, while casually referring to Mexicans as "aliens" and "wetbacks" (*mojados*), she still argued for the humanity and class interests of Mexican workers in the United States.

As a single woman in the early 1930s, Sloss provided rare critiques of women's oppression in the home. She criticized gendered double standards and Latino male privilege. She eventually followed traditional life-cycle patterns of heterosexual women—marriage and children—but she married a modern man to accept her modern ways of gendered selfhood too. Her husband accepted her activism, allowing her true happiness. She found her selfhood as an activist and writer.

Sloss-Vento was a feminist but did not challenge LULAC's homosociality or sexism. She argued against machismo in the home but was silent on machismo in LULAC and other Mexican American organizations. Criticism of sexism in LULAC was taken up instead by Alice Dickerson Montemayor of Laredo in the 1930s.

In the 1940s Sloss-Vento advocated for causes at the local, state, national, and international levels. She wrote numerous essays that were published in newspapers as opinion pieces and letters to the editor. She lobbied state legislators for laws to end racial discrimination. She wrote letters to governors concerning the Good Neighbor policy. She confronted all she disagreed with—governors in Austin and racist local Valley white women and men.

As a woman Sloss-Vento was an unlikely activist and public intellectual. Women were not initially allowed in LULAC, and when they were allowed, they were assigned membership in homosocial chapters. Sloss-Vento resisted prescribed gender ideology, as seen in her writings on machismo. And though she was a married, heterosexual woman in the late 1930s and beyond, she was not fully subordinated in the home. She bore the responsibility of children but managed her children and family so that she could take care of business.

Ironically, domesticity and the home proved Sloss-Vento's political space, where she could be an activist and public intellectual perhaps without the interference or disdain of men or ineffective, time-consuming organizations sometimes filled with difficult personalities. She did not have to rely on male leaders or organizations. Being a writer gave her independence that she could not have through organizational life, especially as a mother and wife. Moreover, LULAC's organizational life was not always supportive of women. Sloss-Vento was a feminist despite not typically working with women in organizations. She avoided membership in Ladies LULAC. As early as the late 1920s she began political relations with men, transcending gender boundaries and operating as a feminist public intellectual based at home.

CHAPTER 3

THE MEXICAN AMERICAN CIVIL RIGHTS MOVEMENT, 1950–1963

Adela Sloss-Vento continued her activism in the Mexican American civil rights movement in the 1950s and early 1960s. The anthropologist Jennifer Najera has pointed out that by the 1940s "inconsistencies and contradictions" had become characteristic of an "accommodated form of segregation" in the Valley.[1] In the 1950s there was still too little change. In 1949 Sloss-Vento began working as a jail matron at the Hidalgo County jail. She was forty-nine in 1950, and her children were nearing their teen years.

In the 1950s Sloss-Vento began advocating for more political representation by Mexican Americans. She wrote US and Mexican presidents to complain about the Bracero Program, and she worked against the program's abuses. She spent time confronting Mexican American male leaders who supported a racist academic study about "wetbacks."[2] She assisted women immigrants. She did all this despite the spastic colon and arthritic pain she experienced in this decade.[3]

In 1960 Sloss-Vento was fifty-nine. Alonso S. Perales died that year, and she began contemplating how his legacy would be documented and preserved. The rise of the Political Association of Spanish-Speaking Organizations (PASSO) followed its establishment in 1962 as a national effort to enhance Latino voting and political empowerment. She had no involvement with LULAC, the American G.I. Forum, or their desegregation legal cases in the decade. More Mexican-descent desegregation cases were being filed and with greater success. Nor was she tied to the American Council of Spanish-Speaking People,[4] the first national civil rights campaign to benefit Latinos as a group that was funded by philanthropic Euro-Americans, specifically the Marshall Trust Fund of New York.

THE 1950S

The Bracero Program

Sloss-Vento opposed the binational Bracero Program that brought contract laborers, mostly men, from Mexico into the United States. The program was a major issue in the post–World War II era. Four million Mexicans crossed the US-Mexico border into Texas and other states through the program. Sloss-Vento's concern was threefold: the exploitation of braceros who were paid below minimum wages, displacement of Valley Mexican American farmworkers, and exploitation of Mexico, which lost workers. She was not anti-Mexican but saw the Bracero Program as another ploy to further exploit Mexican-descent labor. Indeed, organized labor and Mexican American civil rights organizations like LULAC and the American G.I. Forum were *not* invited to negotiations by the United States and Mexico to plan the program. And there was no Mexican American or Latino legal rights organization like the Mexican American Legal Defense and Education Fund, which was founded in the late 1960s and would have provided a Latino and pro-worker perspective on the agreement. In other words, only state actors—governments—were allowed in the negotiations, and it was US agribusiness and other industries, not workers, that benefited.

The 1940s and 1950s complicated relations between Mexican Americans and Mexican immigrants entering the United States. Sloss-Vento's ideas illustrate this evolving and contradictory relationship. While Sloss-Vento typically included Mexican immigrants as part of the political, cultural, and social family of Mexican descent, with the authorization of the Bracero Program from 1942 to 1964, intraethnic dynamics changed, and she made greater distinctions within the political family. In her view the presence of Mexican immigrant laborers, both officially and legally in the United States as braceros and those who were unauthorized, compromised Mexican Americans' status as workers. Sloss-Vento was not anti-Mexican, but she was not entirely pro–undocumented immigrant either. While sympathetic to the exploitation of Mexicans and understanding of their humanity, she also condemned the effects of braceros on the Mexican American community.

The historian Lori Flores has shown that in California, especially in the Salinas Valley, Mexican Americans held walls and mirrors between themselves and Mexican immigrants.[5] She notes,

> Mexican Americans in agricultural regions experienced particularly complex relationships with Mexican immigrants that negatively affected the

> way both groups were treated by the wider public. . . . Wary of braceros and undocumented migrants as labor competition, Mexican Americans grew more resentful when white Americans and immigration authorities targeted them as "foreign" too and challenged their identities and rights as US citizens. Braceros found themselves in a liminal space as unprotected subjects of both their home and receiving countries and sought rights as guest workers with little support from the Mexican Americans around them.[6]

Laura Garza, examining Sloss-Vento's work, suggests that she saw braceros "como invasión mexicana" (like a Mexican invasion) and thought they should return home. Garza finds that the braceros did not belong to Sloss-Vento's concept of nation.[7] Yet, I will note that Sloss-Vento still included them in her concept of a larger community of Mexican descent, La Raza.

Mexican American farmworker migration concerned Sloss-Vento as well. Mexican Americans had to remove their children from school and move to California, Illinois, Michigan, and Oregon. "Mexican-Americans were converted into nomads," she laments.[8] The Tejano diaspora of farmworkers leaving for the Midwest and other regions dated back to the 1920s, and it was amplified in the 1950s with the Bracero Program. The resulting high rate of school dropouts did not foster a future middle class and created an underclass. And a Mexican newspaper reported that Mexico was losing its skilled and semiskilled workers needed for Mexico's economic development.[9] Sloss-Vento cared about the program's impact on Mexico.

Sloss-Vento sought to influence political appointments over bracero issues. Citing his racist remarks and class interests, she tried to void the appointment of James D. Griffin of Mission, Texas, as assistant commissioner of immigration or adviser to the US secretary of labor. In a letter she reports his racist commentary to US Secretary of Labor Martin Durkin and then tells Fidel Velázquez of Mexico's labor union Confederación Obrera Mexicana, "Griffin is also a farmer and naturally he benefits from the slavery of Mexicans on the border."[10] She calls for employer sanctions from Congress "punishing with imprisonment or by paying a heavy penalty to those who keep hiring illegal wetbacks."[11] This was an early call for employer sanctions. She too would use the derogatory language of the day though she still had the interests of "illegal wetbacks" in mind.

Other progressive Mexican Americans had similar concerns. George I. Sánchez, a past LULAC president and University of Texas at Austin educator, referred to "wetbacks" as a "serious problem" and noted that "Spanish-speaking Texans" were being affected.[12] Henry Muñoz of the American Federation of Labor–Congress of Industrial Organizations (AFL-CIO) and the Department of Equal Opportunity in Texas asked why 195,000 braceros were imported when 4,846,000 US workers were unemployed in 1963.[13] The attorney and LULAC member Gus García of San Antonio asked why "thousands upon thousands of South Texas families will continue to be uprooted year after year from their homes and forced to wander about the country, seeking a living or at least a subsistence wage."[14]

The historian Carlos Blanton suggests that Mexican American activists would "sacrifice immigrant sisters and brothers" by opposing the Bracero Program.[15] But the activists were not self-interested or seeking only to benefit Mexican Americans; they cared about immigrants who were part of their larger community. Agribusiness and other capitalists in collusion with the federal government created worker competition and displacement. Braceros benefited minimally, and poor Mexican American workers were displaced. But for braceros the work could have meant the difference between eating and not eating. The 1954 report "What Price Wetback?" by the American G.I. Forum and Texas State Federation of Labor showed that braceros displaced US workers.[16] Bracero Program critics were not blaming braceros but instead pointed to the helplessness of Mexican American workers also victimized by agribusiness and the US government.

Sloss-Vento condemned the Bracero Program in letters to Presidents Truman and Eisenhower.[17] She sent the Republican Eisenhower two articles about the "harmful wetback problem" in the Valley that was causing "exploitation and slavery." In a letter to Eisenhower she advises,

> The best solution . . . is to extend help to Mexico, but that this help be within Mexico's own border. Help for example, in the form of farm machinery, seed, finding markets for the products of Mexico, etc. Another solution is to pass a law to punish those who hire illegals. . . . Another solution is to not to make more bracero contracts for Mexico needs all of its workers at home to develop agriculture and other resources to solve the economic problem of the poor class.[18]

Beyond offering this advice to the US president she suggests employer sanctions for hiring "illegals," yet another derogatory word she used. Operation Wetback entailed the removal of some unauthorized immigrants by the US government in 1954.[19]

In other writings Sloss-Vento denounces low wages paid to braceros and calls for the United States to do more for Mexico: "As good neighbors we should extend help [to] Mexico to solve the economic problem of the poor working class, but this problem must be solved within Mexico's own border."[20]

She writes US Secretary of Labor Martin D. Durkin and suggests punishing employers and hiring US citizens instead.[21] The Mexican consul in McAllen reported that 40 percent of braceros in 1955 were not paid minimum wage.[22]

Perales congratulated her for "having sent valuable information on the subject to President Eisenhower."[23] Perales sent her copies of letters he wrote about braceros. He also suggested that she work with the National Council for Catholic Women, reiterating his belief that women should work along homosocial lines as well as biracially, perhaps as a strategic measure to influence church officials.[24]

Sloss-Vento did attempt to influence church officials about braceros in 1953. She wrote to the liberal Archbishop Robert Lucey and the Bishops Committee for the Spanish-Speaking in Austin to explain her regular contact with immigrants. A Mexican journalist informed her that there were five million braceros out of work. She said farmers, politicians, saloon operators, and packing sheds benefited from them as laborers and customers. *Cantineras* (barmaids) and prostitutes were also among them, women whose work she did not approve. Employment issues needed to "be solved within Mexico's own borders." She suggested fining employers and hiring more Immigration and Naturalization Service employees. She noted that this was owed to "our Communities, to Mexico, to the wetback themselves and to their families."[25] In 1954 she sent Lucey some of her antibracero essays; he passed them to Texas State Representative Madden so he might oppose "Southern Growers and the Texas Congressmen."[26]

Criticizing "the Wetback Pamphlet"

"Wetback" was a new derogatory term for unauthorized Mexican immigrants in the 1950s. The US government popularized the term when it began Operation Wetback and saturated the US media with the slur. Sloss-Vento used the term casually without second thought. However, as a Mexican American she had respect for Mexicans; she considered them her co-nationalists as part of one race. Though she called immigrants "espaldas mojados" (wetbacks) and "illegals," she also called them "nuestros hermanos de raza" (our raza brethren). At the same time, she realized that the Bracero Program had harmful effects on Mexican American workers. Living on the frontera she saw labor exploitation daily, and as a jail matron she had extensive contact with braceros and unauthorized immigrants. She saw braceros in the United States as a problem for Mexico as well.

In the early 1950s Sloss-Vento condemned a University of Texas publication on braceros. Professor George Sánchez oversaw the publication of a study about them in South Texas and wrote the foreword. Written by two Euro-American social scientists, Lyle Saunders and Olen Leonard, the report was also called "The Wetback in the Lower Rio Grande Valley of Texas" or "the wetback pamphlet."[27] The study entailed a social science investigation and interviews with Euro-Texans from Cameron, Hidalgo, and Willacy Counties in the Valley. The title was racist, and many comments were racist but made anonymously and protected by social science methods. One Euro-Texan interviewee declared, "About eighty percent of them have lice in their hair, the women especially, they believe that lice helps them to have babies."[28] Blanton notes that Perales considered the report "racist and insulting" but Sánchez did not.[29] Critics accepted the interviewees' views as false. Perhaps a different title, a better editing job, or intermittent commentary by Sánchez condemning unacceptable racist and sexist comments might have solved the controversy. Its publication by a university press validated racist insults purported as social science and truth. The University of Texas itself in the 1950s had done nothing beneficial for Latinxs, though they were not excluded like African Americans, who could not attend until the 1950s.[30]

Perhaps the most offensive aspect of the ninety-two-page booklet were the anonymous interviews, such as one with a Texas legislator whose quotes include "the local Spanish-speaking people have a gypsy spirit which makes them want to travel"; "the local Spanish-speaking people. . . . They don't like the hard work."[31] He thus rationalized Tejano migration and the need for braceros. Another interviewee referred to Mexicans as "dirty," and one said Mexicans were "lazy." The interviewees reiterated the same traits ascribed to causing "the Mexican problem" of the 1920s.

Mexican American leaders disagreed as to whether the report should have been published. Members at a Texas regional LULAC convention and the American G.I. Forum supported Sánchez, but other community members, among them Sloss-Vento, organized against the pamphlet.[32] Even the English-language press reported on disagreements among leaders. An article in the *San Antonio Light* reports that the forum leader Ed Idar Jr., the son of the LULAC cofounder Eduardo Idar, criticized Perales: "His Committee of One Hundred is a dissident group organized by himself when he could not convince other Latin-American organizations to follow some outdated ideas on what is best for the group."[33] Sloss-Vento, in a moment of paranoia or anticommunist hysteria, wrote Perales wondering, "Don't you think that the authors of that pamphlet are behind something more than racial hatred? What did our friends want—To aggravate Mexico so it joins Stalin?"[34] Sloss-Vento approved of a letter Estella Pérez Contreras, Perales's sister-in-law, wrote to Sánchez condemning the study and his disagreement with Perales; Sloss-Vento called her letter "magnificent."[35]

What was Sloss-Vento's role in campaigning against the pamphlet? She was an organizer and documentarian of a protest event. LULAC founder J. Luz Sáenz came to see her in early January 1951 about a response to its publication.[36] They organized a meeting to inform the community of the pamphlet.[37] She wrote to Perales that she was ready to distribute flyers across the Valley or provide money to Sáenz for the flyers.[38] She sent Sáenz a list of twenty-two people from Edinburg, San Juan, and Mission, including her mother, Roberto Austin of Mission, and Mrs. Leo James of La Joya.[39] Sloss-Vento helped with money and publicity.

On March 9, 1952, Sloss-Vento joined more than three hundred community members from San Antonio, Alice, Corpus Christi, San Angelo, and Valley towns at a conference in Mission in Hidalgo County to condemn the pamphlet.[40] Sáenz encouraged her to "go and raise the spirit of our element."[41] Roberto Austin told her, "We know that we can always count on Doña Josefa Ortiz de Domínguez," a reference to a hero of Mexico's independence movement.[42] Canales, Sáenz, Santos de la Paz, Manuel de la Garza, Conrado Rodríguez, Máximo Guerrero, Raúl Vela, and Mrs. Francisco P. Lozano of Raymondville, another of Perales's sisters-in-law, spoke at the event; Sloss-Vento did not.[43] Lozano was the only woman speaker.

Sloss-Vento recorded the conference proceedings. Her son recalls, "Sometimes, activist Sloss-Vento would imitate a journalist covering an event."[44] She did indeed document the event; her audio recording is archived with the J. T. Canales Papers at Texas A&M University in Kingsville.[45] In her records is her 1959 note saying, "Mrs. Adela S. de Vento tape recorded the eloquent speech by Lic. Canales."[46] Perhaps she believed it necessary to record the LULAC founder Canales's speech as significant to history. Or did she plan to share the speech over the radio? Evidently she downplayed her own potential contribution at the meeting and chose not to speak.

Sloss-Vento's book on Perales is the best documentation of the Mission conference. The conference produced the "Report Adopted by the Latin American Convention, held at Mission, Texas, March 9, 1952," written by Perales, Sáenz, Canales, and others but signed by Santos de la Paz, Roberto Austin, Luis Alvarado, and O. T. Salinas.[47] On March 15 Sáenz wrote to University of Texas Chancellor James P. Hart to condemn the study; university officials apologized and promised not to repeat the offense.[48] Canales, a powerful former legislator and a philanthropist, probably contacted Chancellor Hart as well. Sloss discusses the event in her book and includes responses by activists, some of them critical of Sánchez. She asserts, "Contempt by our people toward Dr. Sánchez was justified."[49]

Blanton has documented conflict between Perales and Sánchez but apparently was unaware of Sloss-Vento's involvement. Perales did not attend the mass meeting but wrote Sánchez of his disgust for the report and demanded that Sánchez give him the names of the racists who were interviewed, especially the Texas legislator. "I want their names so I can sue them for libel so they can learn to respect the Mexican," Perales explains to Sloss-Vento. Sánchez replied with a "cynical and disrespectful response."[50] Perales wrote to Sloss-Vento that Sánchez, Héctor García of the American G.I. Forum, and the attorney Gus García disagreed with him. Perales said the issue was that Sánchez would not name the sources of racist comments, perhaps because of scholarly anonymity.

Sloss-Vento entered the debate to reconcile the Perales and Sánchez camps' differences. She also sought to influence García. In a letter in December 1951 she tells García that he made a mistake in selecting Sánchez to supervise the immigrant study.[51] She reiterates her position about a week later. Always courteous and civil, not servile, she says that she did not mean to offend García and states, "Again, I repeat, I am at your service as a friend and servant."[52] She was a respectful comrade trying to foster unity among male leaders. As a woman she was not afraid to speak her mind and enter the fray among men.

Sloss-Vento also defended braceras and Mexican immigrant women against the publication's racist and sexist depictions, as in this letter to Héctor García:

> I assure you the female wetbacks that are brought to the jail because they crossed illegally are not dirty but clean. They are given soap and towels and they bathe every day. They wash their clothes every day. Female wetbacks including the lost ones know how to sew and embroider the best. They also pray every night. In contrast, the White Trash prisoners are the grossest there are in the entire world. They stink horribly and these do refuse to bathe. And apart from being lost, they don't know how to do anything.[53]

While she expresses a racial and class bias against poor white women, she bravely defends Mexican immigrant women accused of being dirty and full of lice and portrays them as resourceful in gendered tasks. She was the only person to address the study's sexism.

Sloss-Vento wrote to García five days later, perhaps sensing that she may have offended him. She praises him for his unselfish work in the betterment of "nuestro pueblo" (our people). She recognizes his sincere leadership along with that of Perales, Sáenz, Canales, and García. And she praises God for the love God gave him and says, "That great love God has put in the hearts of men like you is part of God's love."[54]

The idealistic Sloss-Vento sought a united front. She wrote Perales that Santos de la Paz, an editor of the Corpus Christi newspaper *La Verdad*, had attacked Sánchez and Idar Jr. She tells Perales, "I responded asking him for peace and because I think there should be harmony between our leaders. . . . Because some [of] our leaders are great and they don't agree with us we ask for an explanation. In my opinion we need an explanation in the free press and in the four winds."[55]

In March 1952 Sloss-Vento responds to the "wetback pamphlet":

> Latin Americans . . . have been exploited for generations. . . . Now, the Anglos of the Valley have the wetbacks to exploit. . . . To call the Mexicans who are our neighbors and friends dirty and cowards in order to illustrate the poverty and living conditions of the wetbacks in the Lower Valley of Texas, is really good ammunition for our enemies, and for those who seek disunity between the people of the Americas. . . . No worker or Mexican is dirty. . . . [M]any of the Anglos of the Valley have grown rich by exploiting both Mexican-American workers and wetbacks. For further proof some of the Anglos of the Valley and some of our Texas politicos in Washington are always ready to oppose any bill that tends to pay better wages in the Valley, or that will punish by law those who keep hiring illegal wetbacks.[56]

The letter appeared in *La Prensa* around March 20, 1952.[57] Sáenz had written a similar letter that was published on November 29, 1951.[58] Even the American G.I. Forum's board of directors eventually passed a resolution for the "elimination of the offensive, anonymous interviews" from the pamphlet.[59]

Well after the pamphlet debacle, Sloss-Vento was still arguing for unity. In 1953 in the manuscript "El precio de la desunión" (The price of disunion) she laments the failure to unite major Mexican American civil rights organizations and the Texas legislature's failure to pass House Bill 909. She calls for unity between the American G.I. Forum and LULAC and likely between Perales versus Sánchez, Héctor García, Idar Jr., and Gus García.[60] She warns that Mexican-descent people and their children, the new generations, would continue to experience injustices until there was a united front. Perales ran her essay in his column in *La Prensa*, "Arquitectos de nuestros propios destinos" (Architects of our own destiny).

Assisting Women Immigrants

Because Sloss-Vento and her husband worked at the Hidalgo County jail she had regular contact with numerous braceros and Mexican immigrants both male and female. In her 1940 manuscript "The Hidalgo County Jail" she observes that the jail was headed by a "conscious and caring Mexican American,"[61] her husband, and she likens it to an orphanage because of its care, cleanliness, order, and equality. Indeed, her son recalls, music entertained inmates, and on Christmas mass was held and tamales and cold drinks were served.[62] She praises incarcerated immigrants: "They almost always act appropriately and when treated right they act even better." She addresses their working-class status and humanity and does not blame them for US problems. She suggests, "We have various problems which impeded our improvement in Texas[,] and when Mexico's working class resolves its problems . . . we can become a united front and solve the problems that affect us."[63] Thus she speaks as a Tejana, Mexican American, borderlander/fronteriza about Mexico and the need for that nation to improve itself.

Sloss-Vento singled out women immigrants for assistance as well.[64] She reports helping penniless, deported, immigrant women and asks, "What could I do? I gave them the funds so they could return to their families." A twenty-year-old barmaid was deported without a peso. Sloss-Vento says, "I did not have the heart to see a near cadaver without funds return to Mexico. I gave her the funds to return home." She concludes, "I have many letters from Mexican mothers who have thanked me."[65] The letters are not in her archive, perhaps suggesting she did not feel the need to document her own generosity.

Sloss-Vento especially cried out for recognition of braceros' humanity. A bracero arrived at her home asking for help since he had no car and his dead child's body needed to be taken to the cemetery. She writes to Perales, "I immediately went and offered my services."[66] She also told Perales that she sent the US secretary of state a letter about a bracero family who were killed in a fire in a shack provided by their employer.[67]

THE 1960S

Perales's Death

Perales died on May 9, 1960, and thereafter, Sloss-Vento had a new mission: to preserve his archive and promote his legacy. She wrote a letter to *La Prensa* about his death, "To Attorney Alonso S. Perales, Defender of Justice and Racial Dignity."[68] In her book Sloss-Vento attests to her enduring admiration for him: "Once again Perales remarked that I was his loyal friend, and whenever someone would say anything against him, I was always there to defend him. And so it was. Who was I to deserve such friendship in view of his dedication during his life time to sacrificing for our welfare, justice and rights?"[69] He was her hero as the most important Mexican American civil rights leader in Texas before World War II.

Sloss-Vento promoted his legacy toward the waning of the Mexican American civil rights movement and during the Chicano movement into the 1970s. In 1961 she penned yet another essay about Perales for *La Prensa* on April 21.[70] It followed one by Luis Alvarado, J. Luz Sáenz's son-in-law. Alvarado wrote "LULAC Landmark of Progress," an early attempt to summarize the history of LULAC's beginnings; he highlights Perales as its major founder.[71] Alvarado was the first LULAC member to bring attention to Perales as its principal founder.

In 1960 Sloss-Vento and/or Alvarado began an effort to honor Perales's legacy with a monument, the Pro-Monumento Alonso S. Perales. In January 1961 Alvarado told Sloss-Vento that San Antonio LULAC councils were using the league for political aggrandizement and were "not concerned with projects such as ours."[72] In May 1961 she joined his campaign to raise funds for the monument. She asked Fortino Treviño of Alice to find ten supporters to donate one hundred dollars each, adding that she would be the first.[73] But the effort failed. She must not have been able to collect one thousand dollars. So she urged the Alice school board to make a "movement toward the erecting of a monument in memory of Alonso S. Perales" since he was born there. But townspeople of Alice ultimately expressed little appreciation or knowledge of him. Her response to the school board president there was that the monument should be placed in San Antonio and "not in the little ungrateful town of Alice, Texas."[74] Not enough people were familiar with his significance, and the school board there was still controlled by European Americans.

Another effort by Sloss-Vento to preserve Perales's legacy was to find a way to keep his archives safe. As an attorney with numerous cases, a civil rights activist who wrote many letters, a columnist with years of newspaper clippings, and a diplomat with official correspondence, Perales had filing cabinets and boxes in the house and a garage full of materials. Sloss-Vento asked his wife to preserve his writings with the ultimate goal of creating scrapbooks and a biography. Three days after Alonso S. Perales died, Sloss-Vento wrote to Marta Perales with this plea: "Martita, I want to ask you for a favor. Don't lose Lic. Perales' writings, newspaper clippings or the rest of his archives. Please gather everything and don't lose anything. Let Father

García and Mr. Alvarado help you put them together and if you like I can help put them in scrapbooks for posterity."[75] She told her that Perales had promised to send her all his archives so she could put them in scrapbooks. She also wrote to enlist Alvarado: "Mr. Alvarado, please do what you can so the archives of Lic. Perales's works are not lost. It is best to preserve them for posterity."[76]

Sloss-Vento had cause for concern about care of the Perales archive, but it would have taken a lifetime to place his documents in scrapbooks. Reportedly, on his deathbed, Alonso S. Perales's preoccupation was his archives, and he cried from worry about their fate.[77] At the time he died in 1960, major university libraries were not seeking to preserve Mexican American history. Marta Perales died in 2000, but the University of Houston acquired the Perales family papers only in 2009.[78]

Political Association of Spanish-Speaking Organizations

The Mexican American civil rights movement was still alive in 1960 but new electoral efforts to maximize national Latinx political clout arose, among them Viva Kennedy clubs and PASSO. Both were new national efforts seeking to exercise Latinx political power with presidential candidates and elect more Latino officials. Viva Kennedy worked to activate Latinos to vote for the presidential candidate John F. Kennedy.[79] Sloss-Vento's archive provides no evidence of involvement in Viva Kennedy, though she did indeed support the Kennedys.

Conceptualized by Héctor Sánchez, PASSO was founded in 1962.[80] Sloss-Vento's support is evident in her response to an opinion piece in the *Houston Chronicle*'s *Texas* magazine on April 12, 1964. In it Ella K. Dagget Stumpf, an ultraconservative from San Antonio and member of the Daughters of the Republic of Texas, writes that "Latins" were "second class citizens and for the most part, voluntary illiterates who just don't want to improve themselves."[81] In the piece Stumpf also opposes the end of the poll tax and attacks the liberal politician Henry B. González and the PASSO president and attorney Albert Peña Jr., both of San Antonio. González was elected to the Texas legislature in 1956 and the US Congress in 1961. Voter registration efforts by LULAC and the American G.I. Forum, men and women, were finally paying off by the 1950s and 1960s. Peña was elected to the Bexar County Commission in 1956 as a progressive Democrat.[82]

Sloss-Vento sent her response to the *Chronicle* and wrote Peña a letter of support.[83] In her letter published in *Texas* magazine, she supports PASSO and calls Stumpf "stupid and insulting." On depriving Latin American people from voting Sloss-Vento retorts, "What a laugh! Mrs. Stumpf forgets that she is not living in Russia but this great Country of ours. . . . In many of our Valley Counties we have half or more than half of the voters. And it is our privilege to vote and elect whoever represents us better." She ends the letter, "It's people as Mrs. Stumpf that makes this Country look small and un-democratic before the eyes of the Americas and of the world."[84]

CONCLUSION

Sloss-Vento emerged even bolder than before in the 1950s and early 1960s. Despite tending to the family home, raising children, attending to her husband, participating in her church, and working as a jail matron after 1949, she advanced her political and intellectual life project. More brazen by the 1950s, she contacted presidents of the United States and Mexico about the Bracero Program. She called for Mexico's sovereignty but suggested that Mexico needed to concern itself with its working class. She sought to stop the bracero flow because the Mexican American working class could not compete with the cheaper, exploited, contracted or uncontracted, Mexican labor.

In this decade Sloss-Vento joined hundreds of others in protesting the publication of a booklet full of racist and sexist statements edited by university professors and published by the University of Texas. In effect the pamphlet condoned white Texans' racist and sexist sentiments. She even challenged George I. Sánchez and Héctor García, Mexican American civil rights leaders associated with the University of Texas and the American G.I. Forum. She defended braceras and Mexican immigrant women as clean and resourceful.

Sloss-Vento expressed her Mexican Americanism in distinguishing the native community from Mexican immigrants. While acknowledging the ties between these "hermanos de raza," she privileged Mexican Americans. She casually used the terms "wetback," "alien," and "illegal" but nonetheless promoted humane treatment of all and fought against labor exploitation. She continued to include Mexican immigrants as part of her Raza nation, and she treated immigrants with compassion.

Sloss-Vento began her mission to preserve Alonso S. Perales's legacy. She not only praised him for decades but also defended him when he was under criticism and attack by other Mexican American leaders. She proved to be a true ally. She wrote about him, and she tried to raise funds for a monument to honor him and more importantly, to save his archives.

Sloss-Vento supported PASSO as an overt effort by Latinxs to assert their racial political authority in electoral politics. Ironically, it was in the 1950s, the era long associated with US women's domesticity and passivity, that she grew bolder. Like numerous African American women in the African American civil rights movement in the same decade, she too waged war on inequality. Writing out of her home, she continued to use the pen as her machete in the comforts of US women's domesticity.[85]

CHAPTER 4

THE CHICANO MOVEMENT OF 1963–1978 AND BEYOND

By the early 1960s the Mexican American civil rights movement in Texas was waning and the Chicano movement was emerging. The historian Mario T. García explains that the Chicano movement "was the continuation of a longer civil rights movement, led initially by . . . the Mexican American Generation of the 1930s through the 1950s that initiated the first major civil rights movement by Mexican Americans in the United States."[1] But since the work to end a racialized class system was incomplete, the next cohort of activists took up the task. The new movement was led by youth fueled by rising expectations and more education and motivated by ideologies of anticolonialism and self-determination.

The Chicano movement in Texas lasted from 1963 to 1978. It began in Crystal City with a major electoral victory by Mexican Americans in the town and died by 1978 with liberalism in decline and Republican ascendance. In Texas and elsewhere, the movement was focused on the political empowerment of La Raza. The historians Juan Gómez-Quiñones and Irene Vásquez have listed the Chicano movement's goals as

> realization of human potential within the community through enhanced education, in particular that of women; maximization of organizations within the community, particularly of women; increased registration and education of voters; enhancement of the legal status of immigrant worker populations; enhanced trade union organization and labor leadership; civic political education and a culturally based project; increased political resources and improved skills of electoral leadership; increased political outreach to select occupational, income, and educational sectors; Spanish-language inclusion in civic matters and promotion of Spanish-language communication materials; and pan-Latino cooperation by

> organizations and their leadership on specific issues and those that drew on interethnic support.[2]

Sloss-Vento welcomed these initiatives, ideas, and tactics.

The Chicano movement involved a renaming and rebranding of the Mexican American people that Sloss-Vento readily supported. The term "Chicano" was itself controversial among older folks, the Mexican American generation, as well as those who were not happy with emerging radical efforts by youth.[3] She was not angered or alienated by the movement but still preferred to call herself an American of Mexican descent rather than a Chicana. In an essay about the terms "Chicano" and "Mexican American," she begins, "To many, the cultural name of Chicano has been disturbing."[4] Of the Chicano movement she says,

> In my opinion it is still a movement of Mexican Americans, American citizens of Mexican descent, Latino descent, Indian and Spanish descent. . . . [W]hat is important is that we are involved. . . . [T]he twenty-one Latin American countries will benefit from this accomplishment and recognition. Our country and our democracy would be enriched by said accomplishment, for greater understanding, friendship, and peace will prevail in the future of the Western Hemisphere.[5]

Here she embraces the multiethnic, multinational aspect of Latino identity and does not even mention whiteness; she also continues to express a hemispheric consciousness tied to Latin America.

Sloss-Vento supported a wide array of causes associated with the Chicano movement—causes championed by labor, youth, students, women, and nationalists. She praised the national leader César Chávez and the United Farm Worker movement in fighting labor exploitation. She supported a high school student protest and walkout in the Valley. She supported the Raza Unida Party (RUP), an alternative to the Republican and Democratic Parties, both controlled by Euro-Texans. She advanced the cultural nationalism of the Chicano movement by advocating for the Spanish language, bilingualism, and the teaching of Chicano history. She continued to promote the legacy of Alonso S. Perales and J. Luz Sáenz, now potential subjects for the emerging field of Chicano history. And she supported the women's movement and young Chicana feminists like me.

At the same time, Sloss-Vento did not comment on other major issues associated with the 1960s and 1970s. She was silent on Vietnam, with the exception of mentioning courageous and loyal Latin American soldiers,[6] and on the African American civil rights movement and gay and lesbian rights. Sloss-Vento limited herself in the 1980s. She retired in 1970 after twenty years of working as a jail matron, but she still wrote until 1990.[7] In her eighties she suffered from osteoporosis and cataracts, and in 1985 she fell, broke her hip, and had a hip replacement that was a "complete failure."[8] In 1990 she wrote her last political letter.

THE 1960S

The Raza Unida Party

By 1963 the first evidence of the Chicano movement appeared in Texas in Crystal City over the election of Mexican American candidates. This would eventually lead to the development of the RUP in the late 1960s. It was formed to seek out and elect Mexican Americans and end their racial exclusion in Texas party politics.[9] In 1967 there were only ten Tejanos, all men, in the Texas legislature, nine in the House and one in the Senate.[10]

The Elsa-Edcouch Chicano Student Walkout of 1967

The Chicano movement was one of resistance by youth and their willingness to use new tactics such as student walkouts. In Texas walkouts occurred in San Antonio, Kingsville, and Elsa-Edcouch in the Valley. In 1967 Elsa-Edcouch students protested a curriculum that excluded Mexican Americans. Sloss-Vento identified with Chicanos and Chicanas as radical youth. Speaking specifically about the walkout and students' demand for the teaching of Chicano and Mexican history, she praised protesters and argued that student rebels should be "complimented, instead of persecuted."[11]

Sloss-Vento wrote a letter published in the *McAllen Monitor* in November 1968 congratulating the civil rights leader and American G.I. Forum leader Héctor P. García and the attorneys and investigators who defended student protesters. She says students

> protested against discrimination for speaking Spanish on the campus, as well as for their demands, to have a course taught in said schools relating to the contributions of Mexican and Mexican Americans in the state and region, including factual account of the history of the Southwest and culture and history of Mexico, etc. . . . There is no harm in this kind of knowledge. This kind of knowledge will bring unity and understanding not only among ourselves, but also among the countries of Latin America.[12]

One of Sloss-Vento's undated manuscripts voices key components of Chicano movement ideology:

> We need to produce more educators, doctors, lawyers, writers, newspaper editors, etc. Politically, we need to elect representatives that will extend justice and representation to the Mexican-American people. We need more patriotic lawyers that could form a Committee to defend Mexican-Americans. That city, county, judges and federal representatives be elected or appointed with the condition that they will represent the people of Mexican descent with justice and impartiality. It is time to say as the new generations of the present Movimiento of Mexican-Americans have said, Basta! Enough is enough! We must never permit that our people be abused and crucified as in the past.[13]

Sloss-Vento was not saying anything new; her themes during the Chicano movement were the same as in the Mexican American civil rights movement. She had participated in the original movement that emerged in the 1920s.

Promoting Perales's Legacy

Perales died in 1960, and by the late 1960s many people had forgotten about him or had never become familiar with his contributions. And there was still no monument honoring him or book about him. Sloss-Vento wrote a letter to the editor of the *San Antonio Express* that the newspaper published in September 1969 as "Monument for Perales."[14] The *Alice Echo* ran an article the same month about a petition drive to name the high school after Perales.[15] Nonetheless, Perales's legacy remained unappreciated and undocumented.

By the mid-1960s LULAC initiated a LULAC Week to celebrate its history. That history was mostly unwritten except for articles in *LULAC News* written by members and a master's thesis in 1951 by Edward Garza that sat on a college library shelf.[16] Chicano history was emerging as a new field, and there were not yet any LULAC archives at any major university in the country. Sloss-Vento knew some of its history after 1927. On February 20, 1968, she wrote to the *McAllen Evening Monitor* during LULAC Week to correct an article that credited J. T. Canales and J. Luz Sáenz as LULAC founders but omitted Perales.[17] She began to revise the narrative.

In 1969 an effort was begun to name a high school after Perales in Alice. In September 1969 Sloss-Vento wrote to the school board to get a school named after him.[18] However, someone else introduced the name of the Euro-Texan Southwestern writer J. Frank Dobie, who had attended high school there.[19] The school was not named for Perales. Finally, in San Antonio—not Alice—the name of Edgewood Elementary School was changed to Alonso S. Perales Elementary School. Sloss-Vento thanked the school officials.[20]

THE 1970S

The full force of the Chicano movement arrived in Texas in the 1970s. Sloss-Vento was excited about the prospects of the movement she referred to as "la Causa" (the cause).[21] She admired the work of César Chávez of the United Farm Workers and Antonio Orendain of the Texas Farm Workers Union. She praised a Chicano political organization in Rio Grande City near the Valley and advocated for Chicano cultural nationalism. She wrote about immigration, which surged in the 1970s. She expressed a more conservative position by that time compared to her call for employer sanctions in the 1950s.

The Chicano movement's goal of better representation of Mexican Americans in education, the professions, and in elected positions was in keeping with Sloss-Vento's early goals in the Mexican American civil rights movement. In 1978 she notes, "We must keep urging our people to complish [*sic*] all the education possible." She calls for "more educators, doctors, lawyers, writers, newspapers [*sic*] editors, etc. Politically, we need to elect representatives that will extend justice and representation to the Mexican-American people. We need more patriotic lawyers that could form a Committee to defend Mexican-Americans."[22] She called for pro-Raza lawyers; apparently she was unaware of the Mexican American Legal Defense and Education Fund, which was founded in 1968 in San Antonio.[23] LULAC and the American G.I. Forum attorneys like Perales, Canales, Gonzales, Gus García, Carlos Cadena, and Albert Peña Jr. acted in this capacity before 1968.

While continuing her work as a public intellectual and activist, Sloss-Vento mainly focused in the 1970s on preserving Perales's memory. But now, instead of establishing a monument or revising LULAC history, she decided she needed to write his biography herself. She also decided to help a young, Chicana, undergraduate student in history—me—to write his history connected to LULAC.

Farmworkers and the Rio Grande City Melon Strike

A Chicano political empowerment organization in Rio Grande City, México-Americanos para Acción Social (Mexican Americans for Social Action), called a strike in 1970. Four hundred strikers were protesting their pay of 40 to 85 cents an hour that should have been $1.25, substandard housing, and illegal working conditions.[24] The strike and the organization gained Sloss-Vento's favor, as she expresses in a letter to its "Estimados hermanos de nuestra Causa" (Dear brothers of our Cause):

> First, I warmly congratulate you for the brave initiators of the "strike" so that one day our progress and well-being will be possible with decent wages in our Democracy. We have to keep fighting to end all that impedes our well-being and progress: the injustices, starving wages, racial discrimination. Politically, we should unite against self-interested politicians who once in office could care less about the suffering Latin America people. I admire the present youth movement and the well-qualified who fight for our organization the solution to our social, economic, and political problems.[25]

Since the early 1960s César Chávez had been fighting for the rights of farmworkers to unionize and receive minimum wage. In 1972 Sloss-Vento wrote a letter to the editor of the *McAllen Evening Monitor* on his behalf after a critic suggested that Chávez was "trying to degrade all Mexicans as well as Anglos." Sloss-Vento responds, "When citizens as Mr. Chávez are interested in the welfare and advancement of American workers, he is an American doing his share in making the principles of democracy work. He is making the great American dream come true under our democracy."[26] She sent a copy of this letter to Chávez, told him how Perales's activism harmed his health, and asked Chávez to avoid sacrificing his own.

The Texas Farm Workers Union leader Antonio Orendain founded that organization after working with the United Farm Workers associated with California.[27] Although he was from Mexico, Orendain decided to focus on farm laborers in Texas and form an independent union. Farmworkers were still common in the Valley in the 1970s, decades after the rise of Valley agribusiness in the 1920s; there were 100,000 farmworkers there in 1979. Unlike Chávez, Orendain organized both Mexicans and Mexican Americans. Chávez only organized US citizens.[28] In 1978 Sloss-Vento wrote a letter of appreciation of Orendain to the editor of the *McAllen Evening Monitor*.[29]

The Bracero Program ended in 1964, but in the 1970s Sloss-Vento was even more convinced of its effects on Mexican American farmworkers. That conviction is evident in her 1972 letter about Chávez:

> For time immemorial Mexican American farm workers were paid very cheap wages along the border in Texas. But it was during World War Two, that the Bracero contracts and hundreds of thousands of illegal aliens from Mexico made their way into Texas and other states. The farmers

> were benefitted by paying very cheap wages, but the native farm workers were forced to flee North with their families in order to survive. . . . Many of our farm workers that migrated North, never came back. Many from the Bracero contracts found ways to stay North and did not go back to Mexico. This was a serious problem for the families in Mexico. The workers of Mexico at the same time that they prevented the Mexican American workers from solving their economic problems, they were also anxious to improve their lot too.[30]

Because of the program's impact on Mexican Americans in the Valley, Sloss-Vento became a critic of Mexican immigration in the 1970s.

Immigration

Immigration was still a major concern of Sloss-Vento. After the Bracero Program ended, Mexican immigration remained an issue in the United States and for the Mexican-descent community. The 1970s brought an increase in the Mexican immigrant population, and US government policies continued to be revised. President Jimmy Carter's administration of 1977–1981 proposed a border wall or "Tortilla Curtain" between Mexico and the United States. Sloss-Vento thought the idea of a "Tortilla Curtain" was insulting and ridiculous; she likened it to the "Frito Bandito" racist TV ad.[31] References to Mexican-descent people as "bandidos" was a sore spot for Tejanos, especially fronterizos who associated the term with a *matanza* (massacre) of Mexican-descent people in the 1910s during the South Texas border war. Many were killed because they were alleged to be bandits.

Sloss-Vento wrote a manuscript she titled "The Illegal Alien Problem" in the 1970s. By then the derogatory term "illegals" had been popularized, just as "wetback" was popular in the 1950s. She contends that immigration was Mexico's problem and that now there were "three generations of Americans from the illegals."[32] However, Mexican immigration actually dated to 1848. Sloss-Vento saw mostly poverty and exploitation in the Valley, and she feared immigration would lead the United States to bankruptcy and the end of Social Security; she expected that the balance sheet of Mexican immigration would have an adverse impact on the US economy. Chicano academic analysis of Mexican immigration in the South Texas press was hard to come by until the late 1970s, so Sloss-Vento was not in tune with critical Chicano studies analysis of immigration. Moreover, *La Prensa* newspaper of San Antonio, which might have included this new analysis, no longer existed after the early 1960s.

The Spanish Language

Sloss-Vento inherited Spanish from her parents. Spanish was spoken in the Lower Rio Grande Valley and northern New Mexico more commonly than anywhere else in the United States.[33] Laura Garza has noted that El Valle (the Valley) has been characterized by its resistance to assimilation.[34] Sloss-Vento's book about Perales was written in English with only his widow's letter and Professor Urbina's poem in Spanish. She wanted to reach the majority of Mexican Americans, so she had to write her book in English in the late 1970s. She promoted the Spanish language although she felt her Spanish was not as good as she wished,[35] a sentiment among many Mexican Americans. She wrote to Perales in 1947 that her "espanol no es muy bueno."[36] Language became a political issue during the Chicano movement. Gómez-Quiñones and Vásquez have noted, "Culturally, the years between 1966 and 1977 were times of notable self-determined revitalizations within the community, self-evident in the energies directed into the arts, education, media, and religious institutions, as well as a period of increased efforts at integration into dominant ways and structures."[37] The Chicano movement asserted the value of the Spanish language after decades of English-only instruction in public schools and the collective toll of linguistic and cultural assimilation. From World War I to World War II, Texas law prohibited the teaching of Spanish, and only in the 1940s was Spanish taught briefly. Bilingual education was not mandated until the 1970s.[38]

By the 1970s and 1980s there were Mexican Americans whose mother tongue had taken a back seat to English. Some spoke and understood no Spanish. The English language in US schools had made many of them more American than Mexican. I was one of the *pochas* (assimilated Mexican Americans), having grown up in Cuero, Texas, away from the Mexican border and in a community with few Mexican-descent people. All of my discussions with Sloss-Vento were in English, although my parents, Mexican immigrants, spoke to us in Spanish.

Sloss-Vento defended the use of the Spanish language. During the Elsa-Edcouch school walkout of 1968, she outlines her reasoning in a letter in a newspaper:

> There are many reasons why we have preserved the Spanish language. First, we are proud to have preserved the Spanish language which one might say it is the first language of Texas and of our ancestors. Second, because a citizen is better prepared by the knowledge of another language. Third, because the Spanish language holds the key to the unity and understanding that our country needs in the Western Hemisphere.[39]

In her first reason she does not acknowledge Native American languages.

In 1970 in writing to a Chicano movement organization she says speaking Spanish is "American," and she requests, "Permit me to write in Spanish, the elegant and beautiful language of our elders. For us it is as American as is English."[40] As the use of Spanish decreased among new generations of Mexican Americans, Sloss-Vento became an avid advocate of bilingualism. In a 1974 letter in the *McAllen Monitor* she proclaims, "Two languages are better than one." She argues that bilingualism made for a better United States and better Latin American countries:

> Several states, including Texas where Spanish was spoken, by an act of war, became a part of the union and their residents became American citizens who are proud to possess both the English and Spanish languages. And since it is the language of our ancestors and the Spanish had been in America first, we feel it is right that our children be taught, in the schools and at home, both Spanish and English.[41]

In 1978 Sloss-Vento's letter "To Speak English and Spanish Means We Are Better Prepared to Know Our Culture" was published in *La Verdad* of Corpus Christi.[42] It is about Canto al Pueblo, a Chicano literary event promoting Chicano and Latino literature and song as well as bilingualism and biculturalism. Canto events were organized to foster cultural revitalization. Sloss-Vento's son was involved in these literary events.[43] In the letter she references Texas's Spanish heritage as revealed in Carlos Castañeda's multivolume *Our Catholic Heritage*.[44] She adds, "The preservation of our culture and the Spanish language does not make us less Americans, on the contrary we are better prepared American citizens."[45] Later that year she reiterates her position on Spanish: "The Mexican American scholars must write in both English and Spanish of the past and present history of our people and specially that of the border."[46] Not only did she stress Spanish, but she also suggested that scholars needed to address both history and contemporary issues; that is, they should be public intellectuals. Here she emphasized the frontera.

Sloss-Vento did not approve of linguistic racism. In her book on Perales she contends that there was "to a great extent discrimination against the Spanish language."[47] On April 16, 1980, she wrote to the Reverend Sebastian Mozos of McAllen about its importance. She writes of the loss of Spanish-language newspapers, "I lament that we can't count on the Spanish newspapers of yesteryear."[48] She also wrote, "We will continue to be incapable because we are losing our culture and language. For me they are rare jewels that we have inherited from our parents and ancestors, and we should instruct others on the importance of these values."[49]

Sloss-Vento tried to educate the assimilated Mexican Americans who frowned upon the Spanish language. Some English-speaking Mexican Americans refused to attend "anything designated to attract only Mexican Americans. That their children speak only English at home." She touts Castañeda's books and adds, "The Mexican in Texas who preserves his culture has nothing to be ashamed of; that is[,] he can lift his head and face the most daring eye to eye, remembering the words of the great poet from Veracruz, Díaz Mirón: 'The bird sings even though the branch may be cracking because he knows what his wings are.'"[50]

Sloss-Vento embraced Mexican American and Chicano identity and at the same time used Latin American, Spanish, and white identities too. In an April 1969 letter to the editor of the *San Antonio Light* she objects to the staff writer Leo Cárdenas's reference to a "brown hand" and asks, "Does this writer know that the Latin American people are recognized as a white race?" She explains, "The Latin American people are descendants of the Spanish and Indian race. The Spaniards is [*sic*] a Caucasian race. To the new race, the Spaniards gave them their language, their customs and their culture."[51] She considered Latin Americans partly of European descent and therefore white. Yet here, she also refers to an "Indian race." Officially, on the Texas 1964 poll tax receipt Sloss-Vento listed herself or was listed as white, not colored, the only two choices.[52]

REVISING LULAC HISTORY

Throughout the 1960s and 1970s Sloss-Vento tried to get LULAC to honor Perales and recognize him as the major LULAC founder. As early as 1961 she tried to set the record straight when Gus García was apparently crediting Ben Garza, the first national president of LULAC, rather than Perales as the key founder.[53] Gus García was fourteen in 1929, when LULAC was founded. By 1970 LULAC did not have a permanent central office in Texas; archives were not collected by LULAC or any Texas archive or library; there was no official historian; the original members had mostly died; and there was little written history. Since Garza of Corpus Christi was the first LULAC president, due in part to Perales's savvy political skills, most assumed he was the founder. Garza died in 1938, so he could not explain his own minor role. In my book *No Mexicans, Women, or Dogs Allowed* I show that eleven men were the key founders in a collective effort. However, it is clear that Perales was the main founder; in my essay on Perales in the 1930s published in 2012

I stress his significance. Recent research by the historian Brandon Mata especially emphasizes Perales as the principal founder.[54]

As early as 1937 Perales realized that Garza was receiving undue credit in LULAC's founding. In his book published that year, *En defensa de mi raza*, he describes the organization's founding and says he had the idea for LULAC in 1919. While he may have had an idea, by 1921 organizers of the Order Sons of America (OSA) in San Antonio, one of the associations that merged to become part of LULAC, had acted on their own ideas and initiated civil rights activism. The OSA constitution was extensive and likely informed Perales as well as J. T. Canales's later writing of the LULAC constitution. Perales's first recorded civil rights action in Texas was in 1922, though he began writing as a public intellectual in 1919.

When LULAC celebrated its fiftieth anniversary in 1979, Sloss-Vento saw yet another opportunity to honor Perales. National LULAC, Texas LULAC, and local LULAC councils commemorated the anniversary. In 1978 Perales's widow and Sloss-Vento wrote to the Texas state LULAC director, Ruben Bonilla of Corpus Christi, suggesting that Perales be honored.[55] LULAC honored Garza and not Perales, the major founder, since LULAC members were not aware of its history and Garza was from Corpus Christi. By 1979 no professional historian had written LULAC's history, and there was still no LULAC archive in any library.[56] Bonilla commissioned some historical writings including a small book by Moisés Sándoval, but they did not emphasize Perales either.[57]

In February 1979 Sloss-Vento wrote a letter to the editor of the Spanish-language newspaper *La Verdad* of Corpus Christi to correct LULAC officials. She noted that Perales—not Garza—should have been honored and 1927, not 1929, recognized as the year LULAC was founded.[58] She believed since LAC was founded in 1927 that it was the true founding date of LULAC. In an essay titled "Alonso S. Perales: Precursor and Founder of LULAC" she declares, "As a living witness, having collaborated with Alonso S. Perales, Attorney J. T. Canales, and Prof. J. Luz Sáenz since the early twenties, I have always been cognizant of the formation and development of the LULAC by Alonso S. Perales." She adds, "Our concern should rest with the question of origination and initiation." Finally, she reiterates, "As I already stated Atty. Alonso S. Perales is the originator of the idea to form the LULAC and therefore, is the true founder of the LULAC."[59] She revisited the issue in a letter published on March 16, 1979, in *La Verdad*.[60]

In a March 1979 letter in the *McAllen Monitor* Sloss-Vento again underscores Perales's major role: "Much has been said during LULAC Week of the different founders of LULAC, but nothing has been said to honor the memory of the true founder of the LULAC, attorney Alonso S. Perales of San Antonio." As early as 1919 Perales, she writes, had the idea to "resolve the problems that prevented our welfare and advancement."[61] She also mentions Perales's books and quotes attorney Gus García's tribute to Perales at his funeral. Agreeing with her was Perales's sister-in-law, Estela Contreras of Rio Grande City, who congratulates Sloss-Vento in a letter to the editor in the *McAllen Monitor*.[62] There is no evidence that any LULAC member responded or listened to Sloss-Vento.

SLOSS-VENTO'S BOOK ON PERALES

With the fiftieth anniversary of LULAC approaching in 1979, Sloss-Vento saw the need for a history of LULAC's origins. In 1972 she wrote César Chávez that she was thinking about writing a book on Perales and wrote her friend Armando Rodriguez in 1974 that she was busy doing so.[63] In her mind the book needed to be published by 1977 to mark the fiftieth anniversary of the Harlingen Convention and the founding of the Latin American Citizens League, one of the organizations that merged to become LULAC two years later. She enlisted the help of her son, Arnoldo Vento, and his wife, Jeanne Lord Vento,[64] and in 1977 she had Artes Gráficas of San Antonio publish *Alonso S. Perales: His Struggle for the Rights of Mexican Americans*. The press had published writings of Perales, Sáenz, and Canales. It cost her $2,400, the equivalent of more than $9,000 today.[65] It was a costly venture but an investment in history.

The book addresses the three men Sloss-Vento treated as the holy trinity of Mexican American civil rights leadership in Texas before World War II—Perales, Sáenz, and Canales.[66] She appears to have been unaware of events and other leaders before 1927. The book has twenty-three short chapters, an appendix, and a bibliography. It includes commentary by Sloss-Vento, biographical information on Perales, documentation of the founding of LAC at Harlingen, and discussion about the founding controversy, the Racial Equality Bill 909, the Texas Good Neighbor Commission of the 1940s, the Bracero Program, the 1952 Mission conference rejecting the "wetback pamphlet," excerpts of Carlos Castañeda's lectures, and the deaths of J. Luz Sáenz and Perales. She promotes Perales's two books, *En defensa de mi raza* and *Are We Good Neighbors?*; her book also includes personal memoirs, letters she wrote, and interviews she conducted.[67]

Sloss-Vento's purpose in writing the book was to document the truth as she saw it, once and for all, as she explains to Marta Pérez Perales the year before it was published: "The book has to help establish the truth—Lic.

FIGURE 4.1. Cover of *Alonso S. Perales: His Struggle for the Rights of the Mexican American*, by Adela Sloss-Vento, 1977. She acknowledged Perales's significance more than that of any other person. Courtesy of Dr. Arnoldo Carlos Vento.

Perales was the founder of LULAC."[68] In the book she states, "This writer hopes that within the humbly written pages of this small book, the new generations will be informed of Alonso S. Perales' struggle in the difficult times of the past." She adds, "It is my purpose to point out three early important and outstanding leaders who worked alone on behalf of our cause."[69] In calling the cause "ours" and not "theirs," she humbly includes herself. Sloss-Vento clearly states her greater goal in writing the book: "My greatest wish is that the new generations will unite and will accomplish additional goals, economically, socially and politically." She asserts, "It is important that they be aware that much of the rights, advancements and welfare we are enjoying today, is due to the sacrifices of leaders like Alonso S. Perales."[70] In her preface she describes how she gathered materials and collaborated with Perales to produce the book. She also thanks the newspapers of the day for their collaboration. Kabalen de Bichara has noted that in the book Sloss-Vento "is also narrating her own life story through her text and epistolary writing."[71] She calls Sloss-Vento's acknowledgments of others "veiled discourse" in "humbly" asserting herself.[72]

The appendix includes letters from family members and colleagues. The first is from the widow Marta Pérez Perales. Other letters came from Santos de la Paz of *La Verdad* of Corpus; the World War I veteran and Perales's close friend Fortino Treviño of Alice; José María Longoria, who organized a LAC council in 1927; Luis Alvarado Sr., the son-in-law of J. Luz Sáenz and a previous LULAC national legislative director; and the World War I veteran and LAC member Felipe García of Mission. The last letter is from Texas Senator Joe J. Bernal of San Antonio. Charles Albidress Sr.'s speech at the 1977 dedication of the Perales Elementary School in San Antonio is printed in the appendix as well. Albidress had joined Perales in LULAC Council 16 of San Antonio in the 1930s and in Perales's group called the Loyal Americans, in the late 1930s and the 1940s. Also in the appendix are a letter from Leo J. Leo of La Joya, Texas, and Professor M. A. Urbina's poem "El defensor de la raza" (The defender of La Raza).

The bibliography lists primary and secondary sources. The primary sources listed include two newspaper essays by Castañeda, the report responding to the "wetback pamphlet," as well as a response from J. Luz Sáenz, newspaper articles about the Harlingen Convention, Perales's books and several of his articles, and one of Canales's books. The bibliography only lists three of her own writings: a 1931 *La Prensa* letter about Perales, a 1952 letter to Perales, and a letter to the *McAllen Evening Monitor* in 1968.[73] While Sloss-Vento's book focused on Perales and included information on Canales and Sáenz, a few passages were autobiographical. Her humility is also seen in a typescript about the book in which she comments, "Ella no es ninguna escritora" (She is no writer).[74] She did not give herself enough credit and prevented others like myself from seeing her greater significance.

Some facts of Perales's life she did not include. She did not mention the controversy related to the exclusion of Mexicans from the Harlingen Convention. She did not mention Perales's founding of Council 16 or his departure from LULAC. She did not mention his Republican leanings in the 1950s. And she did not address his family life, legal work, or stints as a diplomat or consul general of Nicaragua. Moreover, she did not speak of any shortcomings.

Although Sloss-Vento was an amateur historian and did not use footnotes, the book was the first survey of Perales's life and does cite documentation. She provided researchers such as myself and the historians Richard García and Carlos Blanton an outline. Her little red book can only be found in forty-seven libraries today, either in hard copy or as released by her son, Arnoldo Vento, again years later. While it did not make a large splash upon its release in 1977, it is her monument to Perales, and she fulfilled her goal.

Since there was no major publisher behind the book, Sloss-Vento and her son promoted it. *La Red*, a national Chicano studies newsletter, announced the book's publication.[75] On a promotional flyer Vento says the book was written by "a senior citizen and female instrumental in the development of an early and unpublicized twentieth century civil rights movement in South Texas."[76] Indeed, Sloss-Vento was seventy-six when it was published. Vento pointed to her gender, proud of his feminist mother, as she raised him to be.

Sloss-Vento's book was announced in a few newspapers. The *McAllen Monitor* ran the story with the headline "Valleyite Publishes Book,"[77] and Santos de la Paz's article in *La Verdad* of Corpus Christi had the headline "Book on the Life of Alonso S. Perales Tells of Hispanic Leader's Struggle for Human Rights."[78] The *San Antonio Express* writer refers to it as "a small but vital book."[79] Several academics took notice. The historian Richard García had written a book about the Mexican American middle class in San Antonio that involved LULAC; the communications graduate student Donna Tobias wrote Sloss-Vento as well.[80] Sloss-Vento received a few invitations to speak but at age seventy-six already with health issues, she launched no book tour.

Activists in the Chicano movement largely failed to notice the book. In 1977 Sloss-Vento sent the Raza Unida Party founder José Ángel Gutiérrez a copy. In the accompanying letter she writes, "Upon reading my book you will know that I have been a fighter for our Cause before most of the new generation."[81] There is no record of Gutiérrez's thanks or response. He had read Perales's books for his master's thesis, but he would not have known much of the decades-long struggle by LULAC. Chicano movement leaders had little respect for the political generation before them. Gutiérrez did not know Sloss-Vento and in 1977 he apparently did not have enough respect for women or elders. In her book she does not speak enough about herself. Perhaps if she had said more about herself or perhaps if she were a man he might have responded. Interestingly, he wrote a book about himself, *The Making of Civil Rights Leader José Ángel Gutiérrez*.[82]

ASSISTING A YOUNG WOMAN HISTORIAN

Sloss-Vento seized on another opportunity to advance Perales in the late 1970s. Her son, Arnoldo Vento, became a professor of Spanish and Chicano studies in the 1960s, and by the late 1970s he directed the Center for Mexican American Studies at the University of Texas in Austin. I arrived at the University of Texas in Austin in fall 1977. Chicano studies was introduced there in the late 1960s by George I. Sánchez and Américo Paredes. Their colleague Carlos E. Castañeda died before they began the program. In 1978 I took a Chicano history class with the instructor Victor Nelson Cisneros from Brownsville; he was also a graduate student from UCLA. I wrote a thirty-page research paper on the origins of LULAC, an organization that my mother belonged to in Cuero and that had dynamic leadership by its president Ruben Bonilla at the time. While I was a work-study student at the center, Arnoldo Vento became aware of my research interests and arranged a meeting with his mother.

In 1978 Sloss-Vento's chance to further document Perales's history was her encouragement for me to write what she considered a "true" history of LULAC. She advocated for more Mexican-descent women and men professionals, especially historians. She invited me to her Edinburg home and shared some of the archives from her chest but showed me only a few of her own writings. Later she wrote several letters on my behalf and provided the addresses of potential contacts.[83] She wrote Marta Pérez Perales, Alonso Perales's wife, a letter helping me gain access to the Perales archive in San Antonio. Thereafter I wrote a senior honors thesis on the Harlingen Convention and the founding of LULAC largely based on the Sloss-Vento and Perales archives. The senior honors thesis became part of my dissertation and the book *No Mexicans, Women, or Dogs Allowed*.

Ever the intellectual, Sloss-Vento commented on my undergraduate work. In writing this book, I found among her papers a critique of an undergraduate paper I wrote on the Americanization of Mexicans. She says, "In regard to an article written by a young student at the Texas University of the history of LULAC, she asks, . . . Why did Lulac promote Americanization?

. . . I am sure that our leaders as well as our people, never meant for us to forget the Spanish language and customs."[84] Always with great respect, she took on established academicians such as George I. Sánchez as well as up-and-coming undergraduate scholars such as myself. Status did not matter to Sloss-Vento; if she disagreed with someone, she would say so. More importantly, she tried to provide historical context in understanding LULAC and its leaders. In helping me and similar others, she promoted young Chicana professionals. Even in the 1950s, she helped young Lupita Olivares conduct a study of braceros.[85]

CHICANA FEMINISM

Sloss-Vento acknowledged and encouraged Chicana feminism, another part of the Chicano movement. Chicana feminism arose in Texas within the RUP and later at universities. By the 1970s Chicana feminist conferences were held often. Martha P. Cotera was a key activist in the RUP and newly emerging feminist circles.[86] La Conferencia de Mujeres por La Raza (The Conference of Women for La Raza) in Houston in 1971 was an important event in the community. At the University of Texas I helped organize an academic conference for the Chicano Culture Committee at the Texas Student Union in the late 1970s. We organized the Women in Metamorphosis conference; we invited Sloss-Vento, and she accepted. She wrote that the women's conference would be bilingual and about various themes and women's advancement.[87] Sloss-Vento, however, did not attend.

The "Women as Creators of Change" session featured speeches by Rosaura Sánchez, a professor of literature; the playwright Estella Portillo; Marta Tijerina, a TV personality; and Lupe Anguiano, a San Antonio welfare activist. These women emerged during the Chicano movement after Sloss-Vento's decades of activism in the Mexican American civil rights movement. Though she was unable to attend, Sloss-Vento's enthusiasm shines in her letter to the committee: "The women once given the opportunity, not only constitutes a powerful force in all branches of education and advancement, but also is creating a better future, better citizens, the betterment and happiness needed for our people, our Communities and the Nation as a whole."[88] But Sloss-Vento was never "given" opportunity—she made her own opportunities. She proved to be a powerful force as a woman who created a better future, better citizens, better community, and a better nation before and during the Chicano movement. As conservatism began to rise, this movement began to wane by 1978; in 1981 the Republican Ronald Reagan took office to preside over the United States.

CONCLUSION

Sloss-Vento was a Mexican American who supported the Chicano movement of the 1960s and 1970s. She welcomed the movement following the Mexican American civil rights movement from the 1920s to the early 1960s. She embraced new organizations, new leaders, and new tactics by youth, students, labor organizers, and nationalists, male and female. She believed in Mexican American associations like LULAC, the American G.I. Forum, and PASSO and Chicano organizations like the Raza Unida Party and Canto al Pueblo. She was forward-thinking. She embraced new national leaders such as César Chávez and Texas leaders such as Antonio Orendain of the Texas Farm Workers Union. She did not recognize only the older leaders Perales, Sáenz, and Canales. She understood that the empowerment of La Raza required political capital and an end to labor exploitation in the lack of a minimum and living wage.

Chicano nationalists in the Chicano movement advocated for the teaching of Spanish. Previous generations preserved their Spanish-language proficiency because of a high Mexican-immigrant population, Spanish-language newspapers, and segregated schools. By the 1970s assimilation had taken its toll, and Sloss-Vento understood the significance of the decline of this cultural base and the need to advocate for Spanish.

She even praised the new militancy of youth instead of seeing the Elsa-Edcouch student walkout in the Valley as outside of traditional methods of complaint or protesters as troublemakers. Likewise, she approved of the Mexican American farmworkers' melon strike in Rio Grande City. Only on the issue of immigration did Sloss-Vento become more conservative.

Throughout the 1960s and 1970s Sloss-Vento promoted the legacy of Alonso S. Perales. In 1977 she finally published her book about Perales. She had advocated for recognition of his contributions for many years and especially since his passing in 1960. As a grassroots historian and fellow activist, she sought to write the history of Tejano leaders because nobody else had; she even paid for the book's publication at significant cost to herself in time, money, and possibly her health since she was in her seventies.

Chicana feminism arose during the Chicano movement and became more viable after 1970. Sloss-Vento welcomed its rise and enthusiastically endorsed Chicana empowerment through conferences and Chicana professionals in the making like myself. For decades—in fact, since the late 1920s—she was a feminist in asserting a woman's right to work and speak out in the male domains of civil rights, writing, and politics.

PART II

PERSONAS

CHAPTER 5

FEMINIST IN THE GENDERED MEXICAN AMERICAN CIVIL RIGHTS MOVEMENT

Decades before 2000, Adela Sloss-Vento, a feminist, operated in the Mexican American civil rights movement, politics, and public commentary, predominantly masculine domains before the 1970s. During the Mexican American civil rights movement, a number of associations emerged; the extent to which the organizations included women, offered women leadership opportunities, and addressed sexism varied little. Mexican American lawyers, a small cadre almost entirely of men, typically served as leaders of these civil rights groups. Sloss-Vento maintained relations with the LULAC founders Alonso S. Perales, J. Luz Sáenz, and J. T. Canales from 1927 to 1960 and did so in part through correspondence. What were her personal and political relations with these men like, as evidenced in their letters? What does correspondence in the archives reveal about how each man saw her role in the Mexican American civil rights movement? As a movement activist, was she embraced by these male activists? Men's power, influence, and mentorship over Sloss-Vento is worth examining. Finally, how did each male leader feel about her as a person? Letters in the Sloss-Vento, Perales, Sáenz, and Canales archives hold insights into those questions. Fortunately, the archives of Perales, Sáenz, and Canales are now in university libraries. None were in libraries when Sloss-Vento wrote her book. Her correspondence with Perales ran from the 1920s to 1960, with Sáenz primarily in the 1940s, and with Canales mostly in the 1940s and 1950s. The historian Lindsay O'Neill reminds us that letters could sustain all types of networks—social, kinship, intellectual, religious, business, and political.[1]

Few women had the sustained political connections to leading male activists that Sloss-Vento had. The literary scholar Norma Mouton's review of letters in the Perales archive as well as my perusal of the Perales, Sáenz, and Canales archives confirms this.[2] No other Tejana regularly corresponded with these men, and no other Tejana had both personal and political relations with them. These ties were unusual in an era of homosocial relations, of men socializing with men and women socializing with women before the 1970s.

GENDER IN MEXICAN AMERICAN CIVIL RIGHTS ACTIVISM

In California, women crossed gender boundaries in civil rights organizing in the late 1930s. The most important organization nationally was the Congreso de Pueblos de Habla Española (Spanish-Speaking Peoples Congress), a pan-Latinx civil rights and labor organization founded in Los Angeles in 1939. Women and men held leadership positions in the organization since its beginning, in part because many activists had union organizing experience as American Federation of Labor garment workers or Congress of Industrial Organizations cannery workers.[3] The Congreso de Pueblos de Habla Española's agenda was also pro-woman. The Latinas Luisa Moreno and Josefina Fierro de Bright played prominent roles.

In the 1950s and 1960s the Community Service Organization (CSO) was prominent in California and Arizona; women held leadership roles and positions. The historian Lori Flores has found, "The CSO considered women equal members and allowed them to take leadership roles,"[4] although she notes that in the early 1950s, men were typically the organization's presidents and vice-presidents at the national and local levels. In 1956, of twenty-five chapters in California and Arizona, only two had women presidents. In the early 1960s Marguerite Villegas was its national vice president; in 1961 five women were chapter presidents out of thirty-seven chapters. Dolores Huerta, later of United Farm Workers Union fame, headed a number of national CSO committees. Women helped obtain pension legislation under Governor Edmund "Pat" Brown in 1961.[5]

In New Mexico there was both homosocial and heterosocial organizing among Hispanos and Hispanas, as Mexican Americans called themselves there. The New Mexico LULAC in the 1930s, mostly in northern New Mexico, was homosocial with Ladies LULAC.[6] But the Asociación Nacional Mexicana organization founded in the 1950s in southern New Mexico was heterosocial. It had a labor orientation. One of its early leaders was a woman; Isabel González served as its president.[7] Texas was much more homosocial than other states, especially California. Richard Buitrón notes the more liberal California experience: "In Texas, a mentality emerged that was male, politically moderate, middle class, based on history, and integrationist," while California was "more accepting of radical ideologies and female authority."[8]

Texas did not have a large enough population of Latinxs outside of the Mexican-descent community to organize across ethnic nationalities. Mexican American civil rights activism in Texas before 1970 was dominated by men; when women were present, usually they were segregated from men. In the Mexican Catholic church there were Guadalupanas (women honoring Our Lady of Guadalupe) and men's clubs or Knights of Columbus. Perhaps there was more mixing at Protestant churches. A European American scholar who studied Mexican American leadership in Texas has observed homosociality. In her 1949 doctoral dissertation on Mexican ethnic leadership in San Antonio, Frances Jerome Woods finds a lack of Mexican-descent women leaders. She asserts, "Among most minority groups, certainly the Mexican minority, leadership is the prerogative of the males."[9] Woods ignored women's clubs. Among working-class and poor residents of the Alazán-Apache public housing complex in San Antonio she found men's and women's groups and adolescent groups of mixed gender. She comments that among African American groups, "leadership is not restricted to Negro men, nor are women commonly put aside in 'women's auxiliaries.'"[10] Also in the 1940s the writer Pauline Kibbe reports on "the Latin American custom of separating the sexes in all their activities" in Texas.[11] These authors did not see women's social club leadership and Ladies LULAC leaders but made some general observations.

Individual Tejano civil rights activists typically acted in homosocial fashion. In 1953 Perales informed Sloss-Vento about an upcoming conference in Albuquerque, New Mexico, of the Bishop's Committee for the Spanish-Speaking of the Southwest and assures her in a letter, "You will be invited."[12] Her correspondence archive includes no other invitation from Perales. In 1954 Santos de la Paz, the editor of *La Verdad* of Corpus Christi and another of her comrades, wrote of the same-gender tendency. He wrote her about his conflict with the sheriff of Live Oak County in South Texas. He states his request for her help: "I would like you to head up a group of women that could investigate the case soon."[13] His request shows his acknowledgment of her as a capable leader and someone who could confront a sheriff. But once again the homosocial rule prevailed. Could she head up a group of men? Could she lead a mixed-gender group?

Tejano civil rights organizations enacted this homosocial practice, as did LULAC in 1929. LULAC was founded by men for men. Alonso S. Perales was quite conscious of the separation of women from men in LULAC. Besides playing a major role in writing its constitution, he wrote to the co-founder J. T. Canales about the subject in 1933 confirming the idea that separate councils were best.[14] Women in Alice, El Paso, Kingsville, and San Antonio formed ladies auxiliaries. By 1933 women were permitted, but only in Ladies LULAC councils. The groups were composed of single and married women, were assumed to be heterosexual, and typically worked at the local level in towns or cities.[15] Still, they provided leadership opportunities. Chapters addressed racial discrimination, advocated for voters paying their own poll taxes, and advanced women's civic engagement. Ladies LULAC councils were not feminist-inspired, and most members did not express feminist consciousness or openly identify patriarchy, machismo, or sexism as social ills. But they were organized by women and advocated for women's involvement before the US women's movement of the late 1960s and the 1970s.

In LULAC it was typical for women to perform gendered roles at mixed-gender events. Ladies LULAC members interacted with men at some local functions and at annual state and national conventions. They tended convention business like men did. But women also served as hosts and held women's luncheons at the conventions. At no time did women serve as keynote or major speakers before the 1970s. In this sense, women were treated as auxiliary members.

Moreover, gender issues or sexism were rarely addressed in LULAC before the 1970s. Feminist ideology among LULAC women was almost nonexistent between 1929 and 1970. Alice Dickerson Montemayor of Laredo was the only openly feminist participant in LULAC in the 1930s, and she did not rejoin LULAC after World War II. Montemayor was exceptional, much like Sloss-Vento. Montemayor joined Ladies LULAC in the late 1930s and wrote several significant essays for *LULAC News*, including "Women's Opportunity in LULAC" and "Son muy hombres" (They are so male), the latter of which condemned sexism and male privilege in LULAC.[16] Feminist thought was not appreciated in LULAC circles from the 1930s to the 1970s. In November 1936 she wrote to Perales that it "seems like Ladies LULAC Council 15 is about to disorganize" and that the National President Ezequiel Salinas of Laredo was "working underhanded to have our Council disorganize because his mother does not approve of the Secretary of Council 15 and Mr. Salinas himself does not like me personally."[17] After perusing numerous LULAC archives over many years, I have not found any letters or documents written by men that overtly rejected women's presence in LULAC.

Women who were involved in LULAC before 1970 have commented on systemic sexism in the organization. Amada C. Maes Valdez of the long-standing Ladies LULAC of El Paso recalls, "There were some men who did not want women to take part in the organization. They didn't want us to be independent."[18] Isabel Mendez of San Antonio tells a reporter, "When I wanted to get involved with LULAC back in the 1950s it was very difficult because there were a lot of men who didn't want us to be full-fledged members. They wanted us to be an auxiliary to them, but there were women who were real fighters."[19]

The typical manner in which from the 1930s to the 1970s LULAC kept women subordinated was through homosociality. By segregating women, LULAC men did not have to discuss politics with women, consider their intellect, or compete with them for leadership. Men could enjoy socializing with other men, away from women. Surely women who joined Ladies LULAC also enjoyed women's company and believed in women's empowerment. The threat or opportunity of heterosexual sex was absent, though the threat or opportunity of lesbian or gay sex was there. In 1984 San Antonio had seventeen LULAC councils, ten of mixed gender, three all women, and four all male.[20]

While LULAC women worked at the local level since the 1930s, the organization's state leadership was overwhelmingly male, as was the national leadership. Texas LULAC's state directors were all male until 1970, when Dolores Adame Guerrero of Houston was elected. In the 1950s Carmen Cortés of Houston served as national secretary for many years, but men and perhaps women were unable to see her as presidential material. Women did not become national presidents of LULAC until the mid-1990s, when Belén Robles of El Paso won that post years after serving as national secretary. Rosa Rosales of San Antonio and Margie Morán of San Antonio served as national presidents in the 2000s. Women can now readily be elected.

Feminism appeared regularly in LULAC after 1970. It would take the feminist movement to create feminist consciousness in the United States in the 1960s and 1970s; before then it appeared only in a few women and a few moments in the Mexican-descent community. By 1972 *LULAC News* published articles titled "Woman Pushes for Equality," "LULAC Forms Committee to Better Women's Status," and "Women Called Widely Discriminated Against."[21] Overtly feminist councils that chose separatism as a strategy appeared in cities including Houston and Dallas. Even into the 1980s homosociality died a hard and slow death. Corpus Christi women battled men in Council 1 for inclusion in 1984.[22]

NATIONAL AND TEXAS MEXICAN AMERICAN CIVIL RIGHTS ORGANIZATIONS

Between 1929 and 1963 several organizations, commissions, and networks besides LULAC formed to advance Mexican American civil rights efforts in Texas. They included the American G.I. Forum in 1948, the American

Council of Spanish-Speaking People in 1951, the Latin American convention in 1952 in Mission to respond to the "wetback" pamphlet," the biracial Texas Council on Human Relations (also known as the Texas Council for the Study of Human Relations and Texas Good Relations Association) in 1951–1952, the Political Association of Spanish-Speaking Organizations (PASSO) in 1960, and Viva Kennedy–Viva Johnson Clubs in 1960.[23] All were run by men.

American G.I. Forum membership was based on US veteran status; the forum was founded in 1947 by Héctor P. García, a Corpus Christi LULAC member, and spread throughout the Southwest and Midwest. The 1950s saw the rise of the American G.I. Forum Auxiliary for women.[24] Founded in 1956 to formalize women's participation dating back to 1948, the auxiliary held a women's leadership conference in 1957, an unusual act. The historian Ramona Houston has found that auxiliary members participated in parent-teacher councils, conducted desegregation research, and raised money for the organization and litigation.[25] The physician Clotilde García, a sister of Héctor García, played a prominent role in the auxiliary and modeled women's inclusion. She argues that the forum needed women: "The men couldn't go out and do anything by themselves; they needed the family; they needed the women to help."[26] But the men operated successfully alone and with women. Women performed the gendered tasks of organizing picnics, tamale sales, barbecues, dances, and queen contests to raise funds. The historian Julie Leininger Pycior observes in her book *LBJ and Mexican Americans*, "At GI Forum conventions the queen and her court received more attention than any female neighborhood organizers."[27] Beauty was emphasized for women.

Yet Ramona Houston still notes women's role in civil rights work in Texas and several southwestern states, especially in raising money needed for desegregation campaigns. In that way, she concludes, "Women auxiliaries were extremely active in the desegregation of Texas."[28] And queen contests were the most financially rewarding activity, Houston reports, so the forum urged chapters to sponsor them for "the organization, desegregation cases, and the civil rights fund."[29]

The American Council of Spanish-Speaking People was formed in Austin in the early 1950s to end racism, yet it also failed to include women in its leadership. Its impetus came from the Marshall Foundation seeking to fund antiracist efforts for Latinxs. Its goals were to eliminate school and housing segregation, increase Mexican American participation on juries and in public offices, secure equal service in public facilities, and end employment discrimination in government agencies.[30] The council's first leaders included George I. Sánchez and Gus García of Texas;[31] New Mexico Lieutenant Governor Tibo Chávez; Arturo Fuentes of Arizona, president of the Alianza Hispano

Americana; Ignacio López, a publisher in Los Angeles; Antonio Ríos of the Community Service Organization; and Bernardo Váldez, the director of the Community Council in Colorado.[32] Another listing of the council's national leaders included Ralph Estrada of the Alianza Hispano Americana and Ignacio López, the editor of *El Espectador* of Cucamonga, California.[33] In 1953 its board consisted of Tibo Chávez of Belen, New Mexico; Bernard Valdez of Denver; Agustín Serrato of Los Angeles; Edward Roybal of Los Angeles; Ralph Estrada of Tucson; Lyle Saunders of Denver; Arthur L. Campa of Denver; M. C. Gonzáles of San Antonio; and George Garza of Austin.[34] The council died by the late 1950s from a lack of funds, but it had made substantial contributions to supporting civil rights and desegregation cases.

Another organization, the Texas Council on Human Relations, in the 1950s was a response to the defunct Texas Good Neighbor Commission; it also was all-male. Initiated by the Texas state government, it included European Americans. Its first chairman was Robert Everett Smith, and members included George Sánchez, Gus García, Bishop Mariano Garriga, Umphrey Lee, William R. White, and Henderson Coquat. The group sought to form local human relations councils in towns larger than 2,500 residents. It sponsored a state conference in Fort Worth. By mid-1952, it fell apart after criticism from the American G.I. Forum.[35] No women were admitted to the Texas commission.

The Texas Pro Human Relations Fund was then organized, apparently as a scholarship group. When it was organized in Alice in 1952, its chairman, J. T. Canales, apparently did not call upon women to join the effort, although Miriam Domitila García attended the first meeting. Sloss-Vento was not invited or did not attend. Canales appointed three committees—name selection, state organization, and ways and means—and no women's names appeared on the membership list.[36] Hesiquio N. González, Héctor García, Raul Tijerina, Andrés Rivera Jr., and George J. Garza were the men in charge.[37] Canales sponsored Carlos Castañeda as the chairman.[38] Women were mostly absent.

Nevertheless, Sloss-Vento became a leader of the Texas Pro-Human Relations Fund, also known as the Texas Good Relations Association, at the grassroots level. She became a representative in Edinburg, and by 1952 she had raised $251.[39] While several people contributed $5 each and lawyer Juan Noyola of Laredo contributed $12, Sloss-Vento and her mother, Ancelma Garza, each gave $100.[40] A note reads, "Collections by Adela S. Vento for the Texas Good Relations Association an Association to collect funds for Scholarships and formed by Lic. J. T. Canales at Alice, Texas May 4, 1952."[41] She collected money from several more people including M. Cortinas and

E. Torres of Cortinas Studios of Edinburg. Canales succeeded in establishing the Canales Scholarship Foundation, sometimes accessing funds from lower-middle-class folks like Sloss-Vento and her working-class mother.[42] In 1954 Sloss-Vento helped Lupita Olivares of Edinburg receive a scholarship and obtain a $1,200 college loan. Sloss-Vento's contribution was to raise funds but not lead the effort.

Sloss-Vento also tried to help the group get off the ground and saw it as an activist group, not just a fund-raising effort. In June 1952 she wrote to Perales complaining that *La Verdad* newspaper of Corpus Christi hardly had any news about the new organization: "I am announcing the event through the radio here and I sent some flyers that I made" to promote the group, but she said she was running across cowards and selfish people.[43] In October 1952 she complained to Perales that the group leaders needed to occasionally speak to community members.[44]

By the 1950s, according to George I. Sánchez, the "most important and largest, as well as the most effective" Mexican American organizations in the United States were LULAC, the Alianza Hispano Americana, American G.I. Forum, and the Latin American Conference Committee of Colorado. Others he mentions in a letter to an associate director of a New York organization are the Community Service Organization, the Mexican-American Committee of Chicago, and the Casa del Mexicano in Los Angeles. All the contacts he lists for these associations are men.[45]

A national network of Viva Kennedy–Viva Johnson Clubs was organized to help elect John F. Kennedy president in 1960; it was another effort led mostly by men. In California in 1960 the state leadership was also male, with Ed Roybal as chairman, Henry P. López as coordinator, Arthur J. Rendón as treasurer, and Ralph Poblando as secretary. Rendón explains in a letter to Cleofas Callero of El Paso why the leaders were all men: "Celia [likely his wife] doesn't agree with my political interests. However, Cleo we all love our little wives and must be tolerant with their lack of understanding when it comes to active participation in political matters."[46] These condescending beliefs led to the exclusion of women. Clotilde García and the wife of the attorney James de Anda headed the Texas State Ladies Viva Johnson Club, another homosocial group.[47]

The Political Association of Spanish-Speaking Organizations, founded in 1960, was yet another male-led effort. After Kennedy's election as president, this organization took root across the US Southwest. It merged memberships from existing political organizations in California, Texas, and Arizona that included the Mexican American Political Association, the Community Service Organization, and LULAC. In Texas, chapters emerged in Houston, Port

Arthur, Orange, Fort Worth, Dallas, and El Paso. The political brainchild of George I. Sánchez, "it identified with the common man and [asked] nothing from him but everything for him."[48] More research on PASSO is needed, but to date no women's names are associated with it.

Tejano hegemonic homosociality marginalized women. With the rise of the Chicano movement in 1963, slowly but surely and especially after 1970 women began to challenge the gendered status quo. LULAC at the national level and Texas level began to change, but there were holdouts. In 1984 the *Corpus Christi Caller-Times* reported no women among the two hundred members.[49] As late as 2000, the Corpus Christi council had few women among its two hundred members. When Mary Helen Salazar tried to become its president, several male members were upset. The board member Manuel Gonzales is quoted in a news article saying, "This is the first woman president and these men couldn't work with a woman."[50] As a result of her attempted election, Council 4444, a mixed-gender council, was formed.

Unlike many African American women, their Mexican-descent counterparts often did not benefit much by participating in homosocial civic organizations before the 1970s. African American women had the Texas Association of Colored Women's Clubs after 1905 and the National Council of Negro Women after 1935. Teachers could also join the Colored Teachers State Association of Texas, founded in 1884. At the same time, there were no national organizations for Mexican-origin women and no umbrella groups for clubs. There was a Spanish-Speaking Parent Teacher Association in Texas with a predominantly female membership, but it survived only from the late 1920s to the 1930s.[51] African American women also played more prominent roles in the gender-mixed National Association for the Advancement of Colored People (NAACP) and the African American civil rights movement in Texas. The historian Annelise Orleck has suggested that the civil rights movement in the United States was led by women. In a chapter titled "The Civil Rights Movement as a Women's Movement," she argues that "women were also the primary organizers of the main civil rights groups," especially in the 1950s.[52] Such was not the case with Mexican Americans. In fact, civil rights associations in the Mexican-descent community simultaneously functioned as empowering and disempowering institutions for women.

ATTORNEYS AS LEADERS OF CIVIL RIGHTS ORGANIZATIONS

The statewide Tejano civil rights organizations and efforts changed over time, but their leadership continued to be male. Attorneys played a major leadership role in the civil rights movement across decades; they were the

FIGURE 5.1. Mexican American attorneys, all men, celebrate a win in the 1954 Supreme Court ruling in *Hernandez v. Texas* in Corpus Christi. There was only one Tejana lawyer in the 1950s. Dr. Hector P. Garcia Papers; courtesy of the Mary and Jeff Bell Library, Texas A&M University, Corpus Christi.

most educated sector in a time when few graduated from high school. They were also an articulate group. In the 1920s Perales, Canales, and M. C. Gonzales were crucial to LULAC's formation and served as national presidents in the 1930s. There were no Tejana lawyers at this time.

Pre–World War II Mexican American lawyers in Texas were few but were also male. Canales, Perales, Gonzáles, Adolfo Garza, C. N. Quintanilla of San Antonio, and Leo Durán of Corpus Christi were attorneys before the 1940s.[53] Activist lawyers before 1960 included Carlos Cadena, Gus García, Albert Peña Jr., and Richard M. Casillas of San Antonio; Chris Alderete, James De Anda, John J. Herrera, and Judge Alfred Hernández of Houston; Ezequiel Salinas of Laredo; Albert Armendáriz of El Paso; and Homero M. López of Kingsville and Brownsville.[54] By 1970 one of five Texans were of Mexican descent, but only one of twenty-five law students was Mexican American.[55] In 1970 in the United States, 2 percent of lawyers were Mexican American, though Mexican Americans made up 10 percent of the US population.[56]

By the 1940s new male leaders were emerging in LULAC, some who were not attorneys. George I. Sánchez of New Mexico, a professor of education, was a leader in the 1940s. He moved to his new home in Austin, where he became the national LULAC president.[57] The medical doctor Héctor P. García joined LULAC and would go on to found the American G.I. Forum.[58] The new leaders apparently did not know Adela Sloss-Vento or correspond with her. Perhaps her gender and distance from Austin, Corpus Christi, and San Antonio explain this lack of contact.

The law profession was slow to admit women. Two Mexican American women lawyers emerged as oddities, one in the late 1950s and the other in the late 1960s. The first Tejana lawyer was Edna Cisneros Carroll of Raymondville. The press treated her as unusual; a Dallas newspaper reported she was "slim" and "brown-haired," mentioning her cookbooks and her husband's disgust with politics.[59] In the 1960s the second Tejana lawyer, Adela Callejo, began her career in Dallas.[60] The lack of Tejana lawyers hastened the emergence of women as leaders in the Mexican American civil rights movement. Tejana lawyers may have challenged LULAC's homosocial principle and may have served as role models for Tejanas. From the late 1920s on, Sloss-Vento corresponded with Mexican American activist lawyers, all of them male. As late as the 2010s, the political scientist Gabriela Sosa Zavaleta suggests, the Valley's Latina lawyers became "one of the most recent and powerful indicators of the involvement of women in the political dynamics of today's Valley."[61]

SLOSS-VENTO'S MALE COHORT

Activists in the Mexican American civil rights movement belonged to a political generation, a cohort that has been described as almost entirely men.[62] The historian Mario T. García has introduced the idea of a Mexican American generation in which only a few women leaders emerged. García includes Josefina Fierro de Bright of California in the Congreso de Habla Española. Surely the writer Jovita González, the Mexicanist activist María L. Hernández, the LULAC leader Alice Dickerson Montemayor, the labor leader Emma Tenayuca, and Adela Sloss-Vento fit within this generational analysis, but Mario García does not link them to the spirit of the generation's activism in Texas. Later research by María Cotera, John Morán González, Gabriela González, and me added these women.

Sloss-Vento is important to the Mexican American civil rights movement and best associated with a male cohort, particularly with Perales, Canales, and Sáenz. Other than Perales, Sáenz was Sloss-Vento's most important associate in the cause. After serving in World War I, Sáenz co-founded LULAC with Perales and others.[63] He spent most of his life in South and Central Texas working as an activist teacher. He published his diary about his World

War I experience in 1933.[64] He befriended Sloss-Vento in 1927, and they visited and corresponded all their lives until he died in 1953. Canales was a LULAC co-founder, lawyer, state legislator in the 1910s, judge, writer, scholarship benefactor, and Sloss-Vento's third important associate in activism. Canales was the first Latino to graduate from the University of Michigan law school, in 1898, and he wrote several history books.[65] He corresponded with Sloss-Vento in the 1940s and 1950s.

A fourth man from this cohort but who was not Sloss-Vento's close friend was the academic and activist Carlos E. Castañeda. Originally from Mexico, he became a US citizen in the late 1930s. Castañeda was a LULAC member in Del Rio and Austin and spoke at LULAC events in the 1930s.[66] As a professor at the University of Texas in Austin, he collaborated with LULAC, spoke at its events, worked with the School Improvement League in San Antonio, and took a leave of absence to work in Del Rio with the San Felipe School District. He also worked with the Federal Employment Practices Commission, the first federal civil rights agency dealing with employment discrimination. He wrote about Catholic heritage in Texas and other historical topics. He was an acquaintance of Sloss-Vento; she attended several of his talks in Mission and promoted his seven-volume book series *Our Catholic Heritage*.[67] He called her a "valued and esteemed person."[68]

Another activist from this cohort was George I. Sánchez, but Sloss-Vento appears to have had no personal contact with him. Sánchez was born in New Mexico, graduated from the University of California in Berkeley, and became a professor of education at the University of Texas in Austin. LULAC had been embedded in New Mexico since 1936, and he became LULAC's national president in 1940.[69] Blanton originally called him a "service intellectual" but later referred to him as a public intellectual and activist.[70] Sánchez conducted research that he used to challenge racist intelligence tests and desegregation lawsuits. In 1940 Sánchez moved to Austin, where he lived the rest of his life.[71] Since Sloss-Vento mostly lived in the Valley and Sánchez lived in Austin, they probably never met, and they apparently did not write one another.[72] Along with Perales, she condemned his association with the Saunders-Leonard booklet, the "wetback pamphlet," and no friendship developed between them thereafter.

SLOSS-VENTO AS LETTER WRITER

Sloss-Vento used her pen to extend her network outside of San Juan, Corpus Christi, and Edinburg, the towns where she lived. She established this network on her own as one of a shared sociopolitical interest—the Mexican

American civil rights movement. She could have written letters to family members, friends, patrons, business contacts, academics, or intellectual acquaintances. Her archive shows those are not the people to whom she wrote. I saw most of Sloss-Vento's collection that her son shared with me, and it does not include correspondence with family and friends. She corresponded with Perales's wife, Marta, mostly after his death in 1960. Marta became her main correspondent after 1960. Sloss-Vento's friends were political and civic-minded allies. In a 1954 letter to Perales she writes, "I owe responses to Miss Olivares, Mr. de la Paz y many other people."[73] Instead, she chose to write her three friends, all major figures in LULAC and the early Mexican American civil rights movement. She wrote letters not as a feminine (familial) act but as a political act.

Had Sloss-Vento been a traditional woman, she would have corresponded with Marta Perales, not Alonso. Adela Sloss-Vento and Alonso Perales and their spouses and children visited socially, but there are only one or two letters between her and Marta before 1960. Her letters to Alonso Perales typically ask him to say hello to his wife from her and her husband.[74] The two women grew close through letters and phone calls. Both had a shared mission—to save his archives and memorialize his life.

Sloss-Vento's geographic location, gender, and occupation prevented more face-to-face contact with these men. She was not as mobile as men. Although she could drive, she had familial and work obligations. And since she worked after 1949, she could not take off as readily as Perales or Canales, who had offices and secretaries.

The letter was her tool to communicate and activate. O'Neill observes that "letters were the connective tissue that held together widespread networks."[75] In *The Opened Letter* O'Neill explains, "Letters were meant to nurture whole networks, not only intense relationships between two people or an individual sense of self. Recognizing the networking function of letters provides us with a new way to see letters: they are less objects of personal and private meditation and more objects of larger social use."[76] When Sloss-Vento mailed her letters she solidified her network with the three men. Even though she called herself a "collaborator" with these three, all reciprocated and found in her a trusted friend, confidant, and political ally.

SLOSS-VENTO'S CORRESPONDENCE WITH MEN

Among Texas women activists, Sloss-Vento had the closest relations with these three male leaders. They were her colleagues and inspired her for decades.[77] Sloss-Vento's correspondence reveals the extent and nature of these professional and personal ties. Letters referred to recent political and intellectual concerns and hardly addressed family or interior lives; they were typically professional with little chitchat. How do we account for the unique epistolary relations Sloss-Vento had with men? The letters focused on newspaper commentary, legislation, and organizing among Mexican Americans.[78] She called these leaders "co-activists," but they did not use that term. In doing so she included herself as an activist and saw herself as their equal. Still, she did not call herself an "activist" overtly, a sign of gendered constraint.

Before considering these friendships I want to consider sexuality. There is no evidence that Sloss-Vento was infatuated with or interested in any of these men in a sexual way; likewise, to my knowledge none of the men expressed sexual interest in her. No desire can be documented. All were married and none of the letters intimate. The nature of these relationships with regard to power, influence, and mentorship should also be considered. Kabalen de Bichara suggests that Sloss-Vento positioned herself "within the shadow of male leaders,"[79] though she credits her in other ways.

Sloss-Vento acknowledged these men not only as leaders in the Mexican American civil rights movement but also as actors in Mexican American history. Laura Garza says of Sloss-Vento, "Recognition of these Mexican American leaders in the Borderlands represents her national idea."[80] In her book, *Alonso S. Perales*, Sloss-Vento recognizes their leadership and even likens Perales, Sáenz, and Canales to messiahs: "I have always said to myself: 'That great leaders like Alonso S. Perales have been called upon by God for such struggle. Although the struggle is like a "crucification," they know in their hearts that is the only course that can free any people from exploitation and suppression.'"[81] And like Christ, they suffered: "Often, our leaders were persecuted by politicians, Anglos, and in some cases by our own people. But their ideal was as noble as their spirit."[82] She quotes Castañeda, who had called Perales a "prophet."[83] She continues with the analogies: "In the early years of struggle they were also crucified . . . fighting for justice. . . . This was their duty to their dying day."[84] She writes that when Perales died in 1960, the "weather unexpectedly changed to a gloomy dark sky."[85] Of Sáenz she states, "There is no doubt that he was chosen by God to solve our problems."[86] She felt these men were on earth to save La Raza. In her book she does not discuss other leaders from the 1920s through the 1970s. In a manuscript she contends, "Nobody else knew how to sacrifice and fight until the end of their days."[87] Many others did indeed sacrifice and fight, but she did not focus on any of them.

Sloss-Vento and Perales

Of the three, Perales and Sloss-Vento had the most active professional relationship. Perales lived in the Valley briefly in the 1920s but spent the rest of his life in San Antonio. While many of his letters to her were lost by Sloss-Vento over the years or mailed to others by her in her effort to share them, her collection contains twelve envelopes from Perales's law office postmarked in the 1930s through 1950s.[88] Her collection has six letters from Perales in the 1950s.[89] However, the Perales collection has dozens of letters from Sloss-Vento to Alonso S. Perales, especially in the 1950s.

Perales's own family had mostly traditional roles for women. Perales's mother was a homemaker. Perales's wife, Marta, was a homemaker as well; the couple adopted children in the early 1950s. She may have assisted him at his law office, probably ran the short-lived Perales book store, and made several inventions, but mostly she abided by gender rules. She joined the Pan American Round Table, an interracial women's organization interested in

FIGURE 5.2. Alonso S. Perales: attorney, diplomat, public intellectual, author, LULAC principal founder, civil rights activist, and Adela Sloss-Vento's co-activist and the subject of her book, 1960. Courtesy of the M. D. Anderson Library, University of Houston.

US–Latin American relations, but she was not a Ladies LULAC member.[90] Marta Perales accompanied her husband to few LULAC events as his wife.

Alonso S. Perales had traditional ideas of women's place. Mario T. García contends that Perales cannot be fully understood "without understanding the centrality of his Catholic faith," and this Catholicism included traditional gender rules.[91] While he was a "new Mexican-American man,"[92] this new man was not new in gender relations. Perales was largely responsible for the exclusion of women from LULAC; he too was a man of his times and culture. He was aware of gender when he wrote Eduardo Idar in 1928: "Please make another effort to keep the Boys together."[93] Perales did not invite Sloss into LULAC. And he contended that Mexican American women should instead involve themselves in the Spanish-Speaking PTA.[94] Again, in 1933 in a letter to J. T. Canales he reiterates the need for homosocial LULAC chapters.[95]

Sloss-Vento honored Perales in her newspaper writings. She did so in the early 1930s and around March 1952 in *La Prensa* and *La Voz*; the latter was the Spanish-language newspaper of the Catholic Action and Social Justice Center and was published by the San Antonio archdiocese. The government of Spain awarded Perales a Medal of Civil Merit in 1952. Her letter published in *La Prensa* about the honor is titled "Attorney Alonso S. Perales, Champion Defender of Racial Dignity."[96] She declares, "The noble struggle of Alonso Perales will always be great and everlasting. His name will always sound to us as magic music that speaks of hope, faith, honor, justice, and liberty."[97] When he died in 1960 she wrote a tribute to "the great defender, attorney Alonso S. Perales," that *La Prensa* published.[98] In it she again refers to the medal he received from Spain: "The people of Mexican descent in Texas have profound gratefulness and love for Alonso S. Perales, who is regarded as the Champion, the defender of the rights and racial dignity of Mexicanos in Texas. Spain has been the first to recognize Alonso S. Perales. . . . His name will always sound to us like magic music that speaks of hope, faith, honor, justice, and liberty."[99]

She was Alonso S. Perales's biggest supporter. Sloss-Vento documented the life and character of Perales more and better than any other person did. The historian Richard García has found, "Adela Sloss-Vento captures a few of his notable qualities: his intellectuality, his dedication to humanity, his devotion to all Americans of Mexican descent and Mexican workers, and in spite of all his responsibilities, his ability to be and live free." He likewise praises Perales, saying he had all the "qualities of a patriot, a humanitarian, and [was] one who loves justice and seeks to protect the rights of others."[100]

Perales may have seen Sloss-Vento as his near equal, although LULAC initially excluded women and later accepted them only in women's chapters. Kabalen de Bichara has suggested that Perales was Sloss-Vento's mentor, but that was not the case. She contends that he was an "elder" guiding a "novice" and instructed Sloss-Vento on how to open an adult night school in San Juan.[101] Perales was only three years older, and she was not a novice. But sometimes Perales's activist tone was to tell others what to do and how.[102] Kabalen de Bichara interprets Perales's advice to Sloss-Vento to ignore a murder case and get busy with the adult classes as a gendered response. She argues that Sloss-Vento was "speaking outside the limits that were culturally imposed upon women during this time period."[103] That is who Sloss-Vento was, and that is exactly what she did. Perales himself taught adult classes. The only woman Perales mentored was the teenager Vilma Martínez in the 1950s.[104] Her family asked Perales to help her, and he did. Martínez attended law school and in the 1980s presided over the Mexican American Legal Defense Fund, an effort by Latinx lawyers and allies; Martínez would even become a US ambassador to Argentina during the Obama administration.

Laura Garza also contends that Perales heavily influenced Sloss-Vento's ideology: "Because of her close relation to Alonso Perales, she supports and promotes the integration and assimilation of these new settlers to the American hegemonic culture."[105] But Sloss-Vento had her own mind.

Perales appreciated and admired his friend and comrade Sloss-Vento. In 1931 he writes, "My dear Miss Sloss: Again I wish to congratulate you on the splendid service you and your friends are rendering our race and our country in the Lower Rio Grande Valley. Your letter of the 18th instant is more encouraging. I am certain others will follow your good example."[106] In 1947 he acknowledges her "bella y noble labor" (beautiful and noble work) and informs her that he cited her in his June 12, 1947, column in *La Prensa*.[107] He goes on to say, "I have always admired your work and I thank God for giving us people like you who are sincere and not self-interested and who focus on the progress and advancement of our people."[108] He adds that her article was "magnificent." In 1948 his postscript to a letter reads, "I sincerely congratulate you for your beautiful work on behalf of our people. I always read your letters and articles with great interest. Onward. I'm happy, thank God, that we have leaders like you."[109] In 1954 he addresses her in several letters as "Sra. Doña Adela S. de Vento," the "Doña" signifying a title of respect in Mexican culture. In one such letter he proclaims, "Too bad there aren't more people like you who are truly interested in solving the problem."[110] In the same letter he addresses her as "my distinguished and fine friend."[111] After reading an article Sloss-Vento wrote about him, Perales tells her, "I am further deeply indebted to you for this kind gesture."[112]

At no time did Sloss-Vento prove her loyalty to her friend Alonso S. Perales more openly than when he was under public attack for his stance

FIGURE 5.3. Adela Sloss-Vento, Pedro C. Vento, and Alonso S. Perales outside the Alamo Heights Motel, San Antonio, Texas, circa 1950. Courtesy of the M. D. Anderson Library, University of Houston.

on the "wetback pamphlet." Sánchez and Ed Idar Jr. disagreed with him on the publication, and Idar attacked Perales in the press. She tells Perales in a letter dated December 12, 1951, "I have just received your two letters and I'm aware of the gross response by Dr. Sanches [*sic*]. . . . Don't worry. . . . You will always live in the heart of all patriotic citizens."[113]

Perales's public recognition of Sloss-Vento appears in one of his "Arquitectos de nuestro propio destino" columns in *La Prensa*. He writes of her pen and calls her an "articulista" (essayist). He also says, "She is very intelligent, active, enthusiastic, and sincere and her noble work and contributions have earned her the title of excellent civic leader of our community in this nation."[114] He did this in the same column in which he reprints much of her "El precio de la desunión." He included her letter to the editor titled "Cheap Labor Does Not Pay in the Long Run" in his book *Are We Good Neighbors?*[115] He attended an event in San Antonio that honored her, as a photograph documents. She writes in her book that he was planning to acknowledge her—perhaps as a writer, activist, or leader—in *La Prensa* in the early 1960s, but he died before he could do so. She recalls, "He had even asked for a photograph of myself for an article he was writing noting my zeal in collaborating in favor of our cause."[116] She was, in her words, "by his side."[117] Perales might have done more to promote Sloss-Vento. She sent him a book manuscript that he might have edited or helped to get published.

Sloss-Vento and Sáenz

Sloss-Vento also had a friend, comrade, and compadre in J. Luz Sáenz. There is little information about his wife, María Petra Esparza Sáenz, who evidently was busy raising their eleven children. Sáenz was born in 1888 in Realitos in South Texas. He began working at age eleven and traveled with his father to the Texas towns of San Diego, Beeville, and Gonzales. The historian Emilio Zamora describes Sáenz's early work: "Taming horses; clearing the land of brush and hardwood trees with a pick, ax, and shovel under an unrelenting sun; and picking tall cotton plants with sacks that grew heavier with every passing hour taught Sáenz the meaning of hard work."[118] Sáenz benefited from the mentoring of the publisher, teacher, and accountant Eulalio Velazquez, who lived in Alice.[119] Sáenz graduated from high school in 1908 and began teaching at age eighteen. In 1911 he joined the Mexican Protective Association, which organized in San Antonio in response to lynchings and had twenty-five chapters across Texas. Sáenz attended college for a year after World War I, taught for thirty-four years in thirty public schools, and served as a principal at several. He would work on a master's degree in the 1950s at Sul Ross University in Alpine in West Texas, the college his son also attended.

Sáenz volunteered to fight in World War I. He kept a diary of his wartime experiences and taught Mexican and Mexican American fellow soldiers how to read and write. He finally published his diary in the 1930s as *Los méxico americanos en la Gran Guerra*. Sáenz, like Perales, did not access academic presses, probably because they were writing from outside of that network available largely to scholars like Sánchez and Castañeda. In order to self-publish his book, Sáenz asked his collaborators to purchase copies in advance. The book contains a "List of Honor," organized by town, of those early patrons, fellow World War I veterans, and civil rights supporters.[120] Out of the 162 people named, six were women. Along with the name of Zara Thigpen (a Euro-Texan?) was that of Adela Sloss.

Sloss-Vento had little correspondence with Sáenz since she made "frequent trips to his home."[121] He spent decades in the Valley, two of them in McAllen.[122] Only five letters between Sáenz and Sloss-Vento have survived, all in the Sáenz archive. Sáenz did not correspond regularly with other women; archives have one letter to Consuelo Méndez of the Austin LULAC and one to Elena Zamora O'Shea, his Alice teacher who had moved to Dallas.[123]

Sloss-Vento's letters to Sáenz are more personal and familiar than those to Perales. Their letters provide evidence that on several occasions she gave him money and did so without embarrassment. In 1951 she tells him, "You keep making sacrifices and expenses for our defense. . . . I am sending you this $50.00 and use it for expenses of the same cause or how ever you please. Use them to broadcast or for leaflets or expenses incurred with the people. You know better than I what needs to be done."[124] The reference to "however you

FIGURE 5.4. J. Luz Sáenz: teacher, LULAC co-founder, civil rights activist, public intellectual, author, and Adela Sloss-Vento's co-activist, circa 1940s. Courtesy of the University of Texas at Austin, General Libraries, Benson Latin American Collection.

please" was her acknowledgment that she knew he had personal expenses since he had eleven children and frequently lost his job due to activism. Around 1952 she sent him fifteen dollars for advertising; he signs the letter acknowledging it, "Sincerely your friend."[125] Indeed Sáenz was her friend and confidant.

Sloss-Vento told Sáenz that her husband occasionally nagged her about her activism or civil rights expenses. It is likely that Pedro nagged her because of her health or because her funding of activist causes meant less money for the family. Their son, Arnoldo Vento, recounts that his father "believed in saving for a future emergency." He writes, "In the fifties, their pact was to save for the college education of their children. . . . Still, she spends much of her small monthly check on her lifelong Civil Rights Cause."[126]

Sloss-Vento honored Sáenz when he died in 1953. In 1966 a school in Alice was named after him. She published a pamphlet, "In Memory of Professor J. Luz Sáenz, a Great Patriot and Defender of the Latin American people," for the dedication of a portrait for the J. Luz Sáenz Elementary School.[127] She did not speak at the event commemorating the portrait, but her name and those of her family members appear in the program among hundreds of donors as "Friends of J. Luz Sáenz Elementary School."[128] Listed are Mrs. Anselma G. Sloss (Adela's mother), Mr. & Mrs. P. C. Vento, Mr. & Mrs. Pedro Vento, Miss Irma Vento (their daughter), and Mr. Arnoldo Vento (their son). Did Adela send money under these various names? She typically put her money where her mouth was.

Sloss-Vento and Canales

Sloss-Vento's ties to J. T. Canales were professional and friendly. Scholars have called him a Renaissance man, as a landowner, rancher, farmer, lawyer, judge, state legislator, writer, historian, philanthropist, humanitarian, civil rights activist, and political activist.[129] Canales's family had a Spanish land grant and maintained their wealth after 1848 and into the twenty-first century. He attended the University of Michigan law school and saw racial discrimination against African Americans on trains on one of his trips to Michigan in 1897. Though he passed for white because of his light skin, he saw a curtain segregating African Americans and other dark-skinned people from whites for lunch and dinner. When he returned to Texas he saw segregation in railroad stations, theaters, restrooms, and drinking fountains. He experienced racism firsthand despite his light color and US citizenship. And while he was a Texas state legislator around 1910, he was called "the greaser from Brownsville."[130] Canales served as a legislator from 1905 to 1910 and in the late 1910s. As a lawmaker he spearheaded a critical investigation of Texas Rangers' atrocities committed against Tejanos and Mexicans in the 1910s that led to the Rangers' reorganization in 1919. He was a Brownsville city attorney from 1930 to 1937 and a judge.[131]

Perhaps he and Sloss-Vento would have been closer if Canales had been less wealthy, more social, and a consistent Democrat. Canales was rich and as such had much more leisure than she had. Canales feared germs and limited his social contacts. Sloss-Vento was a loyal Democrat, while Canales supported some Republicans.[132] Moreover, he was of Jewish origin, raised Catholic, became Protestant, and studied his various faiths. She was Catholic. He lived in Brownsville and she in San Juan, Corpus Christi, and Edinburg.

Canales was the fellow activist with the most liberal views toward women. He voted for women's suffrage and supported women college graduates. He wrote a pamphlet on the Angel of Goliad, a Mexican woman who saved Colonel James Fannin and other Euro-Americans from death by General Antonio López de Santa Anna of Mexico in the 1830s during the conflict between Texians and Mexico. Upon the passage of a bill promoting a monument to the Angel of Goliad in 1957, Canales explains in a letter, "It is unnecessary for me to tell you that this is the greatest compliment that our State Legislature has ever bestowed on a woman (that is on a Mexican woman) for a noble and merciful Christian act. It is an honor to our race."[133] He also helped fund the construction of a nursing school at Mercy Hospital in Brownsville, an act that especially helped Mexican American women in the Valley.[134] He worked to pass a bill to create a school of nursing for women in each Texas county.

Canales was comfortable with political and intellectual women. His favorite governor was Miriam A. Ferguson, an enemy of the Ku Klux Klan. In the 1930s he became an adviser during her second term.[135] He wrote numerous letters to politicians and historians, but he probably wrote few in a personal way. Canales's biographers Michael Lynch and Carlos Larralde assert, "He valued friendships and generally functioned within a sphere of friends to accomplish his goals."[136] They note, "Among his friends were politicians, statesmen, lawyers, academics, and churchmen."[137] The historian Florence Johnson Scott, a European American woman, visited with Canales in his home.[138] His closest lifelong friend was Carlos E. Castañeda, who grew up in Brownsville,[139] and Sloss-Vento also proved a true friend to Canales.

There is no correspondence in the archives between Canales and Sloss-Vento in the 1920s and 1930s, but there are more than twenty letters between them in the 1940s and the 1950s. Canales wrote her twelve times in the 1950s.[140] The Canales and Vento families did not visit one another. Canales

FIGURE 5.5. J. T. Canales: attorney, judge, LULAC co-founder, civil rights activist, author, and Adela Sloss-Vento's co-activist, circa 1950s. Courtesy of the University of Texas at Austin, General Libraries, Benson Latin American Collection.

married Anne Wheeler, a European American. He supported interracial marriage such as his own and disapproved of laws banning it.[141] Anne Canales did not participate in LULAC or civil rights causes. She was interested in clothes, needlework, and card games, not politics.[142] "Shortly after his marriage to Anne, he realized that his wife was a conformist preoccupied with her house and social graces," Lynch and Larralde contend.[143] Canales does not mention his wife in his letters to Sloss-Vento.

Sloss-Vento supported Canales's historical and intellectual projects in the late 1940s and the 1950s.[144] Like her, he "aimed at increasing knowledge, instructing the ignorant, and correcting perceived wrongs."[145] In 1947 he asked her to prepare two hundred to three hundred pamphlets based on an outline he sent her for his talk about the Mexican Revolution at Teatro Murrillo in San Juan.[146] He asked her in 1953 to distribute one hundred copies of *La Verdad* newspaper of Corpus Christi to judges and lawyers in Edinburg, McAllen, Mission, Weslaco, Pharr, and Mercedes.[147] Canales had secretaries but considered Sloss-Vento a public servant, not his secretary.

Sloss-Vento helped Canales sell two of his history books, *Bits of Texas History in the Melting Pot of America*, published in 1950, and *Juan N. Cortina Presents His Motion for a New Trial*, in 1951; the latter is about his Mexican American relative who resisted Euro-American encroachment after the US-Mexico war.[148] She supported his writing of history because he was a revisionist historian who challenged racial myths and misinformation purported by the Texas State Historical Association (TSHA). Lynch and Larralde assert, "To Canales, the Southwestern Historical Association [TSHA?] was a social and political entity. While it demanded rigorous standards of evidence, it never questioned the mythology of the Alamo that penetrated into textbooks."[149]

Canales admired Sloss-Vento more after she went out of her way to stand up for him. In the 1950s Canales sought disbarment of Fidencio Garza of Jim Hogg County. Later Canales accused District Judge C. Woodrow Laughlin of Alice and District Judge Ezequiel D. Salinas of Laredo of crimes and judicial improprieties.[150] Salinas retired from public office and sued Canales for libel in 1953. Canales agreed not to pursue the matter further; the case had taken a toll on his wife's health and his own.[151] Sloss-Vento came to his support, and in 1954 he thanked her: "You are a dear and faithful friend, whom I greatly esteem."[152]

By the mid-1950s Canales had nothing but praise for Sloss-Vento. In 1952 he tells her, "You have done more and are doing more to help the Latin Americans in Texas than any other person. I wish you were living near me, here in Brownsville, where I could consult with you."[153] He calls Sloss-Vento "the Doña María Josefa Ortiz de Domínguez of Texas," a reference to a heroine of the struggle for Mexico's independence in 1810 who risked her life to undermine Spanish colonialism. Canales was the second activist to call her that. In 1956 Canales tells Sloss-Vento that her daughter, Irma, was fortunate in "having such a mother as you."[154]

The historian Elizabeth Salas has examined the various ways Chicanos and Mexicans, women and men like Canales, have referred to revolutionary women in Mexico. Salas contends, "The struggle of Chicanos in the United States has often been perceived as a war requiring that all male and female Mexicans help fight for cultural integrity and civil rights."[155] She has found that during the Mexican Revolution of 1910–1929, women revolutionaries were considered either "fierce fighters for justice" or "little more than camp followers," the latter known as "Adelitas" or "Las Adelitas" after a woman of the time.[156] Salas says an Adelita is seen as "a sweetheart of the troops, a woman who is valiant, pretty, and [a] wonderful helpmate to the soldier."[157]

Sloss-Vento refers to herself as "La Adelita" in a note in her papers; she knew Mexico's heroines, and she was a woman warrior for La Raza in Texas, not simply a helpmate at the side of men.

While Canales thought highly of Sloss-Vento, it was she who honored him. When a Brownsville elementary school was named after him in 1952, it is unclear if Sloss-Vento attended the event, but she took time to write some notes about him on an envelope accompanying a clipping about the occasion: "He has given thousands of dollars for buildings and schools besides giving thousands of dollars in scholarships for our youth who could not attend college for lack of funds. Is there another soul this patriotic and generous? It does not matter that he was born rich. God had given him a heart of gold and a big soul, generous, full of patriotism and with love for the things God made."[158] When Canales died in 1976 Sloss-Vento honored him with a letter to the editor in the *McAllen Monitor*.[159] A few months later in a letter to the editor about a decline of personal values, she recalls Canales's 1937 essay "Our Responsibilities for the Education of Our Children."[160]

Disaffected LULAC Leaders

Interestingly, another tie between the correspondents was that none of the four was a member of LULAC by the mid-twentieth century. Sloss-Vento evidently never joined Ladies LULAC. Perales, Sáenz, and Canales exited LULAC over time. The men distanced themselves from the organization because of personality and ideological conflicts as well as organizational infighting.

Perales, the principal founder of LULAC, was its most prominent leader throughout the 1930s, but he resigned from LULAC by 1940.[161] He was the major author of LULAC's aims and principles in the original LULAC constitution of 1929. He served as national president in 1930–1931 and held numerous positions and roles until 1937. He founded LULAC Council 16 in San Antonio because he was not happy with Council 2 in the same city. But in 1937 national LULAC voted Council 16 out of existence allegedly since San Antonio already had a council but more so because Perales had rivals.[162] He last served as a LULAC national officer in 1936–1937, as inspector general.[163]

Sáenz also left LULAC. He and Perales had organized the earlier Latin American Citizens League. As a LULAC co-founder, he also helped write its aims and principles. He served on LULAC's board of trustees from 1930 to 1932. From 1932 to 1933 he was a special organizer and may have helped establish the first Ladies LULAC council.[164] His last position in national LULAC was in 1932. He probably quit LULAC when Perales did.

Canales was central to LULAC in several ways before he quit. He helped found LAC in 1927 and wrote most of the 1929 LULAC constitution. He was LULAC's national president in 1932–1933. In 1938 he served as a special organizer in the Valley, where he helped reorganize the chapter in Mission. He collaborated on revising the 1939 LULAC constitution.[165] Beginning in 1938, though, he ran into conflict with other leaders. In 1938 he supported efforts to allow LULAC members to hold political offices; in 1941 he voiced opposition to a rewriting of the aims and principles, and he quit.[166] He also feared LULAC might become a social service club.[167] He exited LULAC after serving as chaplain general in 1940–1941.

Canales explains his resignation in a letter to Perales in 1958 after recapping Perales's own departure from LULAC: "Eventually, you were paid for your noble efforts by being thrown out; or maybe by compelling you to leave the League—the Instrument you had created. In other words, you were paid by ingratitude. . . . I would have been thrown out of LULAC had it not been for the fact that I anticipated the effort against me and sent my resignation requesting my withdrawal from LULAC, at its meeting in Dallas in 1941. Thus, I became with you and Prof. Sáenz, outcasts from LULAC; and of this I am and I feel very proud."[168]

In essence, a tie that bound them had been burned by LULAC, yet they all continued to work independently of the league for decades, still trying to further the cause of the Mexican American civil rights movement. Perales, Sáenz, and Canales came to understand the sting of exclusionary politics, a tradition that Sloss-Vento knew too well as a woman.

CONCLUSION

Mexican American women in Texas were not fully welcomed in civil rights activism from 1920 to 1970. Most civil rights organizations were founded by men and led by men, often male attorneys. Through her actions and life Sloss-Vento rejected the practice, policy, and ideology of homosociality. LULAC first excluded her as a woman, and after 1931, when LULAC created Ladies LULAC, she rejected that option; she understood it to mean she was to be relegated to civil rights homosocial organizational confinement. In her writings she never openly and publicly challenged homosociality as a way to organize La Raza, yet she did not fully abide by its rules. Her activist contacts and friends were men, not women. She had no correspondence with women about civil rights issues.

The relations Sloss-Vento had with Mexican American men provides insight into unique friendships and activist ties during an era of homosociality before 1970. She joined the boys' network at the nexus of politics, ideology, and intellect. She was neither bossed by male leaders nor mentored by them, and she did not stand in their shadows. She was both a political insider and a gendered outsider.

Yet her relations with Perales, Sáenz, and Canales offer insights into male leaders' attitudes toward women that indicate a more liberal tendency than has been shown previously. None of the three men was overtly sexist, patronizing, or condescending to her. They saw her as exceptional, and they collaborated with her. She was her own person, and they respected her. She was an activist, leader, and public intellectual working alongside male leaders for the same cause. Although these male leaders respected her, they did not elevate her to leadership. They did not include her or promote her enough. They were products of their times. More importantly, the men did not see the necessity of critiquing gender segregation. Still, in the world of civil rights, she was unusually free and might have been restrained by these Tejano male political leaders. Other Tejanas of the Mexican American civil rights movement before 1970 were excluded or limited.

Sloss-Vento had unique relations with Perales, Sáenz, and Canales. Perales was her comrade. Sáenz was a comrade and compadre; they had a strong relationship especially since he lived off and on in the Valley. She confided in him and gave him money. She had a more professional relationship with Canales up until the 1950s. After she defended him, he considered her a confidant.

Despite paying homage to these male leaders, Sloss-Vento did not idealize or idolize them. She operated as their equal and a fellow activist. She did not worship men. She honored only men worthy of respect. She sought to fill a void in Chicano history in writing about and advocating for these Mexican American civil rights leaders. She was well aware of the lack of Tejano and Tejana historians and scholars before the 1980s.

When Sloss-Vento referred to herself as a "collaborator" and "co-activist" in her letters, newspaper essays, and book, she inserted herself into the male domain of civil rights. At the same time, her practice of not explicitly calling herself an activist or leader suggests gendered ambivalence. It is more appropriate to call her what she truly was—an activist, leader, and civil rights pioneer. In their book *Chicanas in Charge*, Gutiérrez, Meléndez, and Noyola refer to Mexican American women of the early twentieth century as "trailblazer warriors" and "Adelitas." While "Adelita" has traditionally been used to refer to camp followers during the Mexican Revolution, the authors use it to refer to women warriors. Adela Sloss-Vento was an Adelita in Texas.

Sloss-Vento was unwilling to fight for a more public persona although she was an activist and leader. As a woman in the Mexican American civil rights movement she did not care about recognition of her role. When I was a young woman in the 1970s in the emerging Chicana feminist movement and beginning my career as a historian, I needed to know about her. I wish she had asserted herself as a role model, a pioneer feminist civil rights activist leader. This is another cause she could have served to benefit women in the Chicano movement and others.

CHAPTER 6

PUBLIC INTELLECTUAL

Adela Sloss-Vento was a major civil rights activist and prolific public intellectual. Her son, Arnoldo Vento, has called her a "leading intellectual."[1] She spent much of her time attempting to influence the public and elected officials including US presidents and several presidents of Mexico. She did so primarily through the press and letters. Newspapers were her major medium, and she wrote in two languages. She discussed the important issues of the day, doing so with understanding. Ironically, most of her works today are not particularly public—they cannot be readily accessed on the internet. Moreover, her name is virtually unknown to historians and the general public.

Sloss-Vento may be seen as a public intellectual, given her body of writings across seven decades, particularly in the Spanish- and English-language press in South Texas. During much of that time, few women were published in the US press, and few public intellectuals were recognized for their work in the Mexican American civil rights and Chicano movements.

SOUTH TEXAS NEWSPAPERS

Sloss-Vento effectively partook in the "art of lettered protest" and opinion pieces. Newspapers were to be taken advantage of, offering a place and space where residents or citizens could express opinions, inform, or persuade the public. No newspaper asked for her opinion, and no one asked her to serve as a columnist. Nor was she a trained or paid journalist. Yet, as a citizen she utilized the press. And it was in the home, not the newsroom, that she perfected the craft of political commentator.

South Texas had numerous Spanish, English, and bilingual newspapers. The first Spanish-language newspaper in Texas was published in 1829.[2] In the Valley, Spanish newspapers were many but often short-lived during Sloss-Vento's days. From 1927 to 1970 newspapers included *Diógenes* (McAllen) and *El Defensor* (Edinburg) in Hidalgo County; *El Comercio* (Harlingen) and *El Cronista del Valle* (Brownsville) in Cameron County; Rio Grande City's *El Fronterizo* and *La Revista Hispana* in Starr County; and Corpus Christi's *El Demócrata*, *El Paladín*, *La Verdad*, *El Progreso*, *El Heraldo*, and *Texas Mexican Gazette* in Nueces County.[3] The *Revista Latino-Americano*, edited by Gilberto Díaz and published from 1947 to about 1952 in Mission, Texas, was also important. *La Mañana* of Reynosa, Mexico, close to Brownsville on the border, could be found at Valley street corner stores, but she did not submit letters to it. There were also some short-lived Chicano movement newspapers such as *El Cuáhmil* in the Valley, but Sloss-Vento did not write in any of these.

San Antonio's *La Prensa* prided itself as the most important in serving as the statewide Spanish-language newspaper. Rómulo Munguía, a San Antonio newspaperman and printer, has written about *La Prensa* and *La Época* of that city: "Not only were they major in their local, national, and international influence, their plants far surpassed the physical and mechanical facilities of the *Light* and *Express*,"[4] the major English-language dailies there.

Sloss-Vento mostly wrote letters and longer opinion pieces that were published in Spanish-language newspapers in South Texas. To her, "newspapers were the right arm of our Causa."[5] She read but rarely wrote to Mexican newspapers. During the Bracero Program negotiations in 1954 she tells Perales, "I have been reading Mexican newspapers like the ones here about Bracero negotiations."[6] Although she read Mexican newspapers, her archive does not contain clippings from any. Her nation did not fully cross into Mexico though she cared about its people. Still, she wanted to inform Mexicans about Texas racism and did so through letters to Mexican as well as US government officials.

Sloss-Vento wrote in English-language newspapers especially after 1940. Most were controlled by whites, but African Americans owned a few papers. There were three major Valley newspapers during her writing days, the *Valley Morning Star/Harlingen Star*, *McAllen Monitor*, and *Brownsville Herald*. She did not write to the *Edinburg Daily Review*, which existed by the 1970s.[7] She could influence Euro-Americans and bilingual Mexican Americans after the 1940s; her public was both the Mexican-descent community and the dominant society. Another reason she tended to write in English-language newspapers after 1940 is that fewer Spanish-language newspapers survived the Depression. Munguía surmises that had the dominant *La Prensa* newspaper of San Antonio transitioned into a fully bilingual paper it would have survived.[8] *La Prensa* died by 1963. By 1951 Sloss-Vento lamented "so little

FIGURE 6.1. San Antonio's *La Prensa* newspaper staff dominated by men, 1929. Mexican American women journalists were few. Eleuterio Escobar Collection; courtesy of the University of Texas at Austin, General Libraries, Benson Latin American Collection.

cooperation from the press."[9] One of the few she counted on was *La Verdad* of Corpus Christi.[10] Only with the rise of the Chicano movement was there a resurgence in newspapers for the Raza community.

Before the 1960s the English-language press was mostly biased against the Mexican-descent community. It tended to ignore La Raza except to racialize and demean the community. Perales describes this bias:

> The Anglo-American press has not cooperated in the education of the people against said race discrimination problems. With the exception of the editorials of the distinguished editor Si Cassidy of the *McAllen Monitor* and one editorial [in] "*The Daily Texas*" [*Daily Texan*] by students of the University of Texas, I have never read or known of any newspapers or Anglo-American editorials that have condemned the problem of race discrimination against the people of Mexican origin in the State of Texas.[11]

Cassidy became the editor in the 1950s, and Sloss-Vento took advantage of this access. Outside of the labor union press, the liberal Texas press did not yet exist.

Sloss-Vento also charged several English-language newspapers with class bias favoring agribusiness. She writes in her 1947 manuscript "The Eternal Dilemma of the Wetbacks and Contracted Braceros which Serve Only for Injustice against Mexicans and Mexico":

> Even three newspapers in the Rio Grande Valley (*McAllen Evening Monitor*, *The Morning Star*, and *The Brownsville Herald*) which I believe are owned by one person, continuously side with farmers and are ready to strike a blow to anyone who opposes them. Mexican American workers do

> not have freedom of the press in the aforementioned newspapers; there is never an editorial in favor of their defense. . . . The newspapers alluded to, continuously write editorials against the Department of Immigration; what they desire for Mexico is to open up its borders pouring in thousands of Mexicans to work for nothing.[12]

Agribusiness always needed workers, preferably braceros because they were paid less than US residents. She points out in the essay the disadvantage that arrangement caused and the editorial silence surrounding it:

> In view that there are no editorials in defense of Mexican-American workers who have emigrated to the northern regions of the United States in search of work; in view that this group does not have freedom of the press from the aforementioned newspapers, I will not, under the circumstances, be able to sign my name [to letters to their editors]. What defense does one have who states the truth on the undocumented when these newspapers are opposed to one who brings to the surface the real issues of the exodus of the undocumented?[13]

Sloss-Vento criticizes the *McAllen Evening Monitor* for its silence on the "wetback pamphlet" as well and asks, "Why in 1951 was there an insulting pamphlet regarding all Mexicans and not a word was printed in defense of the wetback or Mexican? . . . [I]t was a study on the wetback but in reality, it was more of a pretext by the media to insult and degrade all Mexicans."[14]

WOMEN'S ACCESS TO THE PRESS

The press, in English and Spanish, suppressed women's voices. European American women in the United States emerged as journalists mostly after the Civil War and especially in the 1880s and 1890s. The historian Alice Fahs quotes a woman journalist describing the attitude in the 1880s: "The average managing editor or city editor will not believe that a woman is capable of handling anything but the latest parties, the latest dresses, the newest bonnets, the latest wedding."[15] Women were expected to cover soft news, topics supposedly of women's interest or human interest and not hard news like politics, crime, and war.

Journalism as a career for women became more accessible after women's suffrage in 1920. The historian Kathleen Cairns notes that from about the 1920s to the 1950s, "women could not break the gender barrier of the all-male press clubs, their salaries were often half those of their male counterparts, and they were not hired nearly as frequently as men."[16] In 1900, of the 30,098 journalists in the United States, 2,193 were women.[17] In 1920 there were 5,730 women journalists, and by 1950 there were 30,000, making up 32 percent of all US journalists.[18] Sloss-Vento was not a journalist by career; however, she was an outspoken commentator, writing opinion pieces and letters. She had her own ideas to promote.

Mexican American women had limited access to getting published in the press. Most newspapers were owned and run by European American men. Mexican American women controlled very few newspapers. There were Mexican-descent women writers before 1970 in the Spanish-language press but not in the English language. Who cared about the opinions of Mexican American and Mexican women in the United States? What ideas, concerns, and hopes did this populace have? To what extent were they the readership of newspapers? Mainstream society and too many Mexican-descent men sought to keep this populace silent and ignorant.

Most newspapers invented a women's page, a society page, or gendered women columnists in seeking to reach a female audience. Women were supposed to be interested in food, family, fashion, home furnishings, marriage, and parenting. According to the historian Julie Golia, between 1895 and 1935 women's sections in newspapers expanded, and "by the 1920s, large, segregated women's sections had become expected and standard parts of a newspaper design."[19] Women were not supposed to be interested in politics or world affairs. *La Prensa* was one such newspaper that reached a broad segment of the Mexican American, Mexican, and Latin American audience but also suppressed women. It too had a women's page that did not interest Sloss-Vento. She turned her attention to essays on politics, immigration, and fascism instead.

MEXICAN AMERICAN AND CHICANO PUBLIC INTELLECTUALS

Sloss-Vento belongs to the category of both Mexican American and Chicano public intellectuals. Scholars have given little attention to Latinx intellectuals. The literary scholar Nicolás Kanellos has written of the Latinx intellectual tradition dating back centuries.[20] The philosopher Eduardo Mendieta suggests that Latinx public intellectuals exist but "have yet to assert their presence within a larger public sphere."[21]

Historians have named a few Mexican American intellectuals from the 1920s to the early 1960s. Mario T. García has identified the intellectuals Carlos E. Castañeda, who was born in Mexico; George I. Sánchez, who was born in New Mexico; and Arturo Campa, who was born in Mexico but spent most of his time in New Mexico.[22] Castañeda was a professor of history at the University of Texas in Austin. Sánchez also was a professor at the University of Texas in Austin. Of these, only Sánchez occasionally wrote for the public. He spent significant time conducting research that was used in legal cases. Olivas also has identified Alonso S. Perales as a public intellectual.[23] The activist Ernesto Galarza of California, who graduated from Columbia University, might have also been added.

García does not name any Mexican American women intellectuals for the period. Jovita González and Emma Tenayuca of Texas would have fit this title. González did try to reach the general public with her co-authored bilingual textbooks for the elementary level. Tenayuca of San Antonio was a brilliant intellectual, as especially can be seen in the insightful essay "The Mexican Question" she co-authored with her husband, Homer Brooks.[24]

Chicana historians have identified a few Chicana public intellectuals. Enriqueta Vásquez was especially active as a public intellectual during the Chicano movement, as was Elizabeth "Betita" Martínez, both of New Mexico.[25] Marc-Tizoc Gonzales has written about Latina/o public intellectuals and identified Dolores Huerta of the United Farm Workers as a public intellectual before and during the internet age.[26]

Sloss-Vento hardly called herself a writer, let alone a public intellectual. Did she see herself as a writer? Yes and no. Writing was both her ambition and profession since the 1920s, though it was unpaid. And as early as 1941 she planned on writing a book, probably following the publication of Perales's 1937 *En defensa de mi raza*.[27] J. Luz Sáenz published his book on his World War I experiences in the early 1930s. In 1953 Sloss-Vento sent Perales a book manuscript, and he passed it on to a professor at Incarnate Word College in San Antonio, but it was not published.[28] Was it lost or forgotten? Did someone discourage her? Or did she not make it a priority?

Sloss-Vento was a writer but ambivalent in calling herself one. She wrote of the "girl" who wrote "without being a writer" and a speaker "without being a public speaker." She was too modest. Finally, in her 1977 book she calls herself a "writer" and "authoress."[29]

DEFINING "PUBLIC INTELLECTUAL"

Defining an intellectual is difficult. Christopher Lasch offers this definition in his 1965 book:

> The intellectual may be defined, broadly, as a person for whom thinking fulfills at once the function of work and play; more specifically, as a person

> whose relationship to society is defined, both in his eyes and in the eyes of society, principally by his presumed capacity to comment upon it with greater detachment than those more directly caught up in the practical business of production and power. Because his vocation is to be a critic of society, in the most general sense, and because the value of his criticism is presumed to rest on a measure of detachment from the current scene.[30]

I will denounce but ignore his gendering of an intellectual as male and focus on the question of detachment. Can an intellectual be attached to his or her subject? Social scientists have long debated the issue of objectivity; for the present purpose I will assume that the nature of an intellectual is subjective. Intellectuals can also be activists not fully detached from their concerns and moved into action in different ways.

Defining a public intellectual is more difficult. In a 2001 essay the critical theorist Edward Said observes that "the definition of who or what a writer and intellectual is has become more confusing and difficult to pin down."[31] The *New York Times* writer Barry Gewen asks, "Who is a public intellectual?"[32] He answers that the intellectual's "public influence" is one criterion and not the intrinsic achievement of having written. The *Library Journal* writer Harry Frumerman defines a public intellectual as "one who plays the role of critical commentator for non-specialist audiences on matters of broad public concern." He names as essential traits "temperament, perspective, character, and knowledge."[33] Daniel W. Drezner has noted, "Public intellectuals pitch their ideas to the general reading public—and their writings appear in newspapers, magazines and books."[34]

Samuel McCormick suggests that a public intellectual is political. He or she is a person "in conflict with public authorities," "rhetorically skilled," and "morally inclined."[35] In *Letters to Power: Public Advocacy without Public Intellectuals*, McCormick says a public intellectual creates "open and often radical opposition to the state."[36] However, a critic can also be in conflict with other entities besides the state—the general public, a specific race, class, gender, or sexual identity. Indeed, public intellectuals fall across the political spectrum.

Some definitions of public intellectuals include character traits. Truthout, a nonprofit news organization offering independent news, suggests that a public intellectual is "fearless" and "independent." The organization's mission and thus perhaps the mission of public intellectuals is "to spark action by revealing systemic injustice and providing a platform for transformative ideas, through in-depth investigative reporting and critical analysis. With a powerful, in-depth voice, we will spur the revolution in consciousness and inspire the direct action that is necessary to save the planet and humanity."[37] But these transformative public intellectuals can be radical or conservative.

Public intellectuals care about their subjects and want to reach the public. Sloss-Vento's subjects included the Mexican people, immigrants, workers, women, and the poor. Gonzales has called public intellectuals like this "gente de corazón" (people with heart) serving "los de abajo" (those at the bottom).[38] Sloss-Vento was a public intellectual serving causes of social justice.

Other questions arise when defining a public intellectual. Who decides who is a public intellectual, and which public confers the title of "public intellectual"?[39] Public influence can be measured by written response, published debate, citations, and documented public acclaim. These are all dependent on a literate public and, in the internet age, Facebook friends, YouTube visits, and tweets. What if public influence through discourse and debate cannot be measured or documented? It is debatable how much or often a public intellectual has to write in order to garner or achieve this status. Some public intellectuals might work in an oral tradition, and their work is not documented. What if the public intellectual stimulates critical thinking, but this too cannot be measured or documented?

Questions about audience and community also emerge. Is a public intellectual one who seeks to influence an audience or community? Sometimes communities are imagined, and some communities' members might be illiterate or literate in only one language or may not read newspapers. What if the writer writes for the distinct community of policy makers, government officials, and people in power or the oppressed community itself? And sometimes the public intellectual is simply seeking self-expression and not public influence or acclaim. Some writers may write for two distinctive audiences or communities divided by language, and perhaps only one community offers recognition or validation. Illiteracy in the Mexican-descent community was a major hurdle. As late as 1948 in San Antonio, with a population of more than 100,000, La Raza accounted for 90 percent of the city's illiteracy.[40] How could a non-Spanish-reading audience know that Adela Sloss-Vento was a critical voice?

Gender defines and influences who is a public intellectual. Perales and Sloss-Vento may be compared as gendered public intellectuals.[41] Olivas has identified Perales as a public intellectual, and Richard García has called Perales a "citizen intellectual."[42] Sloss-Vento was a citizen intellectual, commenting on politics as an informed and intelligent member of society. Perales was a lawyer who graduated from National University in Washington, DC, and wrote hundreds of newspaper columns. Unlike

Perales, Sloss-Vento was not a lawyer, took only a few night classes in college in the 1950s, and yet published numerous opinion pieces and letters to the editors of various newspapers. Gender determined opportunity.

Sloss-Vento also may be compared with J. Luz Sáenz as gendered public intellectuals. Sáenz wrote letters that were published in both Spanish- and English-language newspapers. His writings in Spanish appeared in *La Prensa* (San Antonio), *El Latino-Americano* (Alice), and *La Verdad* (Corpus Christi). His writings in English were published in the *McAllen Evening Monitor* and *Texas Outlook*, a publication of the Texas Education Society.[43] Sloss-Vento could have had her writings published in all these periodicals except *Texas Outlook*, which typically published items by teachers and administrators. But she did not silence herself.

Who was Sloss-Vento's public, and how was she public? Before the rise of the feminist movement of the 1960s and 1970s, women were typically seen only as homemakers. In the borderlands women were especially tied to home and church. Was Sloss-Vento an intellectual, and to what extent is the term "public intellectual" challenged by class, race, gender, sexuality, age, region, marital status, and generation or era? Maybe Sloss-Vento helps to democratize the notion of a public intellectual, or maybe each public intellectual has an audience niche.

ORGANIC PUBLIC INTELLECTUALS

Besides considering Sloss-Vento a public intellectual, one might also call her an "organic public intellectual." Mendieta defines the term as someone who is "rooted in community and [has] addressed the community's concerns and debates, and who at the same time translates these concerns to the larger public and makes his or her specific community of origin aware of these concerns."[44] As a married, working, Mexican American woman with two children in South Texas in the pre–World War II years when college opportunities were limited, Sloss-Vento was an unlikely public intellectual. She operated in a Jim Crow/Juan Crow and patriarchal world.

Ronald N. Jacobs and Eleanor Townsley have asked, "Who speaks in the space of opinion?"[45] Were most public intellectuals before the late 1960s and 1970s college-educated European American men on the East Coast? It is likely that European American men in politics or academia have received more attention and that the diversity of more grassroots public intellectuals is unknown, unwritten, or just not celebrated.

Sloss-Vento was public as an unpaid citizen commentator in newspapers, highly visible and contentious places. She partook in the "art of lettered protest."[46] She did not write just for LULAC or Mexican Americans. In fact, only four articles by her appear in *LULAC News* or any LULAC newspaper affiliate. She sought a broader audience. When she wrote opinions published in *La Prensa* of San Antonio she reached a Tejano, Mexican, and Latin American audience.

Sloss-Vento had all the suggested traits of a public intellectual. As early as 1927 her fellow students called her "brilliant," "smart," and "ambitious." She was also known to be "willing to help everybody" and had the "capacity for hard work."[47] Yet, she was humble, sincere, caring, and diligent. She was a community servant. She was not totally fearless, as she acknowledged constraints on her public intellectual activism. (Who is "fearless"?) Yet she asserted her power as an autonomous force.

Also contributing to Sloss-Vento's identification as a public intellectual is the range of political materials she read. She read numerous local Spanish- and English-language newspapers from across South Texas. She read newspapers from Mexico, thus making her transnational. *El Mañana* of Reynosa, Tamaulipas, near Brownsville was her typical Mexican newspaper. She also read *Novedades* and *Universal Gráfico de Mexico*.[48] Reading *La Prensa* of San Antonio allowed her to be a global citizen, as it included extensive coverage of international news. In his book about Sloss-Vento, her son, Arnoldo Vento, writes, "She is an example of a person that is self-educated constantly improving her mind in all areas."[49]

Sloss-Vento stayed informed of current events and pending legislation. Her public intellectual work was not bookish or theoretical; she was interested in current issues and bettering the lives of others. She sought to inform the general public of injustices, educate the public, and sway politicians. Still, she read books and promoted a few, such as those by Perales, Sáenz, Canales, Castañeda, and their Euro-American contemporary Pauline Kibbe. Which other books she read is unknown, though I do know she admired Sor Juana Inés de la Cruz.

Like Perales, Sáenz, and Sánchez, Sloss-Vento deserves the distinction of being recognized as a public intellectual. Still, factors that affect comparisons are gender, marital status, children, class, and region. As men, they had greater access to education. As men, they had more access to better employment and higher wages. With the exception of Sáenz, who was a teacher but who had eleven children, they had more money than Sloss-Vento. As men, no one questioned their right to be involved in civic life or politics. As men, their wives took care of them. As men, none had to perform housework. As men, none of these men spent the time raising their children that their wives did. As men, they attended meetings at night after work without the responsibility of child care. Their wives allowed them freedom, or the men simply took it.

These Mexican American men were also more mobile than Sloss-Vento.[50] Most men could travel and seek opportunities outside the Valley and beyond Texas, an option fewer women had. Perales traveled to Washington, DC, for his education; he also visited numerous Latin American countries as a US diplomat. Sáenz traveled and worked in Central and South Texas and served in France and other locales during World War I. Canales traveled to Kansas as a young man and attended law school in Michigan. Sánchez was from New Mexico and traveled in the United States, Mexico, and Venezuela. Sloss-Vento traveled only in South Texas and Mexico and perhaps the places her children lived as adults.

Perales and Sánchez were educated professionals, while Sloss-Vento was an organic intellectual, a member of what Antonio Gramsci would call "the thinking groups which every class produces from its own ranks."[51] Raised working class, she and her husband rose to the lower ranks of the colonized Mexican American middle class. She remained in South Texas and mostly the Valley, an area historically suppressed by a lack of access to more and better education for La Raza. She was excluded from the opportunity of a scholarly education. She attended college classes only in the 1950s, studying English and writing to empower herself. Her experience is more impressive because of the gendered obstacles women faced.

Most of Sloss-Vento's male counterparts were conferred honorary titles for their work and intelligence, while she was Mrs. Vento. As attorneys, Perales and Canales had the title "licenciado," designating both education and profession; Sáenz was referred to as "profesor" as a sign of respect for teachers. Canales commanded his title as "judge"; Héctor García had the medical title "doctor"; and Castañeda and Sánchez had doctorates as professors. Only Sloss-Vento had no honorary title. She used "Srita.," "Sra.," or "Mrs." on occasion, perhaps attempting to use traditional gender norms to her advantage. Sometimes "Mrs." or "Sra." or "Mrs. P. Vento" could give her authority as a wife and could work in her favor. Letters she sent to Mexican officials were typically addressed from "Sra. A. S. de Vento," suggesting that she was connected to a husband. She knew gender was also to her disadvantage, but it was a disadvantage that she mostly ignored.

No title or person gave Sloss-Vento authority to speak—she gave herself authority. Kabalen de Bichara has described her as "a woman who demonstrates a capacity to use the written text as a means of contesting those in positions of power, even if it be the President of the United States or of Mexico."[52] Sloss-Vento was bold.

CONSTRAINTS ON SLOSS-VENTO'S ADVOCACY AND ACTIVISM

How do we account for public intellectuals who are activists? Defining "activist" is also difficult. Some self-identify as such, and others do not. Sometimes the label is applied by others. And activists can work for short or long periods and work in different ways. Most of Sloss-Vento's activism was enacted through the art of protest letters and opinion pieces.

Despite crossing homosocial political boundaries and devoting time and thought for decades, Sloss-Vento was constrained in her activism and writing by obstacles of race, gender, and class. She was cognizant of racial, patriarchal, political, and financial constraints on her public intellectual activism. She understood that the dominant society suppressed La Raza; she had no full "autonomy of speech."[53] In a letter to US President Harry Truman in 1952 she acknowledges this lack of speech: "The reason why you probably cannot hear from many of our people is because many of us are under the master's domination economically and to a few politically. Consequently, many of our people are not free to sign their names or to have freedom of the press and freedom of speech."[54] She did not sign the letter in her name but instead as "An American of Mexican descent." Perhaps she feared repression.

Gendered patriarchal constraints were another barrier. The patriarchal way of life in the United States, Mexico, and the borderlands for US women before 1970 was a major constraint. As a heterosexual, married woman with kids, Sloss-Vento was like most women—constrained by domesticity. But she was still able to work outside of the home as a single woman and as a married woman. Yet, her son has said, she felt "trapped."[55]

LULAC played a role in Sloss-Vento's gender constraint. She was not invited to attend the Harlingen Convention or join LULAC before 1933. To my knowledge, besides Eduardo Idar's 1928 invitation she was not invited to speak before any LULAC chapters, men's or women's. She was not asked to serve as a columnist for *LULAC News*. She was never profiled in any of the many biographies in *LULAC News*, which began publication in 1931 and exists to this day.

Sloss-Vento also encountered patriarchal constraints from her husband. Around 1951 she wrote to Sáenz, "You know I do everything because I defend my rights and I have always done so and even in opposition to my husband who has not wanted me to get involved in anything."[56] Her husband, Pedro C. Vento, obviously knew that he married an activist woman. He also knew she would spend money on her causes, though she agreed to save for the children's college fund. Her letters do not indicate the extent of opposition or support he may have shown toward her activism. Overall, their son has said, his father supported his mother's activism.[57] She did not give in.

Sloss-Vento also had class constraints. She was a member of the lower middle class in Mexican American society after 1930; theirs was a colonized middle class. She did not have the luxury of not working after her children entered school, especially because she wanted them to have a college education. In 1949 she began working as a jail matron, a position in which she worked twenty-four-hour shifts. In 1966 she reflects, "My salary for several years deducting the income tec. [*sic*] was $66.00 and after sixteen years of ruining my health, my salary when I quit was raised to $122.00. . . . And all because we had the necessity of educating my son and daughter."[58] She considered her paid work exhausting and debilitating. Her son said she had numerous medical issues but continued working.

There were workplace constraints on Sloss-Vento as well. She had to be careful not to cross the line as a public employee and be fired. She withheld her name from a letter published in the *Harlingen Star* on December 23, 1947, in which she asserts that Valley chambers of commerce were benefiting from undocumented labor.[59] In 1951 she told Perales she had written a response to the "wetback pamphlet" and was ready to publish it. She says of her jail matron job, "It's a job I don't like because it restricts me. You could say I don't have freedom of the press. . . . I can write but I'll get fired. But who cares. I'll find some kind of work."[60] She mentions freedom of the press to mean freedom of speech.

On several occasions Sloss-Vento explained that she was in a "political job." In 1951 she tells Perales, "I am bound hands and feet with this political job [at the jail]. Otherwise I would be the first to speak publicly."[61] She also writes in 1951 to Sáenz, "I am in a political job. . . . Because I am in this type of work I don't want my name mentioned."[62] To Canales also she writes, "I have a political job and I am unable to publish a lot of information, but perhaps you, Judge, [and] Perales had the same kind of complaints."[63] In 1953 she tells Fidel Velázquez, the secretary general of the Confederación Obrera Mexicana (Mexican Workers Federation), "I would appreciate that my name be withheld in future discussions of this information since my job is politically sensitive."[64]

She expressed the lack of her freedom of speech. In 1951 she tells Perales, "I have lived without freedom of the press and it feels like an eternity. You know that jobs in politics lack freedom of the press. I only expect to work a little more and retire from here. I am more buried in the wetback problems than ever. I learn a lot here. It will help me to write when I get out of here."[65] In 1953 she informs the Bishops Committee for the Spanish-Speaking, "I have my hands tied by having a political job, tho [*sic*] in my desire to seek justice, I play the part, one might say, of an undercover agent by writing and keeping records in the hope that others will find the way to end the vices, corruption, crimes, delinquency, broken homes that are taking place in our Communities of the border through vice and the heavy influx of illegal wetbacks."[66] Sloss-Vento explains in her book, "This writer at the time had a political job (and as one knows in most jobs related to politics, ones [*sic*] hands are tied, but not under these circumstances)."[67] She could be fired; writing in the press was not free—her public intellectual work was risky business. Another factor constraining Sloss-Vento was occasional opposition, as her son attests: "In the past, she had received 'ugly letters and threats' from the opposition who were behind the corruption and vice, necessitating her to use a pseudonym."[68] She kept none of these ugly letters.

Sloss-Vento felt censored, so she became in her own words an "undercover agent." She tells Canales in January 1953 about vice and political machines she is tracking in Pharr, Texas, near San Juan: "I have been working as an undercover agent and I have helped and I am helping the Immigration officers in many ways. Not even my husband knows of this kind of work that I am doing."[69] While probably not working to deport everyday immigrants, she could have worked to get rid of criminal immigrants or agents of what she considered vice. Or her undercover work might have been connected to her deputy sheriff status, achieved in January 1, 1953, under Sheriff E. E. Vickers in Hidalgo County.[70] She also used a reference to working "undercover" when writing Perales in 1951 about being in a political job but wanting to advocate against the wetback pamphlet.[71]

Marriage and motherhood were other constraints on her public advocacy. Wifely responsibilities, parenting, and household duties had to be completed. Nonetheless, she took her children to some civil rights meetings.[72] As a working woman, wife, and mother she must have written early in the morning or at night. She sought to assert her power despite motherhood, wifedom, and work. Also as a mother she was instructing her children on civic engagement, civil rights, and the power of the individual and mother.

Sloss-Vento had minimal impact, public influence, or power in her day. In a blog post, the historian, public intellectual, and activist Rodolfo "Rudy" Acuña warns of "illusions of power."[73] Edward Said has noted that public intellectuals have inconsistencies and contradictions based on personal, professional, and public interests.[74] Yet, he outlines their role: "The intellectual's role generally is dialectically, oppositionally, to uncover and elucidate the contest, . . . to challenge and defeat both an imposed silence and the normalized quiet of unseen power wherever and whenever possible."[75] Kabalen de

Bichara contends that Sloss-Vento "gave voice to those who could not speak for themselves."[76] Or who simply did not.

SLOSS-VENTO'S GENDERED SELF-CONSTRAINT

While Sloss-Vento had numerous factors working against her, she also constrained herself. These were not simply individual constraints, but structural, ideological, and gendered constraints that were masked as her tendency to silence herself. She constrained herself by writing in third person, by using pseudonyms, by using variations of her own name, and by not crediting herself. Kabalen de Bichara notes, "Sloss Vento is using a veiled discourse which would seem to be an acceptance of the marginal position imposed upon the female activist during the early period [of] the civil rights struggle."[77]

Sloss-Vento wrote about being persecuted but only in third person. In a 1969 letter to the editor in McAllen she tells the story of a young woman fighting vice and corruption in San Juan in the 1930s. She explains, "This is a tribute to those who are persecuted for seeking justice on behalf of their fellowmen,"[78] thus silencing her own autobiographical note. She goes on to tell of the young woman's work against corruption in the town of San Juan in the 1930s and refers to her as an "outstanding citizen" who worked for justice. She says that someone told others at a meeting the woman was holding, "This lady needs your help and unity, for she is among lions and tigers, etc."[79]

Sloss-Vento constrained herself by using pseudonyms. A letter to the editor published in 1940 was attributed to "Don Salvador Cárdenas"; she also signed letters as "I am an American" and "A Citizen (name withheld by request)."[80] Why a man? Because men were more privileged to speak out. Why "Don"? Because a respected man had more authority. Why an American? (Versus a Mexican?) Her son suggests that she received "ugly letters and threats" that necessitated her use of pseudonyms and prompted fear that her husband might lose his job.[81] "Latin Americans Loyal," an essay about Mexican "aliens" of Brownsville fighting in World War II, was published in 1942 in the *Brownsville Herald* and signed "A citizen of the U.S. of Latin descent, San Juan, Texas."[82] (Versus an "alien"?) It was easier for US citizens to speak out. In 1952 she wrote to the publisher Santos de la Paz in Corpus Christi inquiring whether she could use a pseudonym such as "An American of Mexican Descent" or "La Tejanita" or "La Adelita de Texas."[83] Again, she vacillated while still crediting herself as "La Adelita," a heroine of the Mexican Revolution. Around 1943 she signed a letter as "A Latin American natural born citizen of the United States who will not permit to be classified under any other term but WHITE."[84] She signed a letter to a TV station in Monterrey, Mexico, "Una México-Americana." She signed an essay to a Mexican public official "Una ciudadana Americana de ascendencia Mexicana" (An American citizen of Mexican descent).[85]

Sloss-Vento used a wide range of ways to sign her own name, perhaps to confuse readers about her identity. As a single woman she used "Miss Adela Sloss," "Adela Sloss," and "Srita. Adela Sloss." As a married woman she used "Adela Sloss," "Mrs. P. C. Vento," "Mrs. A. Sloss Vento," "Mrs. Adela S. Vento," "Adela Sloss Vento," "Adela Sloss de Vento," "Mrs. A. S. Vento," and "Mrs. A. S. V." She also used "Mrs. E. de la Garza," another pseudonym. Perhaps with more masks, she could inflict more political damage. After all, she was not writing to create a name for herself.

Sloss-Vento also wrote poetry that she privately published but not in her own name. Her chapbook, *Poemas del alma* (Poems from the soul), however, she signed "Adela Sloss-Vento." The booklet contains seven poems, and there are eight unpublished poems.[86] Most of the poems are about love; "A un arbol de orquídeas" (To an orchid tree) is a tribute to the Perales family.[87] Even in her poetry, she was less than pronounced.

Another way Sloss-Vento constrained herself was to not take credit for her place in history, either in female or activist form or both. She did not seek power, money, or fame. She did not write an autobiography, publish a collected essays book, sell or donate her archive to a library, or organize speaking engagements for herself, all acts suggesting self-importance. In 1978 she asked me how the journalist Gilberto Díaz of *Revista Latina* could sell his papers to a university library, but she did not try to sell her own.[88] She said her son might eventually get them to a university archive.

Her contemporary activist Dolores Huerta explains why people and especially women should take credit for their work:

> You must always stand up for the work you do, so that other people don't steal your thunder. It's hard for women to do this sometimes, because we can be so accommodating. We want to be helpful. We want to be supportive of others. But when it comes to the ideas we have, the good decisions we make, we have to be sure to take credit—even if people think we're being egotistical. I always say to women: It's important that we honor ourselves and our work.[89]

Arnoldo Vento's book on his mother and this one are now giving Sloss-Vento credit for her labor.

INTELLECTUAL ROLE MODEL: SOR JUANA INÉS DE LA CRUZ

Though constraining herself, Sloss-Vento had no problems in following the lead of Sor Juana Inés de la Cruz, a seventeenth-century Mexican nun and intellectual.[90] Sloss-Vento's library was not available for perusal, but it is evident she idolized this Mexican writer. De la Cruz was the first published feminist of the Americas and the "most outstanding writer of the Spanish American colonial period," writing in Mexico City in the mid-1600s, when intellect was discouraged for women.[91] She lived in an era before newspapers. Among Sloss-Vento's papers is the article she wrote, "Distinguished Women of Mexico; Sor Juana Inés de la Cruz."[92] Sloss-Vento's son said she identified with Inés de la Cruz. He notes this passage by Sor Juana that caught his mother's attention:

> Rejoice without fear of fate
> Amidst the course of vigorous age
> And not the death of the morrow
> Can carry away the joy
> You may have known and loved.[93]

In his book Arnoldo Vento writes that this strophe

> illustrates the dilemma of the woman who feels trapped, caught between her heartfelt sentiments and her position. . . . She [Sloss-Vento] also feels trapped. In the case of Sor Juana, it is between what is dear to her art (Arts and Sciences) and her Order and position as a nun. . . . It should be noted that when she wrote this essay on Sor Juana Inés de la Cruz, she was now working as a Jail Matron, restricted by politics and by time for her own work i.e. writing and fighting for the Cause.[94]

Like Sloss-Vento, de la Cruz "thirsted for knowledge."[95] De la Cruz opted for the nunnery, where she could avoid marriage to study, think, and write. On occasion de la Cruz used pseudonyms because it was not common for women to write at that time.[96] But de la Cruz had a space to write in—the nunnery. Sloss-Vento chose marriage and motherhood and so did not have a private space. Yet, whether in her living room or kitchen, Sloss-Vento carved out an intellectual space for herself. Thus, her scholar son was correct in stating, "Her vision is on the grander scale of a Sor Juana Inés de la Cruz or Simón Bolívar."[97]

A PUBLIC INTELLECTUAL YET INVISIBLE

Sloss-Vento sought a public voice though not necessarily a public persona. While she was not a reporter, editor, or columnist, she was intimately connected to newspapers. She sought to assert her voice and succeeded in doing so although she owned no newspaper and was not a paid journalist. She did not seek out a public persona as a writer. Otherwise, she would have signed her name in one way consistently. She wrote for different audiences in different towns and cities. She wrote in English and Spanish. She wrote over the decades. It is doubtful that she herself was a subject of public discussion. Rather, like a sniper she took occasional aim, never seeking to draw attention to herself.

Despite Sloss-Vento's career as a citizen-commentator and public intellectual resisting all types of injustices, she has largely been invisible. Public intellectuals can be seen or heard. Most have a regional or national niche. Yet, some public intellectuals are forgotten.

Fahs finds that many earlier newspaperwomen are invisible today: "After all, they were not powerless. . . . [T]hey left behind a substantial body of published writings in their newspaper articles."[98] All were visible for a day or during their lives. Sloss-Vento also left her name across plenty of newspapers, but that has not made her visible. She published a book, but that did not make her visible either. Gender and her elder status contributed to her invisibility.

The United Farm Workers leader Dolores Huerta also reflects on women's recognition in history:

> It has always been history—*his* story—as you know. Women didn't get as much recognition in the movement as they deserved. I believe, for myself and other women, that acknowledgement was never a priority. Our goal was to make a better life for farmworkers, not to get recognition. We did it to try to accomplish something. We did it to make a better world for working people, for women, or children. That's what matters most.[99]

CONCLUSION

Adela Sloss-Vento was a prolific public intellectual, given the magnitude of her writings, the longevity of her writing career, the intelligence she displayed in the writings, and her spirited will to empower the Mexican-descent community. She rejected gender-defined norms of her era that prescribed society pages for women, especially before the 1970s. Civics and politics, not domesticity or beauty, caught her attention. She worked around racial barriers. She identified social ills and acted to incite the public.

Sloss-Vento lacked the privileges that men, European Americans in general, the middle class, and college graduates had. Men commanded the authority to write and speak. Whites controlled mainstream newspapers and much of the space of public opinion. Elites and the upper middle class assumed they had the right to speak and be heard. College graduates assumed they knew more or were smarter.

Sloss-Vento was an organic intellectual as a member of the lower middle class. She became aware of people like Sor Juana Inés de la Cruz, one of her role models, not in a university but through newspapers and books she read. As a woman and as an activist she did not take full credit for her own intellect and activism. She constrained herself by using a variety of names and pseudonyms. She was too humble. She was unwilling to say that she might be intellectually superior to men. Yet she did not devalue herself.

Ironically, it was in the home that Sloss-Vento could be an autonomous public intellectual and woman warrior. Not owning an office outside of her home, she used the private domain, her house, to write all her letters, opinions, and manuscripts. This autonomous space allowed her to participate in politics. She felt trapped by gender but was also limited by race and class. Still, she was free in a "room of her own," as suggested by the writer Virginia Woolf.

Sloss-Vento was her own agent. At home she was free of organizations, sexist LULAC, sexist and racist men and women, and employment and newspaper deadlines. Yes, there were housework, children, and a husband who occasionally nagged, but there she could enter the public arena, the public dialogue, and comment on public issues. In the midst of domesticity, in her own room, she exercised her prerogative as a public intellectual activist utilizing the free press despite constraints.

CHAPTER 7

•

DEMOCRAT IN THE UNITED STATES AND DEMOCRAT FOR MEXICO

Adela Sloss-Vento was a committed Democrat, with reservations. Her papers provide little evidence of ordinary partisan activities—registering voters, staffing tables, making phone calls, staffing office hours, passing out literature, putting up signs, and lobbying voters. Ordinary party workers leave behind little evidence of this kind of work anyway, and none exists in Sloss-Vento's archives. Instead, the archive includes evidence of an exceptional pioneering partisan leader before the 1970s, as seen through her correspondence to politicians, her public intellectual work, and her activism. Indeed, in 1966 she wrote, "I used to work in politics since I was very young. When I was in High School I became President of a political club."[1] Since she was not typically an organization woman working inside of associations, she largely worked independently.

Sloss-Vento's role with and outside of the Democratic Party as a party activist and not an elected official stretches across the decades from the late 1920s to 1990. From the 1920s on, Sloss-Vento promoted citizens' engagement. A 1929 newspaper article reports that she was working on a political campaign.[2] In the 1930s she worked with the Good Government League in San Juan, Texas, and joined a political party there to bring forth municipal reform.[3] She supported Ladies LULAC and its advocacy for paying the poll tax and thus voting in the 1930s.

The historian Nancy Beck Young argues that the Democratic Party was the only viable party in Texas from 1836 to 1952.[4] Republican ascendance began in the 1950s and solidified in the 1980s. Sloss-Vento threatened to become a Republican because she was "disgusted with the corruption and injustices, the low salaries for the Latin Americans," but she remained a loyal Democrat.[5] Both parties succeeded in disenfranchising and disempowering the Mexican American and African American communities for decades before the 1980s. The poll tax, women's disenfranchisement until 1920, the white primary, white dominance in party politics, and southern sexism fostered disempowerment of all women and people of color.

Sloss-Vento was a Democrat but took several nontraditional political paths to ensure Mexican American political empowerment. Several other political parties existed in Texas besides the Democrats and Republicans. In 1968 Mexican Americans founded the Raza Unida Party (RUP) as a third party, to empower Mexican Americans, elect them to office, and advance Raza interests. Sloss-Vento supported the RUP while also proclaiming loyalty to Democrats. As early as the 1940s she formed an independent political club in Hidalgo County in the Valley to promote Mexican American interests.

Yet another political path Sloss-Vento took was as a transnational citizen addressing politics in Mexico. As a borderlander/fronteriza and Mexican American she concerned herself with the politics of Mexico because of their effects on La Raza in Texas. She wrote to Mexican President Miguel Alemán in 1940, a consul of Mexico in 1943, a Mexican immigration official in the late 1940s, Mexican President Adolfo Ruiz Cortines in 1953, and the head of Confederación Regional Obrera Mexicana, the major labor union in Mexico, also in 1953. She wrote to them about the impact of immigration in Texas, and she offered suggestions for improving conditions in Mexico.

Sloss-Vento's political activism must also be seen in the context of gender politics. Her foray into politics was a struggle against the Texas white male establishment that disdained Mexican Americans and women as party activists and elected officials. In her book *LBJ and Mexican Americans*, Pycior contends, "As in party politics generally, the higher the organizational level, the fewer the women."[6] And the higher the stakes, the fewer Mexican American women.

Using her pen as her primary tool, Sloss-Vento expressed her political audacity. Kabalen de Bichara concludes in her own study of Sloss-Vento,

> She is a woman who demonstrates a capacity to use the written text as a means of contesting those in positions of power, even if it be the President of the United States or of Mexico. Her texts stand as clear evidence of a woman who, in spite of having only a high school education, does not assume a submissive role. Rather, she expresses herself as a woman of conviction, as someone capable of writing herself into the history of civil rights activism, as someone who defends the needs of Mexican Americans, but who was also aware of the plight of the Mexican worker.[7]

TEXAS MEXICAN AMERICAN WOMEN IN THE DEMOCRATIC PARTY AND AS ELECTED OFFICIALS

It is still common to assume that Mexican Americans in Texas became active in politics after World War II, especially given the paucity of elected Mexican Americans before 1945. The political scientist Benjamin Márquez concludes in his study of Mexican Americans in Texas politics, "For their part, Mexican Americans had few resources and little or no access to government at any level through which they could effectively challenge their inferior status."[8] But there had been a long history of Mexican American male officials since colonial times and after 1848 in partisan politics and elected positions at the local and county levels in South Texas. Winning statewide positions was harder. And there was some national politicking. LULAC leaders' first actions after they founded the league in 1929 were to testify before the US Congress in 1930.[9] Perales, J. T. Canales, and the attorney Reynaldo Garza also worked on the presidential campaign of Dwight Eisenhower, a Republican, in the 1950s.

Interestingly enough, Márquez is silent on the access of Mexican American women to electoral politics and their exclusion by white men and men of Mexican descent. The political scientist José Ángel Gutiérrez, also a RUP founder, and his co-authors, Michelle Meléndez and Sonia Noyola, report in their 2007 book, *Chicanas in Charge*, that Mexican American women in Texas were mostly absent from politics before the 1960s, when the RUP was formed. They cite Olga Peña Ramos as an exception.[10] If Mexican American women were active in the 1950s, scholars have assumed they were mostly helpmates to their politically aspiring husbands. Too often it is assumed that Mexican American women were inactive, subject to macho husbands, men's helpmates, and/or devoid of their own political ideologies.[11]

Mexican American women's entrance into Texas politics was slow in the twentieth century and, indeed, occurred mostly after 1970. New Mexican Hispanas were successful much earlier. In the 1920s Adelina Otero Warren of New Mexico ran for Congress, and in the 1930s Concha Ortiz y Pino was elected to the New Mexico legislature. In Texas, Tejanas joined the Democratic Party slowly. In the 1920s Jovita Idar, who was from Laredo and moved to San Antonio, was active in the Democratic Party as a precinct judge; Adela Jaime was a San Antonio precinct chair; and Manuela González Contreras was an active Democrat in Cotulla and San Antonio in 1929.[12] Mexican American women organized a Latin American women's political club to help elect Manuel Bravo in Zapata County in South Texas in the early 1930s. Emma Tenayuca was an avid Communist Party member in San Antonio. In South Texas in the 1940s Josefa M. Gutiérrez chaired Zapata County's Democratic Executive Committee with eight other Mexican American women.[13]

By the 1950s individual Mexican American women were becoming more visible. In the 1950s Olga Peña Ramos was active with Ladies LULAC and the Bexar County Democratic Women's Club, then helped elect her husband, Albert Peña, to the Bexar County Commission four times from the early 1950s to 1972.[14] Clotilde García in Corpus Christi was especially active from the 1950s on.[15] Ladies LULAC and American G.I. Forum auxiliaries conducted the most important electoral work by Mexican American women. Ladies LULAC promoted payment of the poll tax, registered voters, and got out the vote from the 1930s through the 1960s. Mexican American men who won offices did so in part because of women's efforts and votes.

In the 1960s women were involved in the presidential campaigns of John F. Kennedy and Lyndon B. Johnson. Vicente Ximenes, originally of Floresville, Texas, organized the Viva Johnson effort. Pycior lists as campaign advisers Clotilde García of Texas, Francisca Flores of California, and the American G.I. Forum Ladies Auxiliary president Polly Baca of Colorado. Pycior notes Ximenes's view that women were "the best source of grassroots campaign work" and that half of the Viva Johnson volunteers in Austin were women.[16] Peña Ramos was active with this effort in San Antonio.[17]

Pycior asserts, "When it came to political leadership, men largely forged bonds with men, particularly during the Cold War with its male military ethos."[18] By the late 1950s, operatives of the Texas politician Lyndon B. Johnson increasingly recruited women, though "many were chosen not for their own ability but because they were married to political operatives."[19] Pycior cites one of his aides as saying, "You sometimes have problems with women who are active in Democratic politics. There's [a] lot of pride and self-denial among them."[20] Sexism was prominent. Speaking about Mexican American women in politics, Rosie Castro of San Antonio's RUP reflects in a 2015 interview that before the 1970s, "the role that everyone maintained was a support role. . . . It was understood that men would be up front."[21] Yet, historians increasingly are finding examples of individual and collective actions by women in local Ladies LULAC, American G.I. Forum auxiliaries, and Viva Kennedy and Viva Johnson campaigns.

Men did not treat women as intelligent, independent thinkers and actors, and society saw wives as extensions of husbands. Women did not necessarily vote the same way as the men in their lives. Sloss-Vento did not vote the same as J. T. Canales and Alonso S. Perales voted. She received a letter from Canales in October 1952 about his support for the Republican presidential candidate Eisenhower. He enclosed Spanish-language literature prepared by the attorney Reynaldo Garza. In the letter Canales writes,

> I am recommending him [Eisenhower] to our friends because, as Christians, we believe that he will put an end to the Korean War, which Truman has been unable to do and we feel sure that his followers will continue such a war indefinitely. It has been the policy of the Democratic Administrations, ever since Wilson, to use War as a means of bringing prosperity to our Country. In the First World War: Wilson; in the second, Franklin D. Roosevelt; and in the Third, Harry S. Truman got us into this Korean War.[22]

She did not respond. Perales did not support the liberal candidate Ralph Yarborough in the 1950s; Sloss-Vento worked on Yarborough's successful 1964 congressional campaign against George H. W. Bush.[23]

The goal of male politicians from the 1920s to the 1970s was mostly to use Mexican American women as supporters rather than candidates, elected officials, and political thinkers. However, Pycior finds, the presidential candidate Lyndon B. Johnson "wanted to reward Mexican American loyalty by hiring, in his words, 'a talented and goodlooking [*sic*] Mexican or Spanish girl' as a receptionist or secretary."[24] Despite his sexist and demeaning comments, Johnson made federal appointments of two Mexican American women: Francisca Flores and Polly Baca, neither from Texas. Men saw women as secretaries or assistants.

By the 1960s, as the Chicano movement and women's movement emerged, Mexican American women became more involved in politics. At a 1989 Chicano movement reunion in San Antonio, Rosie Castro shared this assessment:

> The role of women in politics has been obliterated, left out. . . . [It is] by and about men. . . .
>
> We too made decisions—Virginia Músquiz, Luz Bazán Gutiérrez. . . . We also ran primaries. We also were election judges. We walked our barrios to gather the petitions. We suffered the separation from family and friends. We made signs and mailers. We proclaimed an idea. We led marches. We organized and empowered people. We worked side by side with our men.[25]

A few Mexican American women, like Sloss-Vento, did some of this even before the Chicano movement.

Most elected officials in Texas still are men, but more women were getting elected by the 1970s. The historian David Montejano has observed, "The public 'official' side of government was essentially male business."[26]

No Mexican American woman ran for state office until the 1960s. To win, women needed male party workers and male voters, but many men were unwilling to support a woman candidate. Women had to believe in themselves and fight condescension from men and even women who believed women's place was in the home; they had to receive endorsements, find volunteers, and obtain funding. In 1972 only 28 of 736 Spanish-surnamed elected officials in Texas were women. By 2005 Mexican American elected women or Latinas numbered 592 of 27,628 officials.[27]

SLOSS-VENTO'S POLITICAL FOUNDATION: PRO-DEMOCRACY AND ANTICOMMUNISM

The most important foundation for Sloss-Vento's activism and ideology was her belief in democracy. In a 1943 letter to the editor she writes, "If we understand what democracy stands for, we must bear in mind that our country not only stands for liberty but also for justice and equality."[28] Most women in the United States gained the right to vote in 1920. Thus, it was Sloss-Vento's right—and in her view, obligation—to seek out the best elected officials. She would later write, "We need able and scrupulous men as leaders, men who are not tied down by political strings that deprive them of practicing justice, which is the principle of Democracy."[29] She refers to men as leaders but would support women leaders too. For a democracy to exist, Americans needed to rid the country of injustices, inequalities, and racism, she asserts: "If Democracy and Christianity are being challenged from the outside, why challenge Democracy from within through hatred, injustice and misunderstanding?"[30] In calling for state legislation to end racial segregation in the 1940s, she writes, "It would be a law that would set [an] example and respect to the young generation of Anglo-descent that the injustices of race discrimination constitute a violation of the rights of the Constitution and of principles of Democracy."[31]

Besides democracy, Sloss-Vento's political ideology encompassed anticommunism, although she did not advocate against the Communist Party in the United States. The party was weak in the 1920s but saw an upsurge in the 1930s. Mexican-descent people in Texas had limited contact with and showed little support for the Communist Party; Sloss-Vento's contemporary Emma Tenayuca of San Antonio was an anomaly.

Sloss-Vento saw communism more as an international threat than a domestic one. Communism emerged in Russia in 1917, in China in 1948, in Korea in the 1950s, and in Cuba in 1958. After 1945 in the post–World War II era Sloss-Vento addresses the international communist threat in her 1947 letter "Christians Must Practice Christianity to Stop Communism,

Valley Woman Says" in the *McAllen Monitor*.[32] While not naming the Russian communist leader Joseph Stalin or discussing his atrocities against the Russian people, Sloss-Vento criticized the undemocratic nature of Russian communism. She did not partake in Senator Joe McCarthy's anticommunist witch hunt in the 1950s. Nor is there evidence she supported Martin Dies, a prominent Texan and staunch anticommunist in the 1950s whom J. T. Canales initially supported. In 1944 she tells Perales, "I heard the speech of Martin Dies. He and the Texas Regulars are one hundred percent for racial hatreds. You know what my answer would be for these War Mongers. I hope they don't get anywhere."[33]

Sloss-Vento expressed anticommunist sentiment again in the 1960s and 1970s. In 1963 she voices her concern to the League of Women Voters state president, JoBetsy Brown of Waco, telling her, "First we need a law requiring all Communists in this country to register. Second, we need to organize clubs to safeguard the safety of our country and to discourage the Communists until they either quit or they leave for Russia."[34] But Sloss-Vento did not organize or join such a club. She asks Brown, "Is the threat of Communism a punishment from God?"[35]

Sloss-Vento wrote to Lyndon B. Johnson, the new vice president–elect, about her concerns. In her November 1960 letter to Johnson she expresses her pleasure that voters elected John F. Kennedy, a Catholic, and says unity could help "exterminate" "our enemy No. 1, 'Communism.'"[36] She suggests, "A conference with all the Americas based on mutual understanding, good faith and sincerity toward ending Communism would be the right step. We shall keep praying that it is not too late."[37] In the early 1960s a reference to communism often was a reference to Cuba and the 1962 Cuban missile crisis.

A decade later, in 1972, Sloss-Vento wrote to Telesistema Del Norte, a Monterrey, Mexico, TV station, applauding it for informing youth about the dangers of communism.[38] She contended that Christianity could curb injustice, selfishness, and discrimination, all of which she associated with communism. In the democratic United States she was also critical of injustice, selfishness, and discrimination.

SLOSS VENTO'S POLITICAL ACTIVISM, 1940S–1990S

The 1940s

Sloss-Vento entered politics in the 1920s but intensified her interest in the 1940s. In that decade she supported the abolition of the white primary in Texas. White primaries had existed in Texas since 1923 to prevent African

Americans and Mexican Americans from voting, depending on the county. On October 19, 1944, she wrote a letter to the editor in *La Prensa* of San Antonio praising President Franklin D. Roosevelt's Good Neighbor policies and his support of the African American community. She writes, "Thanks to the justice and humanity of Pres. Roosevelt, the black race won the privilege they didn't have. This privilege is that the Negro will vote in the primaries."[39] She commented on the 1944 Supreme Court decision in *Smith v. Allwright* to allow African Americans to participate in Texas primaries. She expressed support for equal rights for African Americans when, Lupe Salinas notes, few Mexican Americans favored them.[40] Her support is even more interesting since African Americans were few in the Valley and could not tip the balance of power in an election there.[41] After the *Smith* decision, the number of African American voters more than tripled, from 30,000 in 1940 to 100,000 in 1947.[42]

Sloss-Vento continued to promote Mexican American political empowerment. She writes to an ally in 1947, "We need to organize our people and to keep our people well informed in order to solve the many problems against us. We need several leaders from each town of the Valley. We need to organize our people politically too. If we could count on a Spanish newspaper, a strong one, it will do wonders for us."[43]

Several years after the Ventos returned to the Valley in the mid-1940s, Sloss-Vento presided over the Citizens' Political Club.[44] She served as its first president along with two male officers, so the club was not homosocial. Its heterosocial nature suggests that the club accepted women and men alike as voters to benefit Mexican American empowerment. She could have organized a women's political club but did not. The club's purpose was to "instruct Americans of Latin descent on citizenship and the importance of paying their poll taxes and participating in all elections."[45]

Another goal of the Citizens' Political Club was to elect Mexican Americans to office. In an undated manuscript Sloss-Vento notes, "The great majority of Latinos do not participate politically, we have 500 more votes than the Anglo-American in Hidalgo County."[46] Indeed, Hidalgo County was a place where Mexican Americans were not a minority by 1940. Club members had to pay their own poll taxes, accepted no money from candidates, and paid for socials and speakers.[47] The group's emphasis on self-reliance was to counter Euro-American political patronage and bossism. In earlier decades a boss might control as many as a thousand voters and sway an election.[48]

The idea of an independent political organization, separate from the Democratic Party, was not new among Mexican Americans. San Antonio Mexican American Democrats had organized a similar effort. In 1932 in San

Antonio Henry Guerra, Alonso S. Perales, John Solis, and others founded the Association of Independent Voters to elect Mexican American candidates.[49] Unfortunately, political operatives sabotaged the association. Having worked with the Good Government League in the Valley in the 1930s, Sloss-Vento saw too much Euro-Texan control of the Democratic Party and the need for an independent group in the Valley.

One newspaper published an account of the Citizens' Political Club, and Sloss-Vento wrote an essay about the club. The group vetted candidates on the issue of "proper representation and justice." She notes in the essay that most Latinos did not participate in politics and workers' migration depleted their numbers, but, she says, "we have 500 more votes than the Anglo-Americans in Hidalgo County." She also comments on the poll tax:

> We should not permit anyone to pay our poll tax; we will not allow our people to be tied down. We live in a democratic and free country and as such we should be freed citizens. We need to realize that the vote is a powerful weapon through which we can elect representatives that can assist us in solving our problems. When people are allowed to be deceived or to have their votes misdirected, he or she is causing harm not only to themselves but to their children and the Latin American community in general. It is not sufficient to pay the poll tax; it is requisite to be well informed on politics but one that is not directed by leaders who have personal interests.[50]

She goes on to say that the club would instruct community members on citizenship and constitutional rights:

> We should organize political clubs in all of the barrios and towns. They should be by the people and for the people. And may those who choose its directors or leaders be sincere, patriotic and ask only for the rights and justice of the people. We should be aware that while our people are deceived, confused, divided, without proper information and free choice, we cannot solve our problems that impede our social and economic evolution. While this exists, we cannot hope for the betterment of the Latin American people.

She reiterates the importance of having Latin American elected officials: "What good is it to count on votes if the communities do not properly educate our people so that they can properly enter public office?"[51]

Sloss-Vento first advocated for a US president in 1944, for Franklin D. Roosevelt. In *La Prensa* she writes,

> Roosevelt's justice and humanity is reflected in all of his acts, particularly in the "Good Neighbor Policy," in the brotherhood and cooperation that he has sought with Mexico and the rest of the countries in Latin America. . . . [He] has spoken of the equality between the races . . . [and] has the necessary experience to contribute to those postwar plans that are based on equality, on the dignity and justice of everyone, assuring that there be a durable peace and a better future for all of the countries of the Americas as well as the rest of the world.[52]

Her papers do not contain letters to Roosevelt.

Sloss-Vento wrote to Perales about Roosevelt. She asks him who he supported for president and then declares, "I hope it is our great President Franklin Delano Roosevelt. I think that he is the only person that could give us Justice. I am doing my best for him among my friends."[53]

Beginning in the 1940s Sloss-Vento actively supported candidates for state and national offices. John Garner represented the congressional district for South Texas in the US House of Representatives from 1933 to 1948. He left that office in 1948, thereby opening the way for a new representative—an opportunity for a Mexican American or an ally to take the seat. In 1948 there were no Mexican Americans from Texas in Congress. Four Democrats ran for the office Garner vacated. On January 15, 1948, Sloss-Vento wrote to J. Luz Sáenz about the candidates Phillip "Chick" Kazen; J. T. Ellis Jr.; the businessman and lawyer Augustine Celaya; and the businessman Lloyd Bentsen. After asking Sáenz what he thought about Kazen's platform, she asserts that Kazen was the only one who had the courage to speak about racial discrimination. Kazen was a Lebanese American from Laredo in South Texas, where for decades Mexican Americans had held greater local political power than in the Valley. "Ellis, Celaya and Bentsen did not talk about our problems," Sloss-Vento writes. "We promised to help Ellis and we will help him but after the primaries if Kazen wins we are going with him."[54] Apparently, she had committed to Ellis early or changed her mind about him. Race alone was not enough for Sloss-Vento to support a candidate; otherwise, she would have supported Celaya. She then supported the vocal antiracism candidate.

Arnoldo Vento describes an incident in his mother's candidate vetting: "When Lloyd Bentsen first ran for office, he came to her home seeking her support knowing that she was a political force in the Valley. She refused his request."[55] She rejected his candidacy because he had already been a member of the Good Neighbor Commission, and she considered him white agribusiness's candidate.

During the 1948 House campaign, white voters responded with fear to the growing Mexican American political mobilization. Kazen's campaign advocated for "equal rights and representation for Latin Americans." English-language Valley newspaper publishers tried to avoid an emphasis on race, fearing the loss of white power. Editors wrote of fears of Nazis, with editorials titled "That Racial Issue" and "It's Definitely out of Place."[56] They essentially cried "reverse racism." According to one source, "Bentsen charged that Kazen helped too much on alleged discrimination issues."[57] Ellis and Kazen lost but thanked Sloss-Vento for her help.[58] Bentsen won. In 1953 Sloss-Vento attacked him as a "political boss of the South," especially since he sought to maintain the Bracero Program, a slavelike work program.[59]

Sloss-Vento was critical of Valley agribusiness's political power. The rising commercial associations of packers, canners, farmers, and shippers—all of whom supported politicians such as Bentsen—exploited braceros, and drove Mexican American laborers out of Texas.

Sloss-Vento gave political speeches in the Valley in the 1940s, though she was ambivalent about calling herself an orator. She writes of herself, "And without being an orator, she spoke in political meetings and rallies."[60] Among her manuscripts and papers, a distinct speech cannot be discerned. To describe her oratory, her son, Arnoldo Vento, wrote a likeness of one of her 1948 speeches that he heard as a child:

> It gives me much pleasure to be here with you. And it is an honor to speak to you about the rights of all Mexicans as an American citizen. It has not been that long that our ancestors fought for the human rights of all citizens. Now we have another enemy who does not let us develop, who discriminates against us in the public schools, that is abusing us with bandit American troops, that keeps us in low wage jobs, that protects a corrupt system, that defends crooked lawyers, and that hides behind sell out Mexicans in bars, prostitution halls, and card games.[61]

Unfortunately, no sound recordings remain, and no single document suggests that this was an actual speech Sloss-Vento gave.

Sloss-Vento inserted herself into national politics. In 1948 she sought to influence US president Harry S. Truman (1945–1953), a Democrat.[62] She wrote to him about "the Wetback Problem." She sent him several enclosures, probably her own writings. She then advises him, "Please read it Mr. President for it is God's truth."[63] Sloss-Vento essentially tells President Truman that La Raza was an oppressed people and that she did not feel truly free to tell him so. There is no evidence he responded.

The 1950s

In the 1950s Sloss-Vento continued to write to presidents, especially about the Bracero Program. President Dwight Eisenhower (1953–1960) was the first Republican she wrote.[64] The fact that he was not a Democrat did not keep her from trying to inform or persuade him or speak her mind to him. She begins her 1954 letter to Eisenhower, "I am enclosing two articles dealing with a harmful wetback problem in the Rio Grande Valley of Texas. I am praying Mr. President that you will have the kindness to read these articles. Said problem needs a quick solution for the good of our relations with Mexico and for . . . the good of democracy itself." She suggests that the United States provide Mexico agricultural assistance and impose "a law to punish those who hire the undocumented so that the million and one half or more along the border can be sent back . . . to stop the Bracero contracts since Mexico needs all of its workers at home to develop agriculture and other resources, and to solve economic problems of the poor working class." She mentions jobs for "our many unemployed citizens" as well. She urges, "Let's do what is right for us (our own working class), for our neighbors and for the good of democracy before it is too late."[65] She wrote to Perales that she had sent Eisenhower two articles on the "wetback problem" and adds, "I hope they won't throw it in the wastebasket."[66]

She also continued to lobby for good politicians and condemn the bad. In 1952 she told Perales she did what she could for state legislative liberal candidates Ralph Yarborough and Graham Smedley and that she hoped to see Governor Allan Shivers and state legislator Rogers Kelly of the Valley defeated.[67] In 1952 she also applauded the defeat of three candidates of political machines in Hidalgo County including Ramon Guerra's bid for state representative.[68] In 1953 she wrote Perales that Bentsen and Shivers were in favor of the "wetback problem."[69] In a 1954 column, Perales features an essay in which Sloss-Vento writes, "The politicians in the Texas Legislature keep getting thousands of Latin American votes in all parts of Texas but we don't wake up and unite."[70]

Besides attention to presidential administrations, Sloss-Vento worked on specific campaigns. In 1954 she worked on Fidencio M. Guerra's campaign for district judge in Hidalgo County. In a letter to Perales she writes, "But we have the Anglo-American vote—it united against Latin American candidates. The Anglos get [on] telephones and they come to an agreement and oppose the Latin-American. They don't make any noise and don't make speeches or hand out flyers. They work quietly."[71] She also supported Texas senator and Democrat Hubert R. Hudson, a Euro-Texan, in 1959.[72]

In 1958 Luis Alvarado, Sáenz's son-in-law from San Antonio, asked her to help in the gubernatorial campaign of Henry B. González.[73] Sloss-Vento's archive contains no evidence that she helped. González lost that election but became a state legislator in 1956 and the first Tejano in Congress in 1961. Another Tejano would not join Congress until 1965 (Kika de la Garza), then Solomon Ortiz (1983), and then Albert Bustamante (1985). In 2019 there were sixteen Latino men in the House of Representatives and the Cuban American Republican Ted Cruz in the Senate. Two Tejanas were elected to the House in 2018.

The 1960s

The 1960s saw the rise of the Kennedy family at the national level among Democrats. Sloss-Vento supported them and especially since they were Catholic.[74] She may have been active with the Viva Kennedy effort, though her archive includes no such documents. Viva Kennedy was a national effort by Latinxs to elect John F. Kennedy president of the United States in 1960; it was the first statewide partisan organization of Mexican Americans in Texas.[75] Ignacio García's research on women's participation in Viva Kennedy was minimal, and that was mostly about women's participation in Indiana and Illinois. He explains gender integration: "Lacking money and volunteers, most male-led organizations were happy to allow women to participate at the grassroots level."[76] But women often took their own initiatives. Clotilde García hosted campaign socials and led a Mexican American women's statewide effort to elect Kennedy. These socials were indeed political. More research on Mexican American women's participation in Viva Kennedy is needed. Regardless of women's roles, the Viva Kennedy effort succeeded in Texas going Democratic in the 1960 presidential election, reversing the 1952 and 1956 elections.[77]

Ed Idar Jr., as an American G.I. Forum official, organized Viva Kennedy in Hidalgo County, where Sloss-Vento lived. He invited fifty-nine Mexican Americans to an organizing meeting, men and women. It is unclear if Sloss-Vento was one of them. Ignacio García describes the turnout: "Both men and women were invited, though most who came were professionals and businessmen, or wives of those men."[78] He identifies Clotilde García as an exception, but other women may have attended who were not attached to men at the event.

Sloss-Vento made other pro-Kennedy gestures. In 1963 she congratulated the state president of the League of Women Voters on her speech about President Kennedy's assassination.[79] In 1973 she wrote a tribute to Kennedy in the *McAllen Monitor*.[80] She also saved a 1970 newspaper article about Senator Ted Kennedy's reelection campaign.[81]

In 1966 Sloss-Vento supported a few other politicians. One was the attorney Joe B. Evins, who did not belong to a political machine and lost. She advises him before the election, "It is hard to beat a political machine. I am and have always been for a clean administration and for better salaries for the Latin American people."[82] And she instructed him on how to run a campaign: hire campaign workers, get voters to the polls, use voting machines, and spend money. She tells him, "There are citizens who work for money, very few works [*sic*] as I do only for a good Administration and for the betterment of the Latin American people."[83] She opposed racist white rule and supported enlightened whites.

Sloss-Vento developed ties to the senator and later president Lyndon B. Johnson (1963–1969). In a 1960 letter to him upon his and Kennedy's victory, she expresses her loyalty to Democrats, mentioning her campaign work for him and Kennedy. She says, "As loyal Americans of Mexican descent of the border of Texas, we are also one hundred percent loyal Democrats and we worked hard for your Victory and that of President Elect John F. Kennedy."[84] She complains to Johnson about the racist film *The Alamo*, starring John Wayne. She asserts that the film degraded the dignity of the Mexican people and good neighborliness with Mexico and warns, "It will create more harm than good, for Mexico is our most important neighbor. . . . Everytime the words 'Remember the Alamo' is [*sic*] mentioned, the blood of the Mexican boils. We too have had to suffer the consequences of the hatreds of Texas History." She suggests that Johnson, Wayne, and the film's writer and producers read J. T. Canales's books. She concludes, "Maybe something can be done with the Movie Industry in preventing films that will irritate Mexico and the rest of the Latin Countries."[85] She saw such films as adversely affecting Tejanos and relations with Latin America. She wrote President Johnson or his assistant again in 1964.[86]

The 1970s

The last US president Sloss-Vento wrote was Jimmy Carter (1977–1981). Immigration was still a controversial subject in the 1970s. She tells Carter she is against amnesty for undocumented immigrants and in favor of stiff sentences for them. She argues for more Border Patrol officers.[87] While her position here could be called conservative, it would be a stretch to call her "nativist," especially given her long history of pro-immigrant attitudes and actions.[88] Still, decades of the influx of unauthorized immigrants made more and more Mexican Americans weary of their presence.[89] In contrast, during the Chicano movement, Chicano activists made stronger calls for allying with Raza immigrants.[90] Laura Garza has commented that Sloss-Vento was in an "in-between space."[91]

She supported the Democrat Héctor Uribe for the Texas Senate in 1978.[92] In a letter to the *McAllen Monitor* that year she writes, "It is a sacred duty to get out and vote. . . . We Mexican-Americans by tradition are loyal to our many traditions, one is being loyal to our Party—the Democratic Party."[93] Even though Sloss-Vento claimed loyalty to the Democrats, she still supported the Raza Unida Party. Benjamin Márquez observes, "Few accepted the claim that organizing a Chicano third party in South Texas was consistent with the aims and purposes of the Democratic Party."[94] Yet, Sloss-Vento found that supporting the RUP was indeed consistent with supporting the Democratic Party. She considered the RUP the brown hope.

The RUP offered a unique effort for Mexican American political empowerment. The activists and writers Yolanda Alaniz and Megan Cornish explain,

> La Raza Unida Party was a bold and inspiring step toward Chicana/o liberation. It was the largest independent ethnic challenge to Republicans and Democrats, and it gave voice to Chicanas/os fed up with second-class status. It taught leadership and organizing skills to the grassroots and instilled community activism in the barrio. Its broad social program dramatically demonstrated the bankruptcy of the twin parties of big business. Within the party, Chicanas found unprecedented recognition and opportunities.[95]

The RUP activist Rosie Castro of San Antonio describes the political conditions in Texas that led to the RUP's formation:

> The Democratic Party did not have Latinos or African Americans on their national Democratic committee—same with the state executive committee. You couldn't make those changes within the party, so you had to look to an alternative mechanism. We created [the RUP]. We were the only Latino party around. We knew we weren't going to win governor, if we ran a governor, but we knew that the alternative was to do nothing. And if you did nothing, nothing would change.[96]

Sloss-Vento supported the RUP, though her contact with the party was limited. Juventino Alvarado, the Hidalgo County RUP chair, was the only RUP or Chicano movement activist to contact her. After one of her letters appeared in the *McAllen Monitor*, he reached out to her, writing, "There are a few who take the time to take interest in the important social issues of the day and who take a stand publicity [*sic*], as you did, for the rights of human justice. . . . I was particularly glad for the literature which you mentioned in your letter. . . . Man's inhumanity to man will seem less painful because of such people as César Chávez and you, Mrs. Vento."[97] Her papers include no letters from RUP women in the 1960s or 1970s with the exception of Martha P. Cotera, who wrote her in the late 1970s about Sloss-Vento's archive. Cotera did not include her in her Chicana history book *Diosa y Hembra: The History and Heritage of the Chicana*. Rosie Castro did not know of her.[98]

Sloss-Vento encouraged the RUP. In her reply to Juventino Alvarado's letter to her, she writes, "I also want to congratulate everyone in the Raza Unida for your interest and unity in favor of racial uplift and the complete solution to the problems of Mexican Americans."[99] She kept the news clipping "Raza Unida Delivers Petitions, Party Aiming for Ballot Slot" from the *Corpus Christi Caller-Times* of July 1, 1972.

It was the emphasis on the empowerment of La Raza that she valued. She still supported Democrats and did not publicly denounce them. Sloss-Vento supported progressive whites and was not a narrow nationalist who favored only Mexican American candidates. In a letter to a Rio Grande City Chicano activist she says that in politics "there are good Anglos and bad Anglos."[100] So she could simultaneously support progressive whites and Chicano nationalists in the RUP.

The 1980s and 1990s

Age and poor health were taking their toll on Sloss-Vento by the 1980s, and she became less active. Her last act as a Democrat was to congratulate Ann Richards on her victory as governor of Texas in 1990. Before then, Miriam "Ma" Ferguson was the only woman governor of Texas; she was elected in the 1920s and 1930s. Only Richards's election, as a Democrat and a woman, in November 1990 gave Sloss-Vento enough strength to rally one more time, when she was eighty-nine. A letter to her from Richards says, "It is always gratifying to hear that the people of Texas share my vision for the future of our state and appreciate the changes we are trying to make."[101] This vision was Sloss-Vento's since 1927, working for change. Richards had no idea Sloss-Vento's letter had come from the most active Texas Mexican American woman civil rights leader before the Chicano movement.

Richards befriended the liberal Democrat Lena Guerrero of Mission. Guerrero was another woman who had no idea what she inherited from Sloss-Vento. Guerrero and I were students at the University of Texas and took a women and politics class. We both may have read Cotera's *Diosa y Hembra*. Guerrero presided over the Young Democrats of Texas at the university, while I surrounded myself with Chicano movement activists and academics. In 1985 Guerrero would become the second Tejana elected to the Texas legislature and would serve until 1991. Sloss-Vento could finally rest knowing that a second woman served as governor and that a second Mexican American woman, this one from the Valley, joined the Texas legislature. Arnoldo Vento writes, "By 1992, senior activist Adela Sloss-Vento is ninety-one and is fairly incapacitated."[102]

Sloss-Vento's politics transcended Texas and the United States. She was a borderlander who understood that the fates of Mexican Americans, Mexican immigrants, the United States, and Mexico were intertwined. She contended that Mexico should have self-determination in its politics, but as a fronteriza she sought to provide her opinion to Mexican officials as well. Despite her protests to the Mexican government, she realized that Mexico, like La Raza in the United States, had little power over the US government. In a 1947 letter to Perales she writes, "I would suggest to you that we are lost in these places unless Mexico takes energetic measures so that the thousands of men and women who are in the Valley stay within Mexican territory."[103] A month later she expresses concern to Perales about the United States' increasing power over Mexico: "The way we are going, you wait and see that one day Mexico will pass to Anglo-Americans and what happened to us in Texas will happen to them."[104]

In 1943 Sloss-Vento wrote to the Mexican consulate in Austin. Her letter is not in her archive, but the response from Luis Duplán is. She had written about incidents of segregation and discrimination and enclosed her letter published in the *Corpus Christi Caller* titled "The Problem of Many Texas Towns." Duplán laments that there was not an antidiscrimination law to punish those who acted "through their narrow criteria or subversive ends."[105]

Sloss-Vento wrote in the 1940s to the *jefe de inmigración* (head of immigration) in Reynosa, Tamaulipas state, along the border. Jorge Del Río, the head of immigration, had conducted interviews of undocumented women. She asks him whether she should write to the Mexican secretary of state "so that a solution can be found on the Mexican side that stops and punishes the exodus of illegal working women?" She was concerned with the "serious harm" they caused that also constituted "a disservice to our communities." She cites several specific women and says about one of them, "Those who have known her say that she spends time with all types of men, both single and married."[106]

In 1947 Sloss-Vento wrote to Mexican President Miguel Alemán (1946–1952). While her letter is not among her papers, she tells Perales about "a well-written letter suggesting to President Alemán that he not send braceros to Texas. I sent it yesterday from Reynosa."[107] In 1953 Sloss-Vento wrote to Mexican President Adolfo Ruíz Cortines (1952–1958) about Mexico's problems. She introduces herself as a collaborator of the great defenders of Mexicans and as a jail matron. She tells him she understood Mexico's problems like an open book.[108] She says braceros should not be permitted in Texas and describes the racial discrimination and aggrandizement by "border Anglos" and "corporations." The letter was published in 1953 in *Revista Latino-Americano* in Rio Grande City.[109]

The 1953 letter to Cortines begins with her salutation as "Respetable Sr. Presidente" (Respected Mr. President). She says she hopes "thousands of undocumented workers can contribute to the economic enrichment of Mexico as opposed to the enrichment of Anglos along the border." She offers, "In my estimation, it is the State of Texas that should not allow Braceros along the border of Texas in view that there already exist thousands of wetbacks who are enriching the farmers and their corporations along with their politicians." She adds, "In my opinion, Mexico should not give in to additional Anglo privileges along the border of Texas."[110]

In 1953 she also wrote to Fidel Velázquez, the secretary of the Confederation of Mexican Labor, the largest union in Mexico, on the same subject.[111] She tells him there were two groups of Mexicans arriving in Texas, the hard workers and the criminal element. She says their wages were so low they were not sending money back to Mexico. She suggests, "If the President of Mexico as well as your union would strive to solve the problem by returning the thousands of wetbacks, it would be beneficial for the economic development of Mexico; it would likewise be of great benefit to Mexican Americans along the border."[112] She tells him about "farmers, large agribusiness corporations as well as Washington politicians who own thousands of acres in the Rio Grande Valley." She asks, "Why doesn't the President of Mexico insist that Washington pass a law as a solution which requires that those hiring illegal workers along the border are to be punished?" Here she refers to employer sanctions. She adds, "No one in Texas or in the South should be permitted to contract braceros until thousands of undocumented workers are returned to Mexico." She also mentions that the purpose of the migration was not achieved: "When our brothers from Mexico return home, they arrive without money." The last matter she addresses is the pending appointment of James Griffin of Mission, a racist who opposed the Department of Immigration and favored the flow of "illegal workers." She informs Velázquez that Griffin benefited from the slavery of Mexicans on the border.[113]

CONCLUSION

Adela Sloss-Vento was a pioneering Mexican American Democrat across eight decades; she was not an elite party worker, candidate, or elected official. She was active in partisan politics from the late 1920s until 1990, relying on her own intellect and political will. She utilized resources available to her as a US citizen—paying her poll tax, voting, getting out the vote, lobbying, organizing, participating in partisan organizations, contacting elected officials, writing politicians, giving speeches, and publishing her political opinions.

She sought alternative spaces for Mexican American political empowerment such as the independent club and the RUP, which was critical of the white-controlled Democratic Party. In *The Decolonial Imaginary*, Emma Pérez comments on that kind of third-space feminism, "Historical events . . . show that women's politics may have been subordinated under a nationalist paradigm, but women as agents have always constructed their own spaces interstitially, within nationalisms, nationalisms that often miss women's subtle interventions."[114]

Sloss-Vento addressed the political issues of the day in each decade. In the 1940s she welcomed the end of white primaries in Texas and created an independent political club in the Valley to mobilize support for more Mexican American elected officials. By the 1940s, congressional candidates recognized her as an influential political broker who participated in a heated congressional race and attempted to support the candidate who would best suit La Raza's needs. In the 1950s she spent considerable energy trying to affect policies of the Bracero Program. In the 1970s she favored the rise of the Raza Unida Party so as to empower Texas Mexican Americans; she also backed President Jimmy Carter and wrote to his administration about Mexican immigration, an issue on which she was more conservative. By the 1980s she had quit her work as a Democrat, tired and ill from her job, medications, medical mishaps, and decades of activism. In 1990, her last political act was to congratulate the new Texas Democratic woman governor, Ann Richards.

Sloss-Vento used many means to be an effective partisan leader. She supported national presidential candidates, congressional candidates, state legislative candidates, and local candidates. She contacted presidents, congressmen (no Texas women were yet in office), state legislators, and other elected officials with her complaints, ideas, and solutions. She crossed party lines in her outreach to both Democratic and Republican politicians.

Sloss-Vento contacted at least four US presidents—Truman, Eisenhower, Johnson, and Carter. She also promoted Presidents Franklin D. Roosevelt and John F. Kennedy. She accessed politicians because she was an engaged citizen who believed that although she was a Mexican American and a woman, she still had the right to contact elected officials. In a democracy it was her civic duty to do so. Such acts are important because she took action and because she sought to reach the most powerful person in the US government. Today few Americans contact any public official. Despite her efforts, though, Sloss-Vento had no lasting impact on electoral politics and did not instigate institutional change.

She contacted two presidents of Mexico since her politics were transnational. As a borderlander/fronteriza she professed to understand Mexico "like an open book" and did not feel like a foreigner when she wrote to its officials. She understood the impact the United States had on Mexico and that Mexico had an impact on the fates of Mexican Americans and Mexicans in South Texas. She did not take an imperialistic or superior attitude toward Mexico; she advocated for Mexico's self-determination and economic empowerment. Through the 1970s she privileged Mexican Americans over Mexicans in Texas.

Sloss-Vento assisted candidates who honored the interests of "the people" regardless of race or gender. She helped Mexican Americans and white allies; she was not ethnocentric or a narrow nationalist who cared only if one was of Mexican descent. She praised the end of the white primary that had suppressed African American empowerment. Her declining health and age did not allow her to work on a political campaign for a Mexican American woman.

There is no evidence that Sloss-Vento ever ran for office. She did not put herself on the ballot—she was too humble. It is likely that no one asked her to run for office. Perhaps it would have crossed someone's mind in the Valley in the 1990s, but by then Sloss-Vento was in her nineties.

Sloss-Vento's career in the Democratic Party, inside it or outside of it, was a struggle against male dominance. She worked effectively in politics when it was a boys' club. She did so before the Raza Unida Party and before the women's movement of the 1970s. While some historians continue to focus on Mexican American political exclusion, too often they ignore the exclusion of Latinas by Latinos. To address the democratization of Texas politics in history, Mexican American women must be included, along with other women of color, all people of color, and LGBTQIA communities.

No other Mexican American woman had Sloss-Vento's tenacity and vision as a democrat and Democrat to fight the Texas male establishment, both white and Mexican American. She was a feminist in considering women capable as civic leaders, party leaders, elected officials, and political thinkers. She advocated for women's civic engagement and for women to pay their poll taxes themselves and to vote. By example she showed that women could give speeches, organize, lobby, and write. Women were actors and thinkers, not just secretaries and helpmates, despite what Lyndon B. Johnson thought; women had political intellect. Still, she did write openly against the Democratic Party. Only by example did she assert her critique.

Even in the 2010s not enough women were involved in politics in the United States, Texas, or the Valley. A Texas newspaper headline from 2017 is "Women Still Underrepresented in Legislative Races." This article in the *Texas Tribune* begins, "It remains a daunting political reality in Texas."[115] In 2018 only 20 percent of Texas state legislators were women, while Nevada had 38 percent and California 25 percent. Even more poignant for Latinas was the 2016 article "Texas Has Never Elected a Latina to Congress" in the *Austin American-Statesman*.[116] The story reports that despite five million Latinas in Texas, not one had gone to Congress, while seventeen Latino men had. In 2016 Nevadans elected a Chicana to the US Senate. In 2018 two Tejanas were indeed elected to Congress, and more Latinas joined them. But the Tejana Susana Martínez had to move to New Mexico to become a governor. The political scientist Gabriela Sosa Zavaleta finds, "In the Lower Rio Grande Valley of Texas, the political process continues to be biased against the participation by women. Hispanic culture places low value on women's political participation."[117] Mainstream culture places even lower value on Mexican-origin women. Texas is difficult for Latinas and has been for many decades.

The year 2018 saw more Latinas entering politics and winning offices in part because of the Trump administration. Veronica Escobar of El Paso and Sylvia R. Garcia of Houston won their congressional races to represent Texas districts in the US House of Representatives.[118] Without knowing it, they are following the steps of Sloss-Vento, La Adelita, a political pioneer.

CONCLUSION

Adela Sloss-Vento was one of the most important Mexican American civil rights activists, public intellectuals, political party activists, and feminists of the twentieth century in the United States. Like many others, she was victimized by Jim Crow/Juan Crow, patriarchal Texas, and homosocial civil rights organizing. But as an educated person, a member of the colonized Mexican American middle class, and a beneficiary of modern gendered selfhood, she had the will and tools to resist.

Modern gendered selfhood allowed Sloss-Vento to believe a woman should find her purpose in life despite gendered norms. She was born to be a writer and an activist, two activities not expected of women before the modern women's movement of the late 1960s into the 1970s. Newspapers gave her a public persona also fracturing gender rules. The avenue of civic engagement and writing allowed her to perform her modern gendered selfhood.

Sloss-Vento utilized third spaces to perform her politics. She subverted patriarchy and domesticity by using the separate space of her home to enter into civil rights instead of through LULAC, Ladies LULAC, or any organizational form. She used her public intellectual work instead of submitting herself to the burden of being a columnist in a newspaper, perhaps to avoid the lack of freedom of speech. Finally, in politics she used the independent political club in the 1940s and advocated for the use of the Raza Unida Party in the 1970s during the Chicano movement as third spaces. She employed these strategies to insert herself in a feminist way into the Mexican American civil rights movement and the Chicano movement.

The Mexican American civil rights movement in Texas must not be forgotten or erased. A kind of erasure can be seen in some romanticized post–World War II activism or Chicano movement activism and histories that fail to acknowledge previous struggles. Significant civil rights work took place in the 1910s, 1920s, and 1930s; resistance to European, US, and European American domination began centuries before. Moreover, women's activism in or connected to these efforts must not be ignored. Sloss-Vento has been ignored because she was a woman. Too often historians have seen "No Mexicans Allowed" signs but have ignored actions reading "No Women Allowed."

The Texas Mexican American civil rights movement has focused on male leadership—it is now necessary to add Sloss-Vento to that cohort that includes Alonso S. Perales, J. T. Canales, J. Luz Sáenz, M. C. Gonzales, Carlos E. Castañeda, George I. Sañchez, Gus García, and Héctor P. García in Texas. Mexican American women did not have equal opportunities to become lawyers or doctors as did this leadership cadre. Mexican-origin women did not have the same opportunities to be writers, journalists, or columnists. Nor did they have an equal chance to obtain doctorates in the early twentieth century. Mexican-origin women were not asked to lead or speak, serve as representatives on boards, or act as club presidents. In the 1920s to 1970s they were "dirty" Mexicans and intellectually inferior "ladies" better suited as domestic helpmates, beauty queens, or sexual playmates.

Sloss-Vento's name needs to be added to the early twentieth-century Mexican American leaders associated with LULAC—Perales, Sáenz, and Canales. Not only did she join them in their efforts for Mexican American empowerment, she surpassed these male leaders since she had the burden of gender that also included wifedom and motherhood. With gender came responsibility for a spouse, children, housework, geographic immobility, and prescribed intellectual boredom.

She was active in both the Mexican American civil rights movement and the Chicano movement. While not an organization woman, she invented her own strategy to join the movement—public intellectual activism. She shunned LULAC and Ladies LULAC, found a strategic independent path, and challenged the gender confines of both Mexican American and Chicano nationalism. The scholar Maylei Blackwell reminds us that "narrow definitions of understandings of feminism" will not help excavate narratives of individuals, interventions, or praxis,[1] such as found in Sloss-Vento's life and work. These two movements Sloss-Vento fashioned as her own on her own terms in her own way.

She fought all the abuses associated with the rationale for the Mexican American civil rights movement. This included racial segregation, especially in schools and public places; inequality for Latino soldiers; inferior wages for agricultural workers; exploitation of undocumented workers; abuses of the Bracero Program; and unfair treatment of incarcerated Mexican immigrant women. She also fought for the political empowerment of La

Raza. She promoted voters' purchase of their own poll taxes, supported voting, and worked in numerous campaigns to elect Mexican Americans or Mexican American allies to office. She even founded an independent political club. She provided an example of women's participation in politics and advocated for women's civic engagement in LULAC. And she promoted a living wage for workers and was opposed to forced Tejano migration of workers due to poverty.

Despite analysis that brands Mexican American civil rights activists as "conservative" or "sheepish,"[2] Sloss-Vento was a Chicano movement supporter. Already an elder with health issues and the wear of activism, she could not sustain the level of her involvement once the Chicano movement was in full force in Texas. Still, she was a beacon of light for the few she contacted or supported. Had she lived in Austin or San Antonio, outside of the Valley, she could have been a role model for Chicana feminists of the 1970s and beyond. Unaware of her existence, Chicana feminists of the 1970s did not write her or seek her out as a foremother or mentor.

Sloss-Vento wholeheartedly supported many tenets of the Chicano movement's membership, ideology, and tactics. She applauded new members—youth—as well as their more radical efforts. While not supporting the idea of a separate homeland, Aztlán, she did support Chicano and Chicana power efforts in the United States. She admired the Raza Unida Party, a challenge to the white-controlled Democratic Party. She supported the cultural nationalism of the movement as well, advocating for Chicano history and Spanish language instruction. She applauded both a farmworker melon strike and a Chicano school walkout, the latter a mostly new tactic at the time.

She created her own independent political and intellectual life project as a rebel with a cause. She was bold but could be so only as a politically informed person. Her political project was to empower the Mexican American community using the tools of democracy. She utilized civic engagement, citizen commentary, and the electoral system. Vento's political project included civic action and electoral politics. She raised racial and political consciousness but did much less to raise feminist consciousness. Contrary to the idea that Mexican American women were outsiders to politics before 1970, this study suggests that there were a few exceptional pioneers.

As a woman in partisan politics, Sloss-Vento largely supported the Democratic Party and did so as a leader. However, she supported alternative venues, third spaces, when doing so was expedient to promote La Raza. Since the Democratic Party was controlled by whites she presided over an alternative, independent club in the 1940s and supported the Raza Unida Party, which sought to elect Chicanos and Chicanas in the 1970s. Moreover, her presence in politics as a woman helped to democratize the Democratic Party, a male establishment in Texas before the 1970s. She played a key role as a Tejana non-elite, non-candidate, and non–office holder.

Sloss-Vento's political project required breaking the hegemonic, homosocial, gendered traditions of Mexican American and European American men in Texas. While not openly questioning the homosocial, gendered organizational traditions of LULAC, she subverted this tradition, but only for herself. She did not openly contest LULAC's gendered membership or its lack of focus on sexism. She established key personal heterosocial relationships with activist men so she could take care of business; she utilized correspondence to network. She related to male activists as colleagues, friends, and equals; they were not her bosses or mentors. Perales, Sáenz, and Canales understood her intelligence and significance, but none of them made a strong enough effort to give her due. She outlived all three comrades, so it was she honoring them when they passed, and none could honor her when she died.

Recent work in gender studies has examined positive and negative aspects of homosociality, at least among the genders "woman" and "man." Nils Hammaren and Thomas Johansson have distinguished bonds between men that maintain and defend hegemony (hierarchical homosociality) from those "based on emotional closeness, intimacy and a nonprofitable form of friendship" (horizontal homosociality).[3] In others words, there is nothing wrong with men having male friends and women having female friends—or any kind of gendered friend—but homosociality becomes a problem when it excludes women and maintains patriarchy. In Texas the Mexican American civil rights movement organizations manifested "hierarchical homosociality" versus "horizontal homosociality" and marginalized Latinas in Texas.

The Texas male political establishment worked against women and especially Mexican American women. While most US women were allowed to vote after 1920, it was not common for Mexican American women to be active in electoral politics. Individual women like Jovita Idar and Adela Jaime were active in the Democratic Party in San Antonio in the 1920s and 1930s. By the 1930s Mexican American women in some locales like Zapata County in South Texas were organizing as voters, and Ladies LULAC promoted voting. In the 1940s white men like politician Lloyd Bentsen sought out Sloss-Vento as a Tejana leader with influence in politics. By the 1950s more women like Olga Peña Ramos of San Antonio were involved in political campaigns. Ladies LULAC helped make Raymond Telles mayor in El Paso. And by 1960 Clotilde García and other women were organized at the state level in campaigns to elect John F. Kennedy president and later Lyndon B. Johnson.

The Mexican American male civil rights establishment across the nation also suppressed Mexican American women. In Texas, New Mexico, Colorado, California, and Chicago, national efforts at the political empowerment of Mexican Americans included mostly men until the early 1960s. Mexican American men and European American men had condescending attitudes toward women in politics.

Sloss-Vento critiqued men's privilege in the home, but she did not speak against male-only organizations. Her essay "Why There Is No Happiness in Latino Homes" in 1934 criticizes men's privilege in the question of housework for women. Likewise, she encouraged men to treat women in the home not as "slaves" but as companions. Few Latinas were providing this critique of heterosexual homes in the 1930s. But she did not speak of LULAC men's privilege in organizations.

Though married, Sloss-Vento did not fully accept domesticity as a wife or mother and instead chose a more public persona. Being a wife, mother, or homemaker were not the identities she cherished, though she may have enjoyed these. She accepted wifedom, motherhood, and housework, but when her husband occasionally nagged her, she continued her activism nonetheless. Her husband, Pedro C. Vento, is the "modern man" she writes about in "No Happiness," and he understood she was not ordinary. As a mother she cared for her children, though that sometimes meant sending them to school early and taking them to some meetings. Her gift to her children was not traditional motherhood; instead she taught them political lessons and worked to give them a college education. Her son, Arnoldo, learned the difficulty of farm labor firsthand.

She performed her political and intellectual project as a public intellectual. Her technique was to write numerous opinion pieces and letters to the editor in a broad range of newspapers. Because her writings are located in the press in towns and cities across seven decades in both Spanish and English, no one could see her collective contribution across the twentieth century. Perhaps her regional focus also made her less visible, or perhaps her Latina status made her invisible. Another major reason for her invisibility is that her papers are not yet in a public archive.

She was a feminist; she publicly condemned the domesticity that most women were subjected to in the 1930s, and she patterned her life as a public woman. She took advantage of the modern gendered selfhood available to some US women after 1920, especially those with high school or college educations. Ironically, it was in her home that most of her public contributions were made. There she used the power of her pen to advocate for social change. Even as a paid working woman after 1949 she made time to write. However, she also criticized European American women who sought self-actualization in the 1950s and did not take care of their husbands and families first.

Sloss-Vento's lifestyle modeled a path for feminists based on the idea of modern gendered selfhood. She could be true to herself only inside of the home as an autonomous woman writer and thinker in her own space. She moved toward a new feminist politic that was not available to women before the 1970s by acting in an unladylike manner. She welcomed and praised Chicana feminists, the first generation of semiliberated Mexican American women. She applauded young women professionals in the making like myself. "No Ladies Allowed" signs were coming down. Women in the generations after 1970 have more opportunities.

Still, Sloss-Vento embodied gendered contradictions. Her idea of womanhood was traditional, with taking care of the husband and children as the first priority. Likewise, she was critical of women, particularly sexually active women, outside of traditional patterns of marriage because of her Christianity. She opposed some aspects of women's subordination in the home and in society, but she did not publicly condemn LULAC's or the American G.I. Forum's homosociality that oppressed Latinas in Texas.

Sloss-Vento did not have meaningful homosocial political relations with women. Besides her letter congratulating Governor Ann Richards, she wrote few women about civil rights or politics. While she was active with her church, only a few documents in her archive pertain to her work with the church. She did not join Ladies LULAC and did not work with the women who did. Her political club in Hidalgo County in the 1940s was mixed with men and women. Otherwise, she worked alone. Most of the time she spent with women was either at church or with incarcerated Mexican braceras.

She did not regularly advocate for women; women's rights were not her focus. She did indirectly help women whose husbands frequented prostitutes by advocating the closing of a red light district. She helped women immigrants and braceras. She did not tackle the elephant in the room—LULAC's gender segregation. Nevertheless, she contested the Mexican-descent fraternal order in the United States through her activities. Civil rights organizing, civic engagement, and electoral politics were fraternities closed to ladies. She challenged patriarchal rule in these domains through her actions though not her voice. She questioned the presumptive natural order before 1970 and entered where few women were allowed.

Knowing that no individual makes a movement, Sloss-Vento was nonetheless a movement maker. She was a movement woman thinking beyond individualism, profit, power, acclaim, and fame. As a woman warrior, she did not posture for power. She left no diary, resume, writings list, or archive in a library. She included only three of her own articles in her book, *Alonso S. Perales: His Struggle for the Rights of the Mexican American*, preferring to highlight male leaders. But it was not just his struggle—it was her struggle too. She was a movement team player.

She had gendered ambivalence and did not give herself full credit. More often than not she referred to herself as a "collaborator" or "co-activist," always placing herself next to others, usually men. She was humble, cooperative, collaborative, and supportive, typical postures for women. Yet, she did not place herself behind others. She was not fully self-abnegating. Nor was she male-identified or a hero worshipper. She gave women in civic engagement credit. Her Christianity also made her humble.

Her gendered ambivalence or skill as an activist also explains Sloss-Vento's invisibility. She deflected attention from herself. As a woman she was unwilling to give herself credit for her own work and achievements. As an activist, she did not need attention as an individual; the movement was more important. She was also well aware of the lack of freedom of the press, as she described her own freedom of speech, and political repression. She even told US President Harry S. Truman that Mexican Americans lived under the master's rule. She feared being fired from her job for speaking out.

Still, Sloss-Vento was cognizant of her own collective contribution. So when she died she left her prized possession—her writings—intact in a chest. Like Perales, who cried on his deathbed, worried about the future of his archives and lost history, Sloss-Vento recognized the significance of her own papers. Arnoldo Carlos Vento, the son and academic that she, her husband, and the Chicano movement produced, took over guarding her papers after she died.

She was a self-respecting, self-confident, and self-actualized woman who created her own strategies, tactics, and niche in the Mexican American civil rights movement and the Chicano movement. She succeeded at self-actualization in an era when women had prescribed lives as heterosexual, married mothers caring for their children and tending church activities. She ignored "No Ladies Allowed" signs. Women were to value the communal before the self. She found her calling and purpose in life. Thus, she was not a fully oppressed woman subject to the degradations of social norms before the 1970s. She manifested a strong sense of self, intelligence, and heart. No one granted her access to power—she simply took it. She created her own sphere of influence. She was a confident, strong leader despite or because of sexism, racism, and classism. Sloss-Vento even fought the limitations of aging. She wrote her last letter in 1990, when she was eighty-nine years old.

Sloss-Vento was a self-made woman in the public domain—a leader, organic public intellectual, and trailblazing woman among men in civil rights, public opinion, and politics. An architect of her own destiny, alongside men and women she sought to build a better America, for the betterment of all society. Despite nagging gendered ambivalence, she knew she was somebody. While she was not particularly satisfied with her job as a jail matron, it allowed her to give her children a college education, what she valued most even though she could not attain this for herself.

She had several ambiguous and contradictory identities as a borderlander/fronteriza. She called herself an American, a Mexican American, and a member of La Raza. She was proud of her Mexican heritage. Yet, she did draw a line between the United States and Mexico. Her political work was done as a Mexican American borderlander seeking primarily to have an impact in the United States. She nonetheless wrote several political officials in Mexico because the borderlands felt the impact of Mexican immigrants and Mexico. Only when she believed Mexican immigrants were detrimentally affecting Mexican Americans did she make a distinction and privilege Mexican Americans over Mexicans. She especially felt this way by the 1970s, perhaps being tired of decades of the poverty and labor exploitation that were prevalent in the Valley; "the eternal dilemma" had not ended.[4] The Spanish language, Mexican newspapers, and travel to Mexico allowed her familiarity and solidarity with Mexico. As a borderlander/fronteriza she took political positions that were both pro-Mexican and pro-Mexican American. While she claimed to know Mexico like an open book, she was still a Mexican American. This meant that she did distinguish between the two even as she was pro-Raza, and when forced to choose, she chose Mexican Americans. She continued to refer to "La Raza" (a term revitalized by the Chicano movement), although her political family of La Raza was at times fractured.

Perales, Sáenz, Canales, and Sloss-Vento all deserve more name recognition in Texas, especially in the Valley, and the United States. San Antonio has a Perales Elementary School, but nothing else honors him. In the first paragraph of this book I quote Sloss-Vento that Perales was worthy of being honored with museums, libraries, and monuments. That has still not happened. Alice, Texas, has a Sáenz School, but that is all. Canales has an elementary school in Brownsville, and a Texas marker honors him, but that is all. Nothing yet honors Sloss-Vento besides a small part of a mural in the Midwest.

Sloss-Vento was a public intellectual and wise Latina. Decades before Sonia Sotomayor became a US Supreme Court justice there were smart Latinas. The writer P. J. Pierce interviewed Texas "wise women," including some seven Latinas and Irma Rangel, the first Tejana state legislator.[5] Before there was Rangel there was Sloss-Vento, who had wisdom and intellect. Some wise and smart women did not have access to a college education. In Sloss-Vento's era, high school graduation was the equivalent of a college education for people of Mexican descent in the United States. Besides intellect, she had a moral bedrock due to her Christianity and a strong belief in democracy. Her character traits of tenacity, endurance, and perseverance carried her through her mission across the decades.

Her fellow activists referred to Sloss-Vento as a heroine of Greater Mexico, which encompasses Texas. Roberto Austin of Mission called her a "Josefa Ortiz de Domínguez," in reference to a heroine of Mexico's struggle for independence in 1810, as did J. T. Canales. Gutiérrez, Meléndez, and Noyola have referred to post-1964 Tejana "warrior trailblazers" as "Adelitas."[6] Norma Cantú suggests that there are intellectual Adelitas;[7] Adela Sloss-Vento was such an Adelita in Texas. As an intellectual and writer, she was also a Sor Juana Inés de la Cruz of Texas.

Like others, Sloss-Vento had flaws and interpretations with which others may not agree. She used popular terms like "wetback," "illegals," "aliens," and "white trash" in some of her writings.[8] She saw Mexicans as part of the Raza nation and advocated for them. She supported white allies as well, such as Pauline Kibbe, and white candidates, such as the liberal Ralph Yarborough and several US presidents. Over time she grew more conservative on the question of Mexican immigration; she advocated for employer sanctions as early as the 1950s and spoke out about adverse effects some immigrants were having on the national economy by the 1970s.

On a personal note, I credit Sloss-Vento for helping me in my journey to become a historian. She shared some materials from her chest with me in the late 1970s and acknowledged me as a young woman professional taking advantage of opportunities of which she could have only dreamed. In a letter to me in 1979 she says, "You are very intelligent and I know that one of these days you can write a great book."[9] Forty years after I met her this book is possible, and it is about Sloss-Vento. That "great book" she did not expect to be about her. She would also be pleased to know that I have written a biography of Perales.

Sloss-Vento's extraordinary, unladylike, political, and intellectual project is now documented, so she can take her rightful place among the heroes and sheroes of civil rights activism in the United States. Ironically, she has been "undocumented" despite numerous documents and "invisible" despite being a public intellectual.[10] Her undercover nature helped to marginalize her. But now we know she was a brave feminist intellectual activist who provides a role model for the twenty-first century. Let us honor the legacy of Adela Sloss-Vento with monuments, museum exhibits, libraries, scholarships, literature, art, music, theater, and acts of social justice. More importantly, let us add her to books on twentieth-century civil rights leaders and movement makers in US, southern, western, Texas, Mexican American, Latinx, borderland/frontera, Latin American, world, and women's history so that others may follow in their own ways.

NOTES

INTRODUCTION

1. In Arnoldo Carlos Vento, *Adela Sloss-Vento, Writer, Political Activist, and Civil Rights Pioneer* (Lanham, MD: Hamilton Books, 2017), 65. Since her son, Arnoldo Carlos, used the hyphen in "Sloss-Vento" in his book, I will use it where the two names appear together. She used more than one version of her last name.
2. Cynthia Orozco, "Conflict between Mexican Americans and Mexicans at the Harlingen Convention of 1927: The Genesis of LULAC," senior honors thesis, University of Texas, Austin, 1980.
3. Adela Sloss Vento to Cynthia Orozco, November 3, 1978; Cynthia E. Orozco Papers, Ruidoso, New Mexico (hereafter CEOP). Original text: "Dios quiera que en el futuro surjan mas Cynthias Orozco y Adela Sloss de Ventos, que honren la memoria de Alonso S. Perales." Translations are mine unless otherwise indicated.
4. Orozco, "Conflict." I discuss this research in a radio interview; Cynthia Orozco, "50th Anniversary of LULAC," interview by Armando Gutiérrez, *Onda Latina*, January 25, 1979, Longhorn Radio, University of Texas, http://www.laits.utexas.edu/onda_latina/program?sernum=000524526&term=.
5. Cynthia Orozco to Adela Sloss-Vento, January 25, 1980; carbon copy, CEOP.
6. Arnoldo C. Vento, interview by Cynthia Orozco, April 10, 1991, Austin.
7. Local news items announced the event, among them "LULAC to Hold Scholarship Fund-Raiser," *McAllen Monitor*, February 28, 1999; "LULAC to Honor Adela Sloss Vento," *Advance News Journal*, March 24, 1999; "LULAC Fund-Raiser to Honor Sloss-Vento, *McAllen Monitor*, April 25, 1999.
8. Cynthia Orozco, notes on Arnoldo C. Vento's tribute to Adela Sloss-Vento, 1999, CEOP.
9. Cynthia E. Orozco, *No Mexicans, Women, or Dogs Allowed: The Rise of the Mexican American Civil Rights Movement* (Austin: University of Texas Press, 2009).
10. Donna M. Kabalen de Bichara, "Expressions of Dissent in the Writing of Adela Sloss-Vento," in *Recovering the U.S. Hispanic Literary Heritage*, vol. 9, ed. Donna M. Kabalen de Bichara and Blanca Guadalupe López de Mariscal (Houston: Arte Público, 2014): 191–207.

11. Laura Patricia Garza, "Jovita Gonzalez, Adela Vento y Consuelo Aldape de Vega Hidalgo: Precursoras del pensamiento fronterizo," PhD diss., University of Houston, 2012.
12. Cynthia E. Orozco, "Adela Sloss-Vento: Mexican American Woman, Civil Rights Activist, Feminist, Author, and Public Intellectual in South Texas, 1927–1990," paper presented at the Organization of American Historians, San Francisco, April 2013.
13. Unsigned, to Martita [Perales], June 27, 1979; Adela Sloss-Vento Papers, personal archive of Arnoldo C. Vento, Austin (hereafter cited as ASVP).
14. Cynthia E. Orozco, "Pioneer Woman of Mexican American Civil Rights," *Corpus Christi Caller*, November 14, 2017; Tejano Talks Project, "Adela Sloss Vento," Tejano Talks no. 31, video, Texas A&M University, Kingsville, and Tejano Civil Rights Museum, 2017, https://www.youtube.com/watch?v=ql8wp0LQq0Y.
15. Cynthia E. Orozco, *Alonso S. Perales: Architect of Latino Destiny* (Houston: Arte Público, forthcoming).
16. Michael Omi and Howard Winant, *Racial Formation in the United States: From the 1960s to the 1980s* (New York: Routledge and Kegan Paul, 1987).
17. Omi and Winant, 64.
18. Juan Gómez-Quiñones, *Chicano Politics: Promise and Reality, 1940–1980* (Albuquerque: University of New Mexico Press, 1990).
19. Frances Jerome Woods, "Mexican Ethnic Leadership in San Antonio, Texas," PhD diss., Catholic University, Washington, DC, 1949, 4–5.
20. Woods, 66.
21. Woods, 117.
22. Woods, 86.
23. Elliot Young, "Deconstructing La Raza: Identifying the Gente Decente of Laredo, 1904–1994," *Southwestern Historical Quarterly* 98 (October 1994): 227–259. On nations and imagined communities, see Benedict Anderson, *Imagined Communities: Reflections on the Origin and Spread of Nationalism* (London: Verso, 1983).
24. The historian J. Gilberto Quezada from Laredo argues that the term "Mexican American" did not even exist there in the 1940s or 1950s. He encountered the term for the first time at a university in San Antonio in 1967; J. Gilberto to Cynthia E. Orozco, email, January 5, 2018.
25. Mrs. A. S. Vento to Bishops Committee for the Spanish Speaking, June 20, 1953, Alonso S. Perales Papers, Special Collections, M. D. Anderson Library, University of Houston (hereafter ASPP).
26. Gloria Anzaldúa, *Borderlands/La Frontera: The New Mestiza* (San Francisco: Aunt Lute, 1987).
27. Karen Offen, "Defining Feminism: A Comparative Historical Approach," *Signs* 14, no. 1 (Autumn 1988): 151.
28. Jean Lipman-Bluman, "Toward a Homosocial Theory of Sex Roles: An Explanation of the Sex Segregation of Social Institutions," *Signs* 1, no. 3, Part 21 (Spring 1976): 16.
29. Alice Fahs, *Out on Assignment: Newspaper Women and the Making of Modern Public Space* (Chapel Hill: University of North Carolina Press, 2001), 14.

30. Fahs, 15.
31. Emma Pérez, *The Decolonial Imaginary: Writing Chicanas into History* (Bloomington: Indiana University Press, 1999).
32. Pérez, 33.

CHAPTER 1: CIVIL RIGHTS LEADER, PUBLIC INTELLECTUAL, AND FEMINIST

1. Adela Sloss-Vento, *Alonso S. Perales: His Struggle for the Rights of the Mexican American* (San Antonio: Artes Gráficas, 1977). On Perales, see Cynthia E. Orozco, "Alonso S. Perales," in *New Handbook of Texas* (hereafter *NHOT*), ed. Ronnie C. Tyler, Douglas E. Barnett, and Roy R. Barkley (Austin: Texas State Historical Association, 1996), 4:148–149; Cynthia E. Orozco, *No Mexicans, Women, or Dogs Allowed: The Rise of the Mexican American Civil Rights Movement* (Austin: University of Texas Press, 2009), 111–114. The most complete work on Perales is *In Defense of My People: Alonso S. Perales and the Development of Mexican-American Public Intellectuals*, ed. Michael A. Olivas (Houston: Arte Público, 2012). Arnoldo Carlos Vento, her son, was the first to write about Sloss-Vento; Arnoldo Carlos Vento, "Adela Sloss-Vento, 1901–1998," introduction to Adela Sloss-Vento, *Alonso S. Perales: His Struggle for the Rights of Mexican Americans*, reprint as ebook (Austin: Eagle Feather Research Institute, 2008).
2. On LULAC, see Benjamin Marquez, *LULAC: The Evolution of a Mexican American Political Organization* (Austin: University of Texas Press, 1993); Craig A. Kaplowitz, *LULAC, Mexican Americans, and National Policy* (College Station: Texas A&M University Press, 1995); and Amy Waters Yarsinke, *All for One and One for All: A Celebration of 75 Years of the League of United Latin American Citizens (LULAC)* (Virginia Beach, VA: Donning, 2004); Cynthia E. Orozco, "League of United Latin American Citizens," in *NHOT*, 4:129–131; and Cynthia E. Orozco, "League of United Latin American Citizens," in *Readers Companion to U.S. Women's History*, ed. Wilma Mankiller, Gwendolyn Mink, Marysa Navarro, Barbara Smith, and Gloria Steinem (Boston: Houghton Mifflin, 2000): 378.
3. Alonso S. Perales, *En defensa de mi raza*, 2 vols. (San Antonio: Artes Gráficas, 1937); Alonso S. Perales, *Are We Good Neighbors?* (San Antonio: Artes Gráficas, 1948).
4. Sloss-Vento, *Alonso S. Perales*, 6.
5. Adela S. de Vento, "Grabado . . . Cassette recording," manuscript, November 27, 1973, ASVP.
6. Sloss-Vento, *Alonso S. Perales*, 38–39.
7. Gabriela González, "Jovita Idar: The Ideological Origins of a Transnational Advocate for La Raza," in *Texas Women: Their Histories, Their Lives*, ed. Elizabeth Hayes Turner, Stephanie Cole, and Rebecca Sharpless (Athens: University of Georgia Press, 2015): 225–248; Gabriela González, *Redeeming La Raza: Transborder Modernity, Race, Respectability, and Rights* (Oxford: Oxford University Press, 2018).
8. On Alice Dickerson Montemayor, see Cynthia E. Orozco, "Alice Dickerson Montemayor: Feminism and Mexican American Politics in Texas in the 1930s," in *Writing the Range: Race, Class, and Culture in the American Women's West*,

ed. Elizabeth Jameson and Susan Armitage (Norman: University of Oklahoma Press, 1997): 435–456. On María L. Hernández, see Cynthia E. Orozco, "Maria L. Hernández," in *NHOT*, 3:572–573. On Emma Tenayuca, see Gabriela González, "Carolina Munguía and Emma Tenayuca: The Politics of Benevolence and Radical Reform," *Frontiers: A Journal of Women Studies* 24, nos. 2–3 (2003): 200–229. On Jovita González, see María Cotera, "Jovita González Mireles: A Sense of History and Homeland," *Latina Legacies: Identity, Biography, and Community*, ed. Vicki L. Ruiz and Virginia Sánchez-Korrol (New York: Oxford University Press, 2005): 158–174.

9. On Josefina Fierro de Bright, see Mario T. García, "The Popular Front: Josefina Fierro de Bright and the Spanish-Speaking Congress," in *Mexican Americans, Leadership, Ideology, and Identity, 1930–1960* (New Haven, CT: Yale University Press, 1989): 145–174. On Luisa Moreno, see Vicki L. Ruiz, "Luisa Moreno and Latina Labor Activism," *Latina Legacies: Identity, Biography, and Community*, ed. Vicki L. Ruiz and Virginia Sánchez Korral (New York: Oxford University Press, 2005): 175–192.

10. Isabel González, *Step-Children of a Nation: The Status of Mexican-Americans* (New York: American Committee for Protection of Foreign Born, 1947).

11. Martha P. Cotera to Mrs. Adela Sloss-Vento, February 2, 1979; Mrs. Adela Sloss Vento to Miss Martha Cotera, March 5, 1979, ASVP; Martha P. Cotera, *The Chicana Feminist* (Austin: Information Systems, 1977).

12. Rio Writers, *One Hundred Women of the Rio Grande Valley of Texas* (Waco: Eakin, 1983).

13. José Ángel Gutiérrez, Michelle Meléndez, and Sonia A. Noyola, *Chicanas in Charge: Texas Women in the Public Arena* (Lanham, MD: Altamira, 2007).

14. Adela Sloss-Vento to Ángel Gutiérrez, November 28, 1977, ASVP.

15. F. Arturo Rosales, *Chicano! The History of the Mexican American Civil Rights Movement* (Houston: Arte Público, 1997); F. Arturo Rosales, *Dictionary of Latino Civil Rights History* (Houston: Arte Público, 2007); F. Arturo Rosales, *Testimonio: A Documentary History of the Mexican-American Struggle for Civil Rights* (Houston: Arte Público, 2000); Matt S. Meier and Margo Gutiérrez, *Encyclopedia of the Mexican American Civil Rights Movement* (Westport, CT: Greenwood, 2000).

16. L. Garza, "La concepción de la identidad fronteriza en Jovita González y Adela Sloss Vento," in *Yet More Studies of the Lower Rio Grande Valley*, ed. Milo Kearney (Brownsville: University of Texas, Brownsville, 2015), 29. See also Laura Patricia Garza, "Jovita González, Adela Vento y Consuelo Aldape de Vega Hidalgo: Precursoras del pensamiento fronterizo," PhD diss., University of Houston, 2012.

17. David M. Vigness and Mark Odintz, "Rio Grande Valley," in *NHOT*, 5:588–589.

18. Alberto Rodríguez, "The Making of the Modern Lower Rio Grande Valley: Situating and Reframing Race, Class, and Ethnicity in Urbanizing South Texas, 1928–1965," PhD diss., University of Houston, 2012, 46.

19. Alicia A. Garza, "San Juan," in *NHOT*, 5:863. San Juan's population was 1,203 in 1925 and 2,264 in 1945. The school district was created in 1919.

20. Michael A. Olivas, "The Legal Career of Alonso S. Perales," in *In Defense of My People*, ed. Olivas, 317.
21. Monica Muñoz Martínez, *The Injustice Never Leaves You: Anti-Mexican Violence in Texas* (Cambridge, MA: Harvard University Press, 2018).
22. William D. Carrigan and Clive Webb, *Forgotten Dead: Mob Violence against Mexicans in the United States, 1848–1928* (Oxford: Oxford University Press, 2013), appendix 1, appendix 2.
23. Carrigan and Webb, 31.
24. Everett Ross Clinchy Jr., *Equality of Opportunity for Latin Americans in Texas* (New York: Arno, 1974), 19. This was originally a dissertation from Columbia University in 1954.
25. Aurora E. Orozco, "Mexican Blood Runs through My Veins," in *Speaking Chicana: Voice, Power, and Identity*, ed. D. Letticia Galindo and María D. Gonzales (Tucson: University of Arizona Press, 1998), 109.
26. In Lyle Saunders and Olen E. Leonard, "The Wetback in the Lower Rio Grande Valley of Texas," Inter-American Education Occasional Papers 7 (Austin: University of Texas, 1951), 666.
27. Vicki L. Ruiz, "Working for Wages: Mexican Women in the Southwest, 1930–1980," Working Paper no. 19 (Tucson: Southwest Institute for Research on Women, 1984); Orozco, *No Mexicans, Women, or Dogs*, 23.
28. A. Rodríguez, 70.
29. Irene Ledesma, "Unlikely Strikers: Mexican-American Women in Strike Activity in Texas, 1919–1974," PhD diss., Ohio State University, 32.
30. Vigness and Odintz, "Rio Grande Valley."
31. Fred L. Koestler, "Operation Wetback," in *NHOT*, 4:1157–1158.
32. Steve Taylor, "Farm Workers Have Transformed the Rio Grande Valley," *Rio Grande Guardian*, July 9, 2013.
33. Adela S. Vento to Mr. Dwight D. Eisenhower, President of the United States, February 13, 1954, ASVP.
34. Marc Simon Rodríguez, *The Tejano Diaspora: Mexican Americanism and Ethnic Politics in Texas* (Charlotte: University of North Carolina Press, 2011).
35. Saunders and Leonard, 44, 57.
36. Saunders and Leonard, 48, 53, 55.
37. Saunders and Leonard, 72.
38. A. Rodríguez, 42.
39. Sonia Hernández, *Working Women into the Borderlands* (College Station: Texas A&M University Press, 2014), 94.
40. Orozco, *No Mexicans*, 33.
41. Vento, "Adela Sloss-Vento, 1901–1998," iii–iv.
42. Jennifer Nájera, *The Borderlands of Race: Mexican Segregation in a South Texas Town* (Austin: University of Texas Press, 2015), 116.
43. Nájera, 116.
44. Juanita Luna Lawhn, "Victorian Attitudes Affecting the Mexican Women Writing in *La Prensa* during the Early 1900s and the Chicana of the 1980s," in *Missions in Conflict: Essays on U.S. Mexican Relations and Chicano Culture*, ed.

Renate von Bardeleben, Dietrich Briesemesiter, and Juan Bruce Novoa (Tubingen, Germany: Gunter Narr Verlad, 1986), 65–74.

45. Juanita Luna Lawhn, "María Luisa Garza," in *Double Crossings/Entre Cruzamientos*, ed. Mario Martin Flores and Carlos von Son (n.p.: NJ Ediciones Nuevo Espacio, 2001), 83–96.

46. Evan Anders, *Boss Rule in South Texas: The Progressive Era* (Austin: University of Texas Press, 1982); Evan Anders, "José Tomás Canales," in *NHOT*, 1:953–954; Orozco, *No Mexicans*, 94–97; Cynthia E. Orozco, "Hidalgo County Rebellion," *NHOT*, 3:593; Laura Caldwell, "Baker, Anderson Yancey," *Handbook of Texas Online* (Austin: Texas State Historical Association, 2010, modified October 24, 2018), https://tshaonline.org/handbook/online/articles/fba19.

47. Darlene Clark Hine, "The Elusive Ballot: The Black Struggle against the Texas Democratic White Primary, 1932–1945," in *The African American Experience in Texas: An Anthology*, ed. Bruce A. Glasrud and James M. Smallwood (Lubbock: Texas Tech University Press, 2007), 281.

48. Nasser Momayezi, "Hispanic Representation, Empowerment, and Participation in Texas Politics," *Latino Studies Journal* 11, no. 2 (Spring 2000): 6.

49. Pauline Kibbe, *The Latin American in Texas* (Albuquerque: University of New Mexico Press, 1947), 227.

50. On the LULAC president Belén Robles of El Paso, see Ernestina Muñoz, Alisandra Mancera, Alma Fajardo, Mayra García, and Adriana Alatorre, "El Paso Women Gained Power in LULAC," *Borderlands* 25 (2006–2007), 7.

51. John P. Schmal, "The Tejano Struggle for Representation," Hispanics in Government (Houston: Houston Institute for Culture, n.d.), http://www.houstonculture.org/hispanic/tejano1.html, accessed May 10, 2014.

52. Maggie Rivas-Rodriguez, *Texas Mexican Americans and Postwar Civil Rights* (Austin: University of Texas Press, 2015), 35.

53. Ozzie G. Simmons, *Anglo-Americans and Mexican Americans in South Texas: A Study in Dominant-Subordinate Group Relations* (New York: Arno, 1952), 77.

54. Angela Boswell, "From Farm to Future: Women's Journey through Twentieth-Century Texas," *Twentieth-Century Texas, a Social and Cultural History*, ed. John W. Storey and Mary L. Kelley (Denton: University of North Texas Press, 2008), 114.

55. Nancy Baker Jones and Ruthe Winegarten, *Capitol Women: Texas Female Legislators, 1923–1999* (Austin: University of Texas Press, 2000).

56. Gabriela Sosa Zavaleta, "Women as Political Pioneers in the Rio Grande Valley," in *Yet More Studies in Rio Grande Valley History*, ed. Milo Kearney (Brownsville: University of Texas at Brownsville, 2015), 156.

57. Legislative Reference Library of Texas (LRL), "Barbara Jordan" (Austin: LRL, n.d.), https://lrl.texas.gov/legeLeaders/members/memberDisplay.cfm?memberID=708, accessed March 24, 2019.

58. G. González, "Jovita Idar."

59. J. Gilberto Quezada, *Border Boss: Manuel B. Bravo and Zapata County* (College Station: Texas A&M University Press, 2001), 24.

60. Cynthia E. Orozco, "Ladies LULAC," in *NHOT*, 4:1–2.

61. Rodolfo Rosales, *The Illusion of Inclusion: The Untold Political Story of San Antonio* (Austin: Center for Mexican American Studies, University of Texas, 2000).
62. Rosie Castro to Cynthia Orozco, email, January 10, 2018.
63. S. Hernández, 90.
64. Teresa Palomo Acosta, "Cruz Azul Mexicana," in *NHOT*, 2:429–430.
65. Teresa Palomo Acosta, "American G.I. Forum Women's Auxiliary," in *NHOT*, 1:148.
66. Teresa Palomo Acosta and Ruthe Winegarten, *Las Tejanas: 300 Years of History* (Austin: University of Texas Press, 2003).
67. Britney Jeffrey, "Rangel, Irma Lerma," *Handbook of Texas Online* (Austin: Texas State Historical Association, 2010, modified June 20, 2016), http://www.tshaonline.org/handbook/online/articles/fra85; Nancy Baker Jones and Tiffany J. González, "Irma Rangel," transcript with audio (Austin: Women in Texas History, 1997), https://www.womenintexashistory.org/biographies/irma-rangel.
68. Sosa Zavaleta, 155.
69. Sosa Zavaleta, 156.
70. Megan Seaholm, "Texas Federation of Women's Clubs," in *NHOT*, 6:331–332.
71. Boswell, 114.
72. Simmons, 461, 463.
73. Clinchy, 138.
74. Ramona Alaniz Houston, "African Americans, Mexican Americans, and Anglo-Americans and the Desegregation of Texas, 1946–1957," PhD diss., University of Texas, Austin, 2000, 151.
75. Clinchy, 122–123.
76. Cynthia E. Orozco, "Mexican American Women," in *NHOT*, 4:680–682.
77. Women in Texas History (WITH), "Timeline of Texas Women's History" (Austin: WITH, n.d.), https://www.womenintexashistory.org/learn/timeline, accessed March 24, 2019; Freddie Milam Sanders, "Elena Farías Barrera," *The Rio Writers: One Hundred Women of the Rio Grande Valley* (Austin: Eakin, 1983), 4.
78. A. Rodríguez, 121.
79. On Eduardo Idar, see Cynthia E. Orozco, "Eduardo Idar Sr.," in *NHOT*, 3:814; and Orozco, *No Mexicans*, 101–104.
80. Eduardo Idar to Alonso S. Perales, March 20, 1928, ASVP; G. González, *Redeeming La Raza*, 26.
81. "Una señorita que defiende a la colonia," *La Prensa*, February 20, 1929, ASVP.
82. "Es encomiada la labor del lic. Perales," *La Prensa*, May 20, 1931, 2, ASVP; in her bibliography in *Perales* Sloss-Vento cites this article as "Alonso Perales: Fundador de LULAC," *La Prensa*, May 20, 1931. According to the article "Es encomiada," the newspaper received a letter from Sloss-Vento.
83. Fifth Annual Statewide LULAC Founders' Pioneers and Awards Banquet program, 1968, CEOP.
84. "LULAC Pioneers Due Honor," *San Antonio Express*, November 12, 1968. I thank Jazmin León, a University of Texas at Austin graduate student, for information from "Adela Sloss-Vento," her 2015 draft article for *Handbook of Texas Online*, CEOP.

85. Sloss-Vento, *Alonso S. Perales*, 80–82.
86. Vento, *Adela Sloss-Vento*, 213, 223.
87. "LULAC to Honor the Late Adela Sloss Vento," *McAllen Monitor*, March 24, 1999.
88. Vento, "Adela Sloss-Vento, 1901–1998," iii–iv.
89. Vento, *Adela Sloss-Vento*, xiii.
90. Gerhard Grytz, "German Immigrants in the Lower Rio Grande Valley, 1850–1920: A Demographic Overview," in *Studies in the Rio Grande Valley*, vol. 6, ed. Milo Kearney, Anthony Knopp, and Antonio Zavaleta (Brownsville: University of Texas at Brownsville and Texas Southmost College, 2015), 145–165.
91. Jesse Sloss to Sister Adela and Pete (Vento), September 20, 1966, ASVP.
92. Arnoldo Vento to Cynthia E. Orozco, email, June 4, 2014.
93. Vento, *Adela Sloss-Vento*, xiii.
94. Vento, interview by Orozco, April 10, 1991, CEOP.
95. "Jesse Wilfred Sloss Sr.," *Brownsville Herald*(?), January 2, 1996, ASVP.
96. J. T. Canales to E. D. Salinas, May 2, 1940, folder C, Carlos E. Castañeda Papers, Benson Latin American Collection, University of Texas, Austin (hereafter BLAC).
97. Lyle Saunders, *The Spanish-Speaking Population of Texas* (Austin: University of Texas Press, 1949), 14.
98. Saunders, 14.
99. Vento, *Adela Sloss-Vento*, xv.
100. US Census, 1920, in León, "Adela Sloss Vento."
101. Vento, *Adela Sloss-Vento*, 18.
102. In Cynthia E. Orozco, notes on Arnoldo C. Vento's tribute to Adela Sloss-Vento, April 30, 1999, LULAC Council #4591, McAllen, CEOP.
103. Orozco, notes on Vento's tribute, April 30, 1999.
104. Brandon H. Mila, "Alonso S. Perales and the Creation of the LULAC Spirit," master's thesis, University of North Texas, 2013, 18.
105. Cynthia E. Orozco, "Harlingen Convention," in *NHOT*, 3:463–464; and Orozco, *No Mexicans*, chapter 5.
106. Marta Perales, "Carta para el libro de Mrs. Adela Sloss Vento, Mayo 3, 1977," in Sloss-Vento, *Alonso S. Perales*, 80–82.
107. On the Chicano movement, see Juan Gómez-Quiñones and Irene Vásquez, *Making Aztlán: Ideology and Culture of the Chicana and Chicano Movement, 1966–1977* (Albuquerque: University of New Mexico Press, 2015).
108. Conchita Hassell Winner, "Spanish-Language Newspapers," in *NHOT*, 5:4–5.
109. Sloss-Vento, *Alonso S. Perales*, 22.
110. *La Prensa*, "Una señorita que defiende a la colonia," February 20, 1929.
111. Sloss-Vento, *Alonso S. Perales*, 53.
112. The University of Texas, Austin, has some digitized issues of *LULAC News* from the 1930s and 1940s, and I have copies of most *LULAC News* issues from 1931 to 1965, CEOP.
113. Pedro C. Vento, "Continuation of Dates of Employment," partial employment resume, ca. 1944, ASVP; obituary of Pedro C. Vento, *McAllen Monitor*, n.d., ASVP.

114. Mrs. A. S. Vento to Mrs. Maurice Brown, December 22, 1963, ASVP.
115. Vento, *Adela Sloss-Vento*, 214.
116. Mrs. P. C. Vento to J. W. Sloss, September 24, 1966, ASVP. Original text: "16 años en un trabajo que no era de mi agrado. Eran tantas las horas de trabajo que parece que estaba sepultada viva y perjudiqué un tanto mi salud."
117. "Certification of Deputation," card, Hidalgo County, January 1, 1953, ASVP.
118. J. T. Canales to Mrs. A. S. Vento, February 29, 1956, ASVP.
119. This was during the "Wetback Lift." Vento, *Adela Sloss-Vento*, 213.
120. Mrs. P. C. Vento to J. W. Sloss, September 24, 1966, ASVP.
121. Kabalen de Bichara, "Self-Writing and Collective Representation," 256.
122. Vento, *Adela Sloss-Vento*, 216.
123. "Mrs. P. C. Vento," *Valley Evening Monitor*, May 16, 1948, ASVP.
124. Vento, *Adela Sloss-Vento*, 153.
125. Vento, *Adela Sloss-Vento*, 167.
126. Adela Sloss-Vento, in Vento, *Adela Sloss-Vento*, 226.
127. The essay was "The Problems of Many Texas Towns," published in English in the *Corpus Christi Caller* and originally in Spanish in *El Heraldo* on September 16, 1943; reprinted in Vento, *Adela Sloss-Vento*, 108.
128. Adela S. Vento, "Poverty, TB, and Ignorance to End with Discrimination," letter to the editor, *Valley Morning Star*, December 17, 1947, ASVP.
129. A. S. Vento, "Poverty, TB, and Ignorance."
130. Adela S. Vento, "Christians Must Practice Christianity to Stop Communism, Valley Woman Says," letter to the editor, *Valley Morning Star*(?), November 18, 1947, ASVP.
131. A. S. Vento, "Christians Must Practice Christianity."
132. Unsigned, to George Esqueda, October 21, 1947, ASVP.
133. Original text: "Cartas que a través de largo años se perdieron que guardó los sobres como recuerdo de esa gran lucha de nuestro gran defensor el Lic. Alonso S. Perales. Sobre[s] vacíos—Cartas que se pierden pero que son pruebas evidentes de la larga correspondencia de la Sra. Adela Sloss de Vento con nuestros defensores como el Lic. Perales y el Lic. Jose T. Canales, pero más con el Lic. Alonso S. Perales." Adela Sloss-Vento, note, undated, ASVP.
134. Original text: "No le envié la copia del periódico, porque la que tenía, se la mandé al Señor Héctor Pérez Martínez, Secretaría de Gobernación en México." Adela Sloss-Vento to Alonso S. Perales, November 12, 1947, ASPP.
135. Unsigned, to Senator Franklin Spears, April 16, 1945, ASVP.
136. Mrs. A. S. Vento to the President of the School Board, September 18, 1969, ASVP.
137. Sloss-Vento, typescript notes for *Alonso S. Perales*, ca. 1977, ASVP.
138. Original text: "Voy a comprar un Chest para guardar todo con llave." Mrs. A. S. Vento to Mrs. Martita Perales, May 30, 1960, ASVP.
139. Luis Alvarado to Mrs. Vento, January 1961, ASVP.
140. Vento, *Adela Sloss-Vento*, 67.
141. "The Wetback in the Lower Rio Grande Valley, in Defense of La Raza Mexicana," audio tape recorded by Adela Sloss-Vento, box 438B, J. T. Canales Estate

Collection, Texas A&M University, Kingsville (hereafter JTCEC), and posted online at http://archives.tamuk.edu/uploads/A1999-022.0017.mp3.

CHAPTER 2: THE MEXICAN AMERICAN CIVIL RIGHTS MOVEMENT, 1920–1950

1. Mario T. García, *Mexican Americans, Leadership, Ideology, and Identity* (New Haven, CT: Yale University Press, 1989), 17–18.
2. Kabalen de Bichara, "Expressions of Dissent," 192.
3. Frances Benedict to Adela Sloss, March 25, 1927, ASVP.
4. "Poetry Is Latest Stunt of Seniors," unknown newspaper, 1927, ASVP.
5. Benedict to Sloss, March 25, 1927.
6. Annie Mae Evers to Adela Sloss, ca. March 25, 1927, ASVP.
7. Original text: "Ella leía cuanto libro llegaba a sus manos y *La Prensa* el gran diario de San Antonio era su periódico favorito tanto para leerlo como para escribir en él." Adela S. Vento, "Prólogo," draft, 1977, ASVP.
8. Sloss-Vento, *Alonso S. Perales*; Orozco, "Harlingen Convention."
9. "A los ciudadanos americanos de origen mexicano," unknown newspaper, November 1927, ASVP.
10. "Nuevo Concilio de la Liga de Ciudadanos de Origen Latino" and "Se fundará el Concilio de la Latin-American League," *Diógenes*, November 15, 1927, ASVP.
11. Alonso S. Perales to Adela Sloss, November 7, 1927, ASVP.
12. Alonso S. Perales to Miss Sloss, December 30, 1928, ASVP.
13. On political bossism in Hidalgo County politics in the 1920s, see Orozco, "Hidalgo County Rebellion," in *NHOT*, 3:593. On Zapata County, see J. Gilberto Quezada, *Border Boss: Manuel B. Bravo and Zapata County* (College Station: Texas A&M University Press, 2001), 16–39.
14. Irene Ledesma, "Unlikely Strikers," 28.
15. Abraham Hoffman, *Unwanted Mexican Americans in the Great Depression: Repatriation Pressures, 1929–1939* (Tucson: University of Arizona Press, 1974), 120.
16. Untitled manuscript, ca. 1931, ASVP. This document begins "In order."
17. Original text: "no podían quejarse ni decir nada." Adela Sloss-Vento, untitled manuscript, 1977, ASVP. For a different perspective on prostitution, see Sonia Hernández, "Morality and Gender in Reynosa in the 1920s and 1930s," in *Additional Stories in Rio Grande Valley History*, ed. Milo Kearney (Brownsville: University of Texas at Brownsville, 2008), 349–362.
18. Mrs. A. S. Vento, letter to the editor, *McAllen Monitor*, February 23, 1969, ASVP.
19. Vento, "Adela Sloss-Vento, 1901–1998," 11.
20. Mrs. A. S. Vento, letter to the editor, *McAllen Monitor*, February 23, 1969. She thanks the editor Si Cassidy, who was on the "side of justice." Sloss-Vento, *Alonso S. Perales*, ebook, 13.
21. Adela Sloss, untitled manuscript, ca. 1931, ASVP.
22. Mrs. P. C. Vento to Mr. Joe B. Evins, Atty., May 11, 1966, ASVP.
23. Mrs. A. S. Vento, letter to the editor, *McAllen Monitor*, February 23, 1969.
24. Mrs. A. S. Vento to Mexico-Americanos para Acción Social Inc., Rio Grande City, February 24, 1970, ASVP.

25. Original text: "Entonces la autora de este libro se unió a un partido político con la única condición que limpiara dicho pueblo de todo centro de vicio y sin ser escritora escribió a los periódicos y expuso la quejas del sufrimiento." Mrs. A. S. Vento to Mexico-Americanos para Acción Social Inc.
26. H. L. McCombs to whom it may concern, September 24, 1934, ASVP. In the 1950s Sloss-Vento addressed vice in the Valley town of Pharr. She commended public officials for imposing heavy fines or imprisonment on drunk drivers. She welcomed the closing of "public dances" in the "Latin American" part of town as "dances of prostitutes." Looking at how women and children were affected, she writes that they "have to go without the necessities of life, for this same reason, little children are not sent to school or are drag [*sic*] out of school to go to work in the fields." Sloss-Vento, untitled manuscript beginning with "Two steps," ca. 1950s, ASVP.
27. Sloss-Vento, "Prólogo," ASVP, 130.
28. Original text: "no solo a los norteamericanos de ascendencia Mexicana, sino también a los ciudadanos de México, residentes en los Estados Unidos." *La Prensa*, "Una señorita que defiende a la colonia," February 20, 1931, ASVP.
29. Vento, *Adela Sloss-Vento*, 19.
30. Untitled document, begins "La Senora Adela S. de Vento del Valle del Rio Grande de Texas," ca. 1960, ASVP.
31. "Carta de felicitación," *El Paladín*, June 25, 1931, copy at Chicano Studies Research Center, University of California, Los Angeles (hereafter CSRC). Perales again congratulated her for these efforts; Alonso S. Perales to Srita. Adela Sloss, June 13, 1931, and June 20, 1931, ASVP.
32. Cynthia E. Orozco, "Del Rio ISD v. Salvatierra," *NHOT*, 2:578–579; Richard R. Valencia, *Chicano Students and the Courts: Mexican American Legal Struggle for Educational Equality* (New York: New York University, 2010).
33. Michael A. Olivas, "The Legal Career of Alonso S. Perales," in *In Defense of My People*, ed. Olivas, 318. On M. C. Gonzales, see Cynthia E. Orozco, "Manuel C. Gonzales," in *NHOT*, 3:227; and Orozco, *No Mexicans*, 104–107.
34. Cynthia E. Orozco, "Alonso S. Perales and His Struggle for the Civil Rights of La Raza through the League of United Latin American Citizens (LULAC) in Texas in the 1930s: Incansable Soldado del Civismo Pro-Raza," in *In Defense of My People*, ed. Olivas, 2–28.
35. Some of her early tributes to Perales are found in Adela Sloss, "L. Unidad de Ciudadanos," *El Paladín*, Boletín no. 3, January 2, 1931, CSRC; "Nuestra gratitud y estimación hacia el autor de la Liga de Ciudadanos Unidos Latino-Americanos," *Diógenes*, 1931, ASVP; "Es encomiada la labor del lic. Perales," *La Prensa*, May 20, 1931, Dolph Briscoe Center for American History, University of Texas, Austin (hereafter BC); "Importancia de la Liga de Ciudadanos Unidos Latinoamericanos," *LULAC News*, December 1932, 15, BC.
36. Adela Sloss, "Nuestra gratitud y estimación."
37. Adela Sloss, "Es encomiada la labor del lic. Perales," *La Prensa*, May 20, 1931, ASVP.

38. Constitution, League of United Latin American Citizens, 1929, 2–4, Oliver Douglas Weeks Papers, BLAC.
39. *El Paladín* ran from 1925 to 1939 and was edited by Eulalio Marín of Corpus Christi. Cynthia E. Orozco, "Eulalio Marín," in *NHOT*, 4:508; "Display in White Library Honors Former Local Activist," *Del Mar College Campus News*, October 5, 2007.
40. Adela Sloss, "Importancia de la Liga de Ciudadanos Unidos Latino Americanos," *LULAC News*, December 1932, 15, BC.
41. J. T. Canales to M. C. Gonzales, March 26, 1932, J. T. Canales Estate Collection, box 436, folder 20, South Texas Archives, James C. Jernigan Library, Texas A&M University, Kingsville (hereafter JTCEC).
42. Cynthia E. Orozco, "Spanish-Speaking PTA," in *NHOT*, 6:13–14.
43. "Brief Resume of the Work Accomplished at the Del Rio Annual Convention," *LULAC News*, May 1933, BC.
44. Adela Sloss, "The Butterfly," *LULAC News*, May 1932, 12, BC.
45. "Boletin #3," *El Paladín*, January 2, 1931, CSRC.
46. "Se instala otro concilio auxiliar LULAC de Damas en Alice, Texas," *LULAC News*, April 1933, 18–19, BC; Orozco, "Ladies LULAC."
47. "Organización de concilios de mujeres," *La Prensa*, April 9, 1933; León, draft of "Adela Sloss Vento."
48. Orozco, "Ladies LULAC."
49. Orozco, "Ladies LULAC."
50. "Sixth Annual Convention, the League of United Latin American Citizens Program," *LULAC News*, May 1934, 13, 16, Paul S. Taylor Collection, Bancroft Library, University of California, Berkeley (hereafter PSTC); "Ninth Annual LULAC Convention Program," June 5, 6, 1937, CEOP.
51. Sloss-Vento, "La mujer americana y el marido latino-americano," in Vento, *Adela Sloss-Vento*, 138.
52. Alice Dickerson Montemayor, "Son muy hombre," *LULAC News*, March 1938, Alice Dickerson Montemayor Papers, BLAC.
53. Montemayor, "Son muy hombre"; Alice Dickerson Montemayor, interview and videotape by Norma Cantú with questions by Cynthia Orozco, Laredo, January 26, 1981, CEOP.
54. Cynthia E. Orozco, "Alice Dickerson Montemayor: Feminism and Mexican American Politics in Texas in the 1930s," in *Writing the Range: Race, Class, and Culture in the American Women's West*, ed. Elizabeth Jameson and Susan Armitage (Norman: University of Oklahoma Press, 1997): 435–456.
55. Adela Sloss, "Por que en muchos hogares no hay verdadera felicidad," *LULAC News*, May 1934, in PSTC.
56. J. Reynolds Flores, "How to Educate Our Girls," *LULAC News*, December 1932, 6, BC.
57. Adela Sloss, "El barco LULAC," *La Avispa*, Del Rio, May 15, 1933, ASVP.
58. Original text: "de mujeres abnegadas dispuestas a poner un ejemplo de voluntad y de energía." Adela Sloss, "El barco LULAC."
59. Vento, *Adela Sloss-Vento*, 20.

60. Adela Sloss, "Por qué en muchos hogares latinos no existe verdadera felicidad," *LULAC News*, March 1934, 31–32, box 12, folder 39, PSTC. I thank Maria Brandt for her assistance in copying this essay.
61. Vento, *Adela Sloss-Vento*, 20.
62. Vento, interview by Orozco, 1991, CEOP.
63. Emilio Zamora, *Claiming Rights and Righting Wrongs in Texas: Mexican Workers and Job Politics during World War II* (College Station: Texas A&M University Press, 2009); Matthew Gritter, *Mexican Inclusion: The Origins of Anti-Discrimination Policy in Texas and the Southwest* (College Station: Texas A&M University Press, 2012); Guadalupe San Miguel, *Let All of Them Take Heed: Mexican Americans and the Campaign for Educational Equality in Texas, 1910–1981* (College Station: Texas A&M University Press, 2000).
64. Sloss-Vento, *Alonso S. Perales*, 33.
65. Original text: "Los ideales y el futuro de la América deber ser antes que todo: . . . Debemos de deshacernos de malas a injustificadas actitudes. Debemos evitar que se forme una segunda Europa en nuestro continente, llena de odios y de malas interpretaciones." Adela Sloss-Vento, "Mi súplica a todos las naciones de la América," *La Prensa*, June 21, 1940. León, draft of "Adela Sloss Vento."
66. Sloss-Vento, "Mi súplica a todos las naciones."
67. Thomas A. Guglielmo, "Fighting for Caucasian Rights: Mexicans, Mexican Americans, and the Transnational Struggle for Civil Rights in World War II Texas," *Journal of American History* 92, no. 4 (March 2006): 1212–1237; Emilio Zamora, "Connecting Causes: Alonso S. Perales, Hemispheric Unity, and Mexican Rights in the United States," in *In Defense of My People*, ed. Olivas, 287–313. See also González, *Redeeming La Raza*.
68. Original text: "Hay que comprender que las teorías peligrosas de Alemania y la de sus aliadas, Italia y Rusia, son contrarias a nuestros teorías democráticas." Sloss-Vento, "Mi súplica."
69. Adela S. Vento, "The Awakening of the Real Needs of Our Country and of America," letter to editor, *Brownsville Herald*, October 16, 1940, ASVP.
70. A. S. Vento, "Awakening of the Real Needs of Our Country."
71. José E. Limón, *Américo Paredes: Culture and Critique* (Austin: University of Texas Press, 2013), 1; Richard A. García, *Rise of the Mexican American Middle Class: San Antonio, 1929–1941* (College Station: Texas A&M University Press, 1991), 231.
72. Adela Sloss-Vento to Mrs. Maurice Brown, December 27, 1965, ASVP. Sloss-Vento told Brown she traveled to Mexico City.
73. Adela Sloss-Vento, "A Latin American Speaks," letter to the editor, *Brownsville Herald*, October 1943, ASVP.
74. Sloss-Vento, "A Latin American Speaks."
75. Adela Sloss-Vento, "Latin Americans Loyal," letter to the editor, *Brownsville Herald*, September 22, 1942, ASVP.
76. Richard Pattee to Mrs. Vento, August 5, 1940, ASVP. He was the acting assistant chief of the Division of Cultural Relations in Washington, DC. In the letter he repeats her assertions.

77. Don Salvador Cardenas [Adela Sloss-Vento pseudonym], letter to the editor, *Brownsville Herald*, October 8, 1940. She also mentions Clark in Adela S. Vento, "The Problems of Many Texas Towns," *El Heraldo*, September 16, 1943, ASVP.
78. Sloss-Vento, "A Latin American Speaks."
79. Sloss-Vento, "A Latin American Speaks."
80. Sloss-Vento, "Latin Americans Loyal."
81. Sloss-Vento, "Latin Americans Loyal."
82. George N. Green, "Good Neighbor Commission," in *NHOT*, 3:240.
83. John Weber, *From South Texas to the Nation: The Exploitation of Mexican Labor in the Twentieth Century* (Chapel Hill: University of North Carolina Press, 2015), 199.
84. Original text: "Ojalá y México pusiera a todos estos Condados del Valle en la lista negra y evitara la pasada del mojados. Sería un paso hacia adelante." Adela Sloss de Vento to Alonso S. Perales(?), letter fragment, ca. 1942, box 5, folder 8, ASPP.
85. Adela Sloss-Vento, "Discrimination Defeats Idea of the Good Neighbor Policy," *Corpus Christi Caller*, September 4, 1943, ASVP.
86. Sloss-Vento, "Discrimination Defeats Idea."
87. Adela Sloss-Vento, "Legislative Action as Well as a Campaign against Race Discrimination against Latin Americans Is Needed," opinion piece, *Corpus Christi Caller*, ca. 1945, ASVP.
88. Sloss-Vento, "Legislative Action"; Adela S. de Vento to Consul de México Luis Duplán, October 22, 1943, ASVP.
89. Adela Sloss-Vento, "Governor Praises Corpus Christian for Interest in Good Neighbor Policy," letter to the editor, *El Heraldo*, September 16, 1943, ASVP.
90. Adela Sloss-Vento, untitled document beginning "The present Governor," June 1944, ASVP. She seems to have meant to date this 1943.
91. Maurice E. Turner to Mrs. Adela S. Vento, ca. August 29, 1943(?), ASVP.
92. Sloss-Vento, "Legislative Action."
93. Clinchy, 147.
94. Clinchy, 163.
95. Pauline R. Kibbe to Mrs. Adela S. Vento, letterhead, May 22, 1947, ASVP.
96. Sloss-Vento, "Legislative Action."
97. Mrs. Adela S. Vento, letter to the editor, "Says Good Neighbor Commission Real Need," 1947, ASVP.
98. Kibbe, *Latin Americans in Texas*. See also Cynthia E. Orozco, "Pauline R. Kibbe," in *NHOT*, 2:1084–1085.
99. Sloss-Vento, *Alonso S. Perales*, 14, 17.
100. Adela Sloss-Vento, open letter to Sr. Governor Beauford Jester, *La Prensa*, October 1947, ASVP.
101. Carlos Kevin Blanton, *George I. Sánchez: The Long Fight for Mexican American Integration* (New Haven, CT: Yale University Press, 2015), 79.
102. Clinchy, 41.
103. Clinchy, 5–6.
104. Clinchy, 19.
105. Sloss-Vento only credits Perales, while Guglielmo also credits M. C. Gonzales. Sloss-Vento, *Alonso S. Perales*, 28; Guglielmo, 1219.

106. "Aboga porque se dicte una ley sobre igualdad racial en Texas," *La Prensa*, ca. April 26, 1943, ASVP. *La Prensa* included her letter in this news article.
107. Fagan Dickson to Mrs. Adela S. Vento, May 7, 1941; Homer Leonard, House Speaker, to Mrs. Adela Sloss-Vento, May 6, 1941, ASVP; Alonso S. Perales to Distinguida y muy estimada Señora de Vento, May 1, 1941, ASVP; Alonso S. Perales to Distinguida y muy estimada Señora Vento, postcard, May 1, 1941, ASVP. Perales mentions that he received a letter from her that day.
108. In "Aboga por que se dicte un ley."
109. In Rogers Kelley, Texas State Senate, to Mrs. Adela S. Vento, June 29, 1941, ASVP.
110. In Kabalen de Bichara, "Expressions of Dissent," 196.
111. Guglielmo, 1220.
112. Sloss-Vento, *Alonso S. Perales*, 28.
113. A. Sloss-Vento, "El precio de la desunión," *La Prensa*, June 21, 1953, ASVP.
114. Sloss-Vento, "El precio de la desunión."
115. Sloss-Vento, "El precio de la desunión."
116. Guglielmo, 1120–1121. He also mentions the Victory War Mothers Club of San Antonio, a group of two hundred Mexican American women that wrote to the governor, 1226; Sloss-Vento, 28.
117. Sloss-Vento, "Governor Praises Corpus Christian."
118. J. Franklin Spears to Mrs. A. S. Vento, April 18, 1945, ASVP.
119. Adela Sloss Vento to Clarence La Roche, c/o *Brownsville Herald*, April 14, 1945, ASVP.
120. Sloss-Vento, "El precio de la desunión."
121. Adela Sloss-Vento, "The Problems of Many Texas Towns," *El Heraldo*, September 16, 1943, ASVP.
122. Sloss-Vento, "The Problems of Many Texas Towns."
123. Alonso S. Perales, *Are We Good Neighbors?* (San Antonio: Artes Gráficas, 1948).
124. According to the writer Dionicio Morales, Perales said "racism in Texas was even more intense in rural towns and smaller cities, from one side of the state to the other." Dionicio Morales, *A Life in Two Cultures: An Autobiography* (Houston: Arte Público, 1997), 141.
125. Vento, *Adela Sloss-Vento*, 23.
126. Sloss-Vento, letter to the editor, *Brownsville Herald*, September 14, 1943, ASVP.
127. Vento, *Adela Sloss-Vento.*
128. Mrs. A. S. Vento, "Segregation Hurts Educational Chances for Latin-American Child, Says Reader," letter to the editor, *McAllen Monitor*, June 16, 1948, ASVP.
129. Sloss-Vento, "Segregation Hurts Educational Chances."
130. Sloss-Vento, "Segregation Hurts Educational Chances."
131. Adela Sloss-Vento, letter to the editor, *Brownsville Herald*, October 9, 1940.
132. Club Social Amigos to Sra. Adela S. Vento, July 7, 1944, ASVP. The club members thanked Sloss-Vento for her letter.
133. Sloss-Vento, "Tolerant People," letter to the editor, *Valley Morning Star*, November 2, 1947, ASVP.
134. Original text: "ella atacaba a tres cuartos partes de los Latinoamericanos." In L. Garza, "Jovita González, Adela Vento y Consuelo Aldape de Vega Hidalgo," 44.

135. Adela S. Vento, "Better Conditions," letter to the editor, *Valley Morning Star*, December 17, 1947, ASVP.
136. Adela S. Vento, "Poverty, TB, and Ignorance"; Harvey Anderson to Mrs. A. S. Vento, May 17, 1947, ASVP.
137. Arnoldo Vento, in conversation with the author, July 2015.
138. Sloss-Vento, "El club político que trabaja por la organización de política bien dirigida y por el mejoramiento del pueblo latinoamericano" (A political club organized for the betterment of the Latin American people), ca. mid-1940s, ASVP.
139. Sloss-Vento, "Problems in the Lands of America," ca. 1948, in Vento, *Adela Sloss-Vento*, 97.
140. Sloss-Vento, "Problems in the Lands," 97–98.
141. Sloss-Vento, "Problems in the Lands," 98.
142. Sloss-Vento, "Problems in the Lands," 100.
143. Sloss-Vento, "Problems in the Lands," 101.
144. Una méxicoamericana, Valle de Río Grande en Texas, "El problema de explotación y odio racial puede tener una solución más pronto no enviando braceros al estado de Texas," letter to the editor, *El Mañana*(?), Reynosa, Mexico, 1947, ASVP.
145. Adela Sloss de Vento, "Cheap Labor Does Not Pay in the Long Run," letter to the editor, *Valley Evening Monitor*, April 27, 1947, ASVP; Carlos Blanton, "The Citizenship Sacrifice: Mexican Americans, the Saunders-Leonard Report, and the Politics of Immigration, 1951–1952," *Western Historical Quarterly* 40, no. 3 (Autumn 2009): 306.
146. Sloss de Vento, "Cheap Labor."
147. Sloss de Vento, "Cheap Labor."
148. A citizen (name withheld by request), "Political Problem," letter to the editor, *Harlingen Star*, December 23, 1947, ASVP.
149. Sloss-Vento, *Alonso S. Perales*, 32.
150. Sloss de Vento, "Cheap Labor."
151. Sloss de Vento, "Cheap Labor."
152. A citizen, "Political Problem."
153. A citizen, "Political Problem."

CHAPTER 3: THE MEXICAN AMERICAN CIVIL RIGHTS MOVEMENT, 1950–1963

1. Jennifer N. Najera, *The Borderlands of Race: Mexican Segregation in a South Texas Town* (Austin: University of Texas Press, 2015), 84.
2. On the Bracero Program, see Ernesto Galarza, *Merchants of Labor, the Mexican Bracero Story: An Account of the Managed Migration of Mexican Farm Workers in California 1942–1960* (San Jose: Rosicrucian Press, 1964); Deborah Cohen, *Braceros: Migrant Citizens and Transnational Subjects in the Postwar United States and Mexico* (Chapel Hill: University of North Carolina Press, 2011); Mireya Loza, *Defiant Braceros: How Migrant Workers Fought for Racial, Sexual, and Political Freedom* (Chapel Hill: University of North Carolina Press, 2016).
3. Vento, *Adela Sloss-Vento*, 53.

4. Cynthia E. Orozco, "American Council of Spanish-Speaking Peoples," in *NHOT* 1:146–147.
5. Lori A. Flores, *Grounds for Dreaming: Mexican Americans, Mexican Immigrants, and the California Farmworker Movement* (New Haven, CT: Yale University Press, 2016). The phrase "walls and mirrors" comes from the historian David Gutiérrez, *Walls and Mirrors: Mexican Americans, Mexican Immigrants, and the Politics of Ethnicity in the Southwest 1910–1986* (Berkeley: University of California Press, 1995).
6. Flores, 5.
7. L. Garza, "La concepción de la identidad fronteriza," 44, 47.
8. In L. Garza, "La concepción de la identidad fronteriza," 44.
9. L. Garza, "La concepción de la identidad fronteriza," 37. No specific newspaper is named; the date Garza cites is January 21, 1954.
10. Original text: "Griffin es agricultor tambien y naturalmente les conviene la esclavitud de los Mexicanos en la frontera." Sra. A. S. de Vento to Fidel Velásquez, Confederación Obrera Mexicana, May 6, 1953; Mrs. A. S. Vento to Hon. Martin P. Durkin, April 27, 1953, ASVP.
11. Mrs. A. S. Vento to Durkin, April 27, 1953.
12. George I. Sánchez, foreword to "The Wetback in the Lower Rio Grande Valley of Texas," by Lyle Saunders and Olen E. Leonard, Inter-American Education Occasional Papers VII (Austin: University of Texas, 1951), 3.
13. John Weber, *From South Texas to the Nation: The Exploitation of Mexican Labor in the Twentieth Century* (Chapel Hill: University of North Carolina Press, 2015), 215.
14. In Weber, 216.
15. Blanton, "Citizenship Sacrifice," 319.
16. Blanton, "Citizenship Sacrifice," 319.
17. Blanton, "Citizenship Sacrifice," 316, 318; An American of Mexican Descent to Mr. Harry S. Truman, February 15, 1952, ASVP.
18. Mrs. Adela S. Vento to Mr. Dwight D. Eisenhower, President of the United States, February 13, 1954, ASVP.
19. Juan R. García, *Operation Wetback: The Mass Deportation of Mexican Undocumented Workers in 1954* (Westport, CT: Greenwood Press, 1980).
20. Adela Sloss-Vento, "La lucha de un pueblo valiente," manuscript, ASVP.
21. Mrs. A. S. Vento to Martin D. Durkin, Secretary of Labor, April 27, 1953, ASVP.
22. Weber, 213–214.
23. Sloss-Vento, *Alonso S. Perales*, 36.
24. Kabalen de Bichara, "Self-Writing and Collective Representation," 256. Her source is Perales to Sloss-Vento, September 15, 1947, microfilm 2309, reel 27.
25. Mrs. A. S. Vento to Bishops Committee for the Spanish Speaking, June 20, 1953, ASVP.
26. Alonso S. Perales to Mrs. P. C. Vento, February 26, 1954, ASVP.
27. Lyle Saunders and Olen W. Leonard, "The Wetback in the Lower Rio Grande Valley of Texas," Inter-American Education Occasional Papers VII (Austin: University of Texas, 1951).

28. Cited in Saunders and Leonard, 68.
29. Carlos K. Blanton, "George I. Sánchez, Ideology, and Whiteness in the Making of the Mexican American Civil Rights Movement, 1930–1960," *Journal of Southern History* 72, no. 3 (August 2006): 585. Perales responds to the pamphlet in his column, "Arquitectos de nuestros propios destinos," *La Verdad*, December 14, 1951, reel 14, ASPP.
30. Dwonna Goldstone, *Integrating the Forty Acres: The Fifty-Year Struggle for Racial Equality at the University of Texas* (Athens: University of Georgia, 2012).
31. In Saunders and Leonard, 66, 70.
32. Carl Allsup, "American G.I. Forum of Texas," in *NHOT*, 1:147–148.
33. "Study Attack Draws Retorts," *San Antonio Light*, December 9, 1951, ASVP.
34. Original text: "¿No cree Ud. que dichos autores con ese folleto que escribieron está atrás algo más que odio racial? ¿Qué quieran dichos amigos, agraviar a México para que se una a Stalin?" Adela S. Vento to Lic. Alonso S. Perales, December 17, 1951, box 5, folder 8, ASPP.
35. Adela S. Vento to Lic. Alonso S. Perales, January 3, 1952, box 5, folder 8, ASPP.
36. Adela S. Vento to Lic. Alonso S. Perales, January 3, 1952, ASVP.
37. Adela S. Vento to Lic. Alonso S. Perales, January 9, 1952, box 5, folder 8, ASPP.
38. Adela S. Vento to Lic. Alonso S. Perales, December 17, 1951, box 5, folder 8, ASPP.
39. List, no title, no date, box 5, folder 8, ASPP.
40. Adela Sloss-Vento, letter to the editor, *La Verdad*, February 23, 1979, CEOP; J. Luz Sáenz to Chancellor James P. Hart, March 15, 1952, box 33, folder 1, George I. Sánchez Papers, BLAC (hereafter GISP). Sáenz was elected president of La Convención Latinoamericana del Sur de Texas, Canales vice president, and Gilberto Díaz secretary. Other responses to the wetback pamphlet are found in Wetback Report—Responses, 1951–1952, box 62, folder 8, GISP.
41. Sloss-Vento, *Alonso S. Perales*, 40.
42. Sloss-Vento, *Alonso S. Perales*, 39.
43. "'Latinos' Traits Pamphlet Blasted," *Brownsville Herald*, March 11, 1952, https://texashistory.unt.edu/ark:/67531/metapth250234. Sloss-Vento recalls the following people in attendance: Luis Alvarado, O. T. Salinas, Gilberto Díaz, and Rodolfo Villarreal. Sloss-Vento, *Alonso S. Perales*, 41.
44. Vento, *Adela Sloss-Vento*, 48.
45. "Wetback in the Lower Rio Grande Valley," audio recording, JTCEC and http://archives.tamuk.edu/uploads/A1999-022.0017.mp3.
46. Mrs. Adela S. Vento, note, January 1959, ASVP. The untitled note is about the 1952 convention in Mission.
47. "Report Adopted by the Latin American Convention, Held at Mission, Texas, March 9, 1952," Latin American Convention of South Texas, San Antonio, ca. 1952, ASVP. The convention committee consisted of Santos de la Paz as chairman, Roberto E. Austin, Luis Alvarado, and O. T. Salinas. The Reynosa, Mexico, newspaper *El Mañana* published a critique of the pamphlet; it was reprinted in a bilingual Corpus Christi newspaper. "Editorial tomado del periódico diario 'El Mañana' de C. Reynosa, Tamps., México," ca. 1951, ASVP; Sloss-Vento, *Alonso S. Perales*, 45.

48. A. S. Vento, note, January 1959.
49. Sloss-Vento, *Alonso S. Perales*, 41.
50. Original text: "Quiero los nombres para demandarlos por defamación para que aprendan a respetar al mexicano." Alonso S. Perales to Sra. Adela Sloss de Vento, December 14, 1951, ASVP.
51. Adela Sloss de Vento to Dr. Héctor García, December 17, 1951, ASVP.
52. Original text: "Me repito a sus órdenes como su amiga y servidora." Adela Sloss de Vento to Dr. Héctor García, December 22, 1951, box 5, folder 18, José de la Luz Sáenz Papers, BLAC (hereafter JLSP); Sloss-Vento, *Alonso S. Perales*, 41.
53. Original text: "Le aseguro que las mujeres mojadas que traen a la cárcel por cruzar ilegalmente no son sucias sino limpias. Se les da jabón y toalla y se bañan todos los días. Ellas lavan su ropa todos los días. La mujeres mojada aún incluyendo las pérdidas saben coser y bordar de lo mejor. Rezan también todas las noches. En cambio las prisioneras White Trash es de lo más asqueroso que hay en el mundo. Apestan horriblemente y éstas sí que se rehúsan a bañarse. Y aparte de ser pérdidas no saben hacer nada." Sloss de Vento to García, December 17, 1951, ASVP.
54. Original text: "Ese gran amor que Dios ha puesto en los corazones de hombres como Ud. es parte del amor de Dios." Sloss de Vento to García, December 22, 1951, JLSP.
55. Original text: "Yo le contesto por la paz y porque creo que debe haber armonía entre nuestros líderes. ¿Qué piensa Ud. de esto?" and "Porque siendo tan ilustres algunos de los nuestros no están de acuerdo que el pueblo necesita una explicación. Em [*sic*] mi opinión se necesita una explicación en tribuna libre y a los cuatro vientos." Adela Sloss Vento to Lic. Alonso S. Perales, December 13, 1951, box 5, folder 18, JLSP.
56. Mrs. Adela S. Vento, letter to editor, March 20(?), 1952, ASVP.
57. Perales wrote to Sloss-Vento after reading the letter. Alonso S. Perales to Sra. Adela S. Vento, March 20, 1952, box 5, folder 8, ASPP; Mrs. Adela S. Vento, untitled, March 1953, ASVP. Her book includes a letter from Estela Pérez de Contreras, Perales's sister-in-law, to Sánchez condemning him and the pamphlet. Sloss-Vento, *Alonso S. Perales*, 46–47.
58. J. Luz Sáenz, letter to the editor, *McAllen Monitor*, November 29, 1951, ASVP. See also Sloss-Vento, *Alonso S. Perales*, 49–50.
59. Michele Hall Kells, *Héctor P. García: Everyday Rhetoric and Mexican American Civil Rights* (Carbondale: Southern Illinois University Press, 2006), 147. Kells and Blanton underestimate the magnitude of the Mission meeting.
60. A. S. Vento, "El precio de la desunión."
61. Original text: "casi siempre se portan bien y siendo que se les trate bien son más buenos todavía." Sra. Adela S. de Vento, "La cárcel del condado de Hidalgo," manuscript, 1940, box 2, folder 13, JLSP.
62. Vento, *Adela Sloss-Vento*, 213–215.
63. Original text: "Nosotros tenemos varios problemas que impiden nuestros mejoramiento en Texas y cuando la clase trabajadora de México resuelva sus problemas aquí y deje de vagar de una punta de México hasta la otro . . . podremos

nosotros más fácilmente hacer un sólido frente y resolver los problemas que nos afectan." Vento, *Adela Sloss-Vento*, 213–215.

64. "En breve el problema de mujeres ilegales," ca. 1950s, ASVP. On gendered Mexican immigration, see Pierette Hondagneu-Sotel, *Gendered Transitions: Mexican Experiences of Immigration* (Berkeley: University of California Press, 1994); Denise A. Segura and Patricia Zavella, eds., *Women and Migration in the U.S.-Mexico Borderlands: A Reader* (Durham, NC: Duke University Press, 2007).
65. Original text: "¿Qué podía hacer yo? Les di el pasaje para que se hicieran llegar con sus familiares. No podía yo tener Corazón de ver a casi un cadáver y sin recursos que volviera a México. Le di el pasaje hasta su casa. . . . Tengo muchas cartas de madres en México que me han mandado dar las gracias." Sra. Adela S. de Vento, "La cárcel del condado."
66. Adela Sloss-Vento to Alonso S. Perales, November 12, 1947, box 5, folder 8, ASPP.
67. Adela S. Vento to Lic. Alonso S. Perales, January 3, 1948, box 5, folder 8, ASPP.
68. Sloss-Vento, *Alonso S. Perales*, 30. Her recollection of the Perales's memorial is titled "Memorias del fallecimiento del gran defensor, lic. Alonso S. Perales, el día (9 de Mayo 1960) por la Sra. Adela Sloss de Vento, Edinburg, Texas," ASVP.
69. Sloss-Vento, *Alonso S. Perales*, 66.
70. Adela Sloss-Vento, letter to the editor, *La Prensa*, April 21, 1960, ASVP.
71. Luis Alvarado, "LULAC Landmark of Progress," typescript, ca. 1961, ASVP.
72. Luis Alvarado to Mrs. Vento, January 1961, ASVP.
73. Mrs. A. S. Vento to Sr. Fortino Treviño, May 20, 1961, ASVP. See also Santos de la Paz, "Proposed Monument for Alonso S. Perales, in Alice, Is Unanimously Supported throughout Texas," *La Verdad*, July 8, 1960, ASVP.
74. Mrs. A. S. Vento to President of the School Board, Alice, Texas, September 18, 1969, September 18, 1969, ASVP.
75. Original text: "Martita, quiero pedirle un favor. Que no se pierda nada de sus escritos, recortes de periódicos y demás archivos del Lic. Perales. Por favor que se recoja todo sin que se pierda nada. Que Father García y Mr. Alvarado le ayuden y los pongan juntos y si Ud. gusta los puedo yo poner en orden en 'scrap books' para la posteridad." Mrs. A. S. Vento to Sra. Martita P. de Perales, May 12, 1960, ASVP.
76. Original text: "Por favor Mr. Alvarado haga por que no se pierde nada de los archivos de sus trabajos del Lic. Perales. Es preciso guardarlos para la posteridad." She then commented that she admired lawyer Gus García and hoped he would write Perales's biography. Adela Sloss-Vento to Mr. Luis Alvarado, May 11, 1960, ASVP. While García was qualified, he was an alcoholic and died shortly after Perales in 1964. Moreover, Sloss-Vento knew Perales before García did and perhaps better. On Gus García, see Cynthia E. Orozco, "Gustavo C. Garcia," in *NHOT*, 3:84; Anthony Quiroz, "'I Can See No Alternative Except to Battle It Out in Court': Gus Garcia and the Spirit of the Mexican American Generation," in *Leaders of the Mexican American Generation, Biographical Essays*, ed. Anthony Quiroz (Boulder: University Press of Colorado, 2015), 209–228. Isidro Aguirre is writing a book about García.
77. "An Interview with Mrs. Perales," *Chicano Times* (San Antonio), February 14–February 28, 1975, box 14, folder 11, ASPP.

78. Araceli Pérez Davis, "Marta Pérez de Perales," *El Mesteño*, newsletter, October 2000, 16–17.
79. Ignacio M. García, *Viva Kennedy: Mexican Americans in Search of Camelot*; Cynthia E. Orozco, "Viva Kennedy–Viva Johnson Clubs," in *NHOT*, 6:769–770.
80. Teresa Palomo Acosta, "Political Association of Spanish Speaking Persons," in *NHOT*, 5:256.
81. Ella K. Dagget Stumpf, typescript copy of "Latins No," *Texas*, magazine of the *Houston Chronicle*, April 12, 1964, ASVP.
82. Rodolfo Rosales, *The Illusion of Inclusion: The Untold Political Story of San Antonio* (Austin: Center for Mexican American Studies, University of Texas Press, 2000). On Peña, also see a repost of the Associated Press obituary of July 9, 2006, and commentary of Stace Medellin, "RIP: Judge Albert Peña–Chicano Activist and Leader," Dos Centavos blog, https://doscentavos.net/2006/07/09/rip-judge-albert-pena-chicano-activist-leader.
83. Mrs. Adela S. Vento, letter to the editor, *Texas*, April 14, 1964, ASVP; Adela Sloss-Vento to Albert Peña Jr., April 16, 1964, ASVP.
84. A. S. Vento, letter, *Texas*, April 14, 1964.
85. I use "machete" with a nod to Catriona Rueda Esquibel, *With Her Machete in Her Hand: Reading Chicana Lesbians* (Austin: University of Texas Press, 2006), who refers to Américo Paredes, *With His Pistol in His Hand* (Austin: University of Texas Press, 1958).

CHAPTER 4: THE CHICANO MOVEMENT OF 1963–1978 AND BEYOND

1. Mario T. García, introduction to *The Chicano Movement: Perspectives from the Twenty-First Century* (New York: Routledge/Taylor and Francis, 2014), ed. Mario T. García, 2. See pages 1–17 for more definitions and explanations of the movement.
2. Juan Gómez-Quiñones and Irene Vásquez, *Making Aztlán: Ideology and Culture of the Chicana and Chicano Movement, 1966–1977* (Albuquerque: University of New Mexico Press, 2014), xvi.
3. José Limón, "The Folk Performance of Chicano and the Cultural Limits of Political Ideology," in *And Other Neighborly Names: Social Process and Cultural Image in Texas Folklore*, ed. Richard Bauman and Roger D. Abrahams (Austin: University of Texas Press, 1981), 197–225; Cynthia E. Orozco, "Folk Usage of 'Chicano' in Cuero, Texas," unpublished paper in Mexican folklore class taught by Américo Paredes, 1979, 9, CEOP.
4. Adela Sloss-Vento, "Sobre el nombramiento 'Chicano' y el nombramiento 'México-Americano'" (Concerning the names "Chicano" and "Mexican-American"), in Vento, *Adela Sloss-Vento*, 132. This was written for her book but was not included in it.
5. Sloss-Vento, "Sobre el nombramiento," 132.
6. Adela Sloss-Vento, letter to the editor, *McAllen Monitor*, November 24, 1968, ASVP.
7. Vento, *Adela Sloss-Vento*, 63.
8. Vento, *Adela Sloss-Vento*, 69.

9. On the Crystal City revolt, see John Staples Shockley, *Chicano Revolt in a Texas Town* (Notre Dame, IN: University of Notre Dame Press, 1977); on the Raza Unida Party, seeIgnacio M. García, *United We Win: The Rise and Fall of La Raza Unida Party* (Tucson: University of Arizona Press, 1989).
10. Benjamin Márquez, *Democratizing Texas Politics: Race, Identity, and Mexican American Empowerment, 1945–2002* (Austin: University of Texas Press, 2014), 1.
11. Sloss Vento, letter, *McAllen Monitor*, November 24, 1968.
12. Sloss Vento, letter, *McAllen Monitor*, November 24, 1968.
13. Adela Sloss-Vento, untitled manuscript, begins "But regardless of our hard earned progress," ca. 1970s, ASVP.
14. Adela Sloss Vento, "Monument for Perales," letter to the editor, *San Antonio Express*, September 25, 1969, ASVP.
15. "Petition Recommends High School Be Named for Alonso S. Perales," *Alice Echo*, September 9, 1969, ASVP.
16. Edward Garza, "LULAC: The League of United Latin American Citizens," master's thesis, Southwest Texas State Teachers College, 1951.
17. Sloss-Vento, *Alonso S. Perales*, 23.
18. Sloss-Vento, *Alonso S. Perales*, 23.
19. Francis E. Abernathy, "James Frank Dobie," in *NHOT*, 2:662–663.
20. Mrs. A. S. Vento to School Trustees of Edgewood Elementary School, San Antonio, November 24, 1974, ASVP.
21. Sloss-Vento, *Alonso S. Perales*, viii. Among her papers is the article "Chicanos Are Being Viewed with Respect in Mexico City," *McAllen Monitor*, March 5, 1972, ASVP.
22. Adela Sloss-Vento, untitled notes on the Chicano movement, ca. 1978, ASVP.
23. Maggie Rivas-Rodriguez, *Texas Mexican Americans and Postwar Civil Rights* (Austin: University of Texas Press, 2016).
24. Kristian Hernández, "Remembering the 1966 Rio Grande City Melon Strike," *McAllen Monitor*, May 9, 2016.
25. Mrs. A. S. Vento to México-Americanos para Acción Social, Rio Grande City, February 24, 1970, ASVP.
26. Adela Sloss-Vento, letter to the editor, *McAllen Evening Monitor*, May 28, 1972, ASVP.
27. Teresa Palomo Acosta, "Texas Farm Workers Union," in *NHOT* 6:379. See Timothy Bowman, "What About Texas? The Forgotten Cause of Antonio Orendain and the Rio Grande Valley Farm Workers, 1966–1982," master's thesis, University of Texas, Arlington, 2005.
28. "UFW Rally Seen as Start of New Struggle in Texas," *McAllen Monitor*, March 4, 1979, ASVP.
29. Adela Sloss-Vento to *McAllen Evening Monitor*, March 30, 1978, ASVP. This is a request to publish the letter to the editor.
30. A. S. Vento, letter, *McAllen Evening Monitor*, May 28, 1972.
31. Adela Sloss Vento to *McAllen Monitor*, ca. 1977, ASVP. This note might have been intended as a letter to the editor.
32. "The Illegal Alien Problem," typescript, ca. 1978, ASVP.

33. Saunders and Leonard, "Wetback in the Lower Rio Grande Valley," 20.
34. L. Garza, "Jovita González," 5–6.
35. Adela Sloss-Vento to Lic. Alonso S. Perales, December 6, 1947, box 5, folder 8, ASPP.
36. In Kabalen de Bichara, "Expressions of Dissent," 201.
37. Gómez-Quiñones and Vásquez.
38. Rodolfo Rodríguez, "Bilingual Education," *Handbook of Texas Online* (Austin: Texas State Historical Association, 2010, modified July 5, 2017), http://www.tshaonline.org/handbook/online/articles/khb02.
39. Sloss Vento, letter, *McAllen Monitor*, November 24, 1968.
40. Original text: "Permítame que les dirija estas líneas en el idioma español, en ese elegante y hermoso idioma de nuestros mayores, y que para nosotros es tan American como lo puede ser el idioma inglés." A. S. Vento to México-Americanos para Acción Social, February 24, 1970.
41. Adela Sloss-Vento, "Two Languages Are Better than One," letter to the editor, *McAllen Monitor*, n.d., 1984, ASVP.
42. Adela Sloss-Vento, "To Speak English and Spanish Means We Are Better Prepared to Know Our Culture," letter to the editor, *La Verdad*, June 23, 1978, ASVP.
43. Vento, *Mestizo*, 237–242.
44. Sloss-Vento, "To Speak English and Spanish"; Carlos E. Castañeda, *Our Catholic Heritage in Texas, 1519–1936*, 7 vols. (Austin: Von Boeckmann-Jones, 1936–1958).
45. Sloss-Vento, "To Speak English and Spanish."
46. Adela Sloss-Vento, typescript, ca. November 28, 1978, ASVP. This might be a copy of a letter to the editor of the *McAllen Monitor*.
47. Sloss-Vento, *Alonso S. Perales*, 11.
48. Original text: "Lamento que no contamos como antes con periódicos en Español." Adela Sloss de Vento to Rev. Sebastián Mozos, April 16, 1980, ASVP.
49. "Debemos de seguir haciendo incapié porque perdure nuestra cultura e idioma. Para mí son como rara joyas, que hemos heredado de nuestros padres y de nuestros antepasados, y debemos orientar a los demás sobre la importancia de esos valores." Sloss de Vento to Mozos, April 16, 1980.
50. Sloss-Vento, "To Speak English and Spanish."
51. Adela Sloss-Vento to the editor of the *San Antonio Light*, April 1, 1969, ASVP. It is not clear if it was published.
52. Poll tax receipt, 1964, Mrs. P. C. Vento, January 30, 1965, ASVP.
53. Mrs. A. S. Vento to Hon. J. T. Canales, March 29, 1961, ASVP.
54. Cynthia Orozco, "Americanization and Mexicans," undergraduate history paper, ca. 1980, CEOP; Brandon H. Mila, "Hermanos de Raza: Alonso S. Perales and the Creation of the LULAC Spirit," master's thesis, University of North Texas, 2013.
55. Marta Pérez Vda de Perales to Lic. Ruben Bonilla, December 1978, ASVP; Mrs. Francisca Pérez Lozano to Mr. Ruben Bonilla, January 16, 1979, ASVP.
56. Cynthia E. Orozco, "Bernardo F. Garza," in *NHOT*, 3:105; Orozco, *No Mexicans, Women, or Dogs*, 115–117. LULAC published *LULAC: Fifty Years of Serving*

Hispanics, Golden Anniversary, 1929–1979 (Corpus Christi: Texas State LULAC, 1979) to commemorate the anniversary.

57. Moisés Sándoval, *Our Legacy: The First Fifty Years* (Washington, DC: LULAC, 1979).
58. Adela Sloss-Vento, letter to the editor, *La Verdad*, March 2, 1979, CEOP.
59. Adela Sloss-Vento, "Alonso S. Perales: Precursor and Founder of LULAC," ca. February 1979, ASVP.
60. Adela Sloss-Vento, "Chismes—no me defiendas, compadre," letter to the editor, *La Verdad*, March 16, 1979, JTCEC.
61. Adela Sloss-Vento, letter to the editor, *McAllen Monitor*, March 5, 1979, CEOP.
62. Estela P. Contreras, letter to the editor, *McAllen Monitor*, March 26, 1979, CEOP.
63. Adela S. de Vento to César Chávez, June 1, 1972; Adela S. de Vento to Sr. Armando Ramírez, April 22, 1974, ASVP.
64. Adela S. de Vento to José María Longoria, March 13, 1974, ASVP.
65. Roland Ramírez, bill from Artes Gráficas, San Antonio, 1977, ASVP.
66. On Canales, see Evan Anders, "José Tomás Canales," in *NHOT*, 1:953–954; Richard Ribb, "José T. Canales and the Texas Rangers: Myth, Identity, and Power in South Texas, 1900–1920," PhD diss., University of Texas at Austin, 2001; and Michael Lynch and Carlos Larralde, *Judge J. T. Canales, Latino Civil Rights Leader, an Intimate Portrait* (London: Lambert Academic, 2015).
67. Adela S. de Vento to José María Longoria, March 13, 1974, ASVP. Here Sloss-Vento mentions her interview of Longoria.
68. Adela Sloss-Vento to Mrs. Martita Perales, September 21, 1976, ASVP.
69. Sloss-Vento, *Alonso S. Perales*, 2.
70. Sloss-Vento, *Alonso S. Perales*, vii.
71. Kabalen de Bichara, "Expressions of Dissent," 204.
72. Kabalen de Bichara, "Expressions of Dissent," 198.
73. Sloss-Vento, "A Selected Bibliography," *Alonso S. Perales*, 100–101.
74. Adela Sloss-Vento, untitled manuscript, 1977, ASVP.
75. Adela Sloss-Vento to Mrs. Martita Perales, September 21, 1978, ASVP.
76. Flyer for Sloss-Vento's book, *Alonso S. Perales*, ASVP.
77. "Valleyite Publishes Book," *McAllen Monitor*, January 29, 1978, ASVP.
78. Gilberto Díaz, "Juicio crítico sobre el libro 'Alonso S. Perales: His Struggles for the Right of the Mexican American' de la señora doña Adela Sloss de Vento," *Sun Valley News*, June 14, 1978, 43, ASVP; Santos de la Paz, "Book on the Life of Alonso S. Perales Tells of Hispanic Leader's Struggle for Human Rights, *La Verdad*, August 1978(?).
79. Clarence La Roche, "Perales, the Fight for Equality," *San Antonio Express-News*, March 19, 1978, ASVP.
80. Richard A. García, *Rise of the Mexican American Middle Class: San Antonio, 1929–1941* (College Station: Texas A&M University Press, 1991); Adela Sloss-Vento to Mrs. Donna Tobias, May 4, 1979, ASVP. Later, Tobias sent her a questionnaire about Perales's public speaking style, and Sloss-Vento responded with observations on his vocal delivery, physical delivery, and preparation. She

describes his stance as erect, his gestures animated, and his speeches mostly extemporaneous, adding that "his involvement and sense of mission gave his [*sic*] the needed inspiration, energy and spirit." Tobias died before completing her work.

81. Adela Sloss-Vento to Mr. Ángel Gutiérrez, November 28, 1977, ASVP.
82. José Ángel Gutiérrez, *The Making of Civil Rights Leader José Ángel Gutiérrez* (Houston: Arte Público, 2005).
83. Adela Sloss de Vento to Sr. Tomasito Hinojosa, September 11, 1978, ASVP. Here, she introduced him to me.
84. Adela Sloss-Vento, critique of Orozco, "Americanization and Mexicans," ASVP.
85. Unsigned (Adela Sloss Vento) to Alonso S. Perales, March 9, 1953, box 5, folder 8, ASPP.
86. Mary Ann Villarreal, "The Synapses of Struggle: Martha Cotera and Tejana Activism," *Las Obreras: Chicana Politics of Work and Family*, ed. Vicki L. Ruiz (Los Angeles: Chicano Studies Research Center, University of California, Los Angeles, 2000), 273–295.
87. Original text: "sobre varios temas y el adelanto de la mujeres." Sloss-Vento, untitled manuscript, ca. 1980, critique of Orozco undergraduate history paper.
88. Adela Sloss-Vento to Chicano Culture Committee, April 14, 1980, ASVP.

CHAPTER 5: FEMINIST IN THE GENDERED MEXICAN AMERICAN CIVIL RIGHTS MOVEMENT

1. Lindsay O'Neill, *The Opened Letter: Networking in the Early Modern British World* (Philadelphia: University of Pennsylvania Press, 2015), 6.
2. Norma Adelfa Mouton, "Changing Voices: Approaching Modernity from Mexican to Mexican American to Chicano," in *In Defense of My People*, ed. Olivas, 226. Perales asked readers of his column "Arquitectos de nuestros propios destinos" to send in affidavits of discriminatory incidents. Mostly men responded.
3. Kenneth C. Burt, *The Search for a Civic Voice: California Latino Politics* (Claremont, CA: Regina, 2007), 61.
4. Lori Flores, *Grounds for Dreaming: Mexican Americans, Mexican Immigrants, and the California Farmworker Movement* (New Haven, CT: Yale University Press, 2016), 121–122. Flores mistakenly noted that LULAC limited its membership to women in auxiliaries.
5. Flores, 122–123.
6. Cynthia E. Orozco, "Regionalism, Politics, and Gender in Southwest History: The League of United Latin American Citizens' Expansion into New Mexico from Texas, 1929–1945," *Western Historical Quarterly* 29 (Winter 1998): 459–483.
7. On the Asociación Nacional Mexicana, see Mario T. García, *Mexican Americans: Leadership, Ideology, and Identity* (New Haven, CT: Yale University Press, 1989), 199–230; Julie Leininger Pycior, *LBJ and Mexican Americans: The Paradox of Power* (Austin: University of Texas Press, 1997), 62.

8. Richard A. Buitrón Jr., *The Quest for Tejano Identity in San Antonio, 1913–2000* (New York: Routledge, 2004), 53.
9. Woods, 81.
10. Woods, 120.
11. Kibbe, *Latin Americans in Texas*, 25.
12. Alonso S. Perales to Mrs. Adela S. Vento, June 12, 1953, ASVP.
13. Original text: "Yo desearía que Usted encabezara un grupo de mujeres e investigara en caso debidamente." Santos de la Paz to Sra. A. S. Vento, September 10, 1954, ASVP.
14. Alonso S. Perales to J. T. Canales, April 8, 1933, ASPP.
15. Orozco, "Ladies LULAC."
16. Orozco, "Alice Dickerson Montemayor," in *NHOT*, 4:798; Orozco, "Alice Dickerson Montemayor," in *Writing the Range*.
17. Mrs. F. I. Montemayor to Alonso S. Perales, November 15, 1936, box 4, folder 1, ASPP.
18. In *San Antonio Express*, "No Sexism, Sort Of," March 9, 1984.
19. In John Gutiérrez-Mier, "The Hispanic Brotherhood," *San Antonio Express News*, April 19, 1989.
20. *San Antonio Express*, "No Sexism, Sort Of."
21. *LULAC News*, January, March, and December 1972, BLAC.
22. Gloria Padilla, "LULAC Here Bars Women," *Corpus Christi Caller-Times*, February 19, 1984; *Nuestro*, "Women, LULAC Collide," April 1984, 9.
23. Orozco, "American Council"; *San Antonio Light*, "El Paso Ladies LULAC Council 9 Set to Mark Its Golden Anniversary," February 16, 1984.
24. Palomo Acosta, "American G.I. Forum Women's Auxiliary."
25. Houston, 102–103.
26. In Pycior, 61.
27. Pycior, 95.
28. Houston, 102.
29. Houston, 104.
30. Kay Briegel, "Alianza Hispano-Americana and Some Mexican-American Civil Rights Cases in the 1950s," in *The Mexican-Americans: An Awakened Minority*," ed. Manuel P. Servín (Beverly Hills, CA: Glencoe, 1970), 179.
31. On García, see Cynthia E. Orozco, "Gustavo C. Garcia," in *NHOT*, 3:84; Quiroz, "I Can See No Alternative."
32. Orozco, "American Council."
33. José Ámaro Hernández, *Mutual Aid for Survival: The Case of the Mexican American* (Malabar, FL: Robert E. Krieger, 1983), 52–53.
34. Newsletter, American Council of Spanish Speaking People, April 1953, 3, box 20, George I. Sánchez Papers, BLAC.
35. Pycior, 95.
36. Membership list, 1952, STAD box 0437, folder 25, JTCEC.
37. Inventory, STAD box 0437, JTCEC.
38. Michael Lynch and Carlos Larralde, *Judge J. T. Canales, Latino Civil Rights Leader: An Intimate Portrait* (London: Lambert Academic, 2015), 36.

39. J. M. Castellano, Treasurer, to Mrs. A. S. Vento, November 25, 1952, ASVP.
40. Adela Sloss-Vento, "List of Members," n.d., ASVP.
41. "Collections by Adela S. Vento," note, n.d., ASVP.
42. J. T. Canales to Alonso S. Perales, November 26, 1954, ASVP.
43. Original text: "Yo estoy anunciando por la Radiodifusora de aquí, y hice unas hojas sueltas que estoy mandando." Adela Sloss-Vento to Alonso S. Perales, June 6, 1952, box 5, folder 8, ASPP.
44. Mrs. A. S. Vento to Lic. Alonso S. Perales, October 22, 1952, box 5, folder 8, ASPP.
45. George I. Sánchez to Mr. Yaroslave J. Chyz, Associate Director, Common Council for American Unity, New York, June 30, 1954, George I. Sánchez Papers, box 37, BLAC.
46. Arthur J. Rendón to Cleofas Callero, October 28, 1960, Cleofas Callero Papers, C. L. Sonnichsen Special Collections Department, University of Texas, El Paso.
47. Orozco, "Viva Kennedy."
48. Palomo Acosta, "Political Association," 256.
49. Gloria Padilla, "LULAC here bars women," *Corpus Christi Caller-Times*, February 19, 1984, CEOP.
50. "Corpus Christi's LULAC Council on the Verge of Splitting," *Lubbock Avalanche-Journal*, ca. September 9, 1999. Nancy Vera, a past president of Council 4444, says women integrated into LULAC Council #1 in the late 1990s. Vera, phone interview by the author, March 31, 2019.
51. Cynthia E. Orozco, "Spanish-Speaking PTA."
52. Annelise Oreleck, *Rethinking American Women's Activism* (New York: Routledge, 2015), 69.
53. Michael A. Olivas, *Colored Men and Hombres Aquí: Hernández v. Texas and the Emergence of Mexican American Lawyering* (Houston: Arte Público, 2006).
54. On Carlos Cadena, see Martin Donell Kohout, "Cadena, Carlos Cristian," *Handbook of Texas Online* (Austin: Texas State Historical Association, 2010), http://www.tshaonline.org/handbook/online/articles/fcaas. On John J. Herrera, see Thomas Kreneck, "Mr. LULAC: The Fabulous Life of John J. Herrera," in *Leaders*, ed. Quiroz, 229–251. On Armendáriz's work in civil service in El Paso, see Maggie Rivas-Rodriguez, *Texas Mexican Americans and Postwar Civil Rights* (Austin: University of Texas Press, 2015). James De Anda's archive was destroyed in a fire. Further research is needed on the work of Judge Alfred Hernández. Ramona Houston mentions the lawyers Homero López and Richard Casillas; Houston, 101. My second cousin Abel Toscano Jr. became a lawyer in the 1950s but was not involved in civil rights activism. See Laura Toscano González, "In Loving Memory of Our Friend, Husband, Father, and Grandfather Abel Toscano, Jr., 1926–2005," in *Once upon a Time/Más Antes: Family Stories of the Rio Grande Valley*, ed. Alonzo Cavazos Jr., Ofelia Olsson, and Santos V. Canales (Harlingen, TX: Rio Grande Valley Hispanic Genealogical Society, 2014), 265–270.
55. Olivas, *Colored Men and Hombres*, 46. In California most Mexican American lawyers were men. The attorney Herman Sillas reports on the Mexican American Lawyers Club founded in California most likely in 1961; he finds that the club

had an auxiliary composed of "wives and friends." Herman Sillas, "Mexican American Lawyers Club," *Somos Primos*, August 2015, http://www.somosprimos.com/sp2015/spsep15/spsep15.htm.

56. Goldstone, *Integrating the Forty Acres*, 137.
57. Blanton, *George I. Sánchez*.
58. Kells, *Héctor P. García*; Carl Allsup, "Dr. Héctor Pérez García: Giant of the Twentieth Century," in *Leaders*, ed. Quiroz, 191–208; Carl Allsup, *The American G.I. Forum: Origins and Evolution*, Monograph 6 (Austin: Center for Mexican American Studies, University of Texas, 1982); Henry A. J. Ramos, *The American G.I. Forum: In Pursuit of the Dream, 1948–1983* (Houston: Arte Público, 1998).
59. *Dallas Times Herald Magazine*, "Prosecution and Preserves," April 26, 1964. I thank the attorney and scholar Michael Olivas for this information.
60. Acosta and Weingarten, *Las Tejanas*.
61. Gabriela Sosa Zavaleta, "Women as Political Pioneers in the Rio Grande Valley," in *Yet More Studies in Rio Grande Valley History*, ed. Milo Kearney (Brownsville: University of Texas at Brownsville, 2015), 159.
62. M. García, *Mexican Americans*.
63. On J. Luz Sáenz, see Emilio Zamora, "José de la Luz Sáenz," *El Mesteño*, April 2000, 4–5; Emilio Zamora, "Fighting on Two Fronts: The WWI Diary of José de la Luz Sáenz and the Language of the Mexican American Civil Rights Movement," in *Recovering the Hispanic Literary Tradition*, vol. 4, ed. José F. Aranda Jr. and Silvio Torres-Saillant (Houston: Arte Público, 2002), 214–239; Benjamín Olguín, "Sangre Mexicana/Corazon Americano: Identity, Ambiguity, and Critique in Mexican American War Narratives," *Journal of American Literary History* 14, no. 1 (Winter 2002): 83–114; Orozco, *No Mexicans, Women, or Dogs*, 97–100.
64. José de la Luz Sáenz, *The World War I Diary of José de la Luz Sáenz*, ed. Emilio Zamora, trans. Emilio Zamora with Ben Maya (College Station: Texas A&M University Press, 2014).
65. Canales's writings include J. T. Canales, *Bits of Texas History in the Melting Pot*, parts 1 and 2 (San Antonio: Artes Gráficas, 1950 and 1957); J. T. Canales, *Juan N. Cortina: Bandit or Patriot?* (San Antonio: Artes Gráficas, 1951); J. T. Canales, *Ethics in the Profession of Law* (San Antonio: Artes Gráficas, 1953); J. T. Canales, *The Tragic Quadrangle* (San Antonio: Artes Gráficas, 1958); J. T. Canales, *Character Builders and Leaders of Men* (San Antonio: Artes Gráficas, 1959); J. T. Canales, *La Guerra de Tejas* (San Antonio: Artes Gráficas, 1959). On Canales, see Orozco, *No Mexicans, Women, or Dogs*, 94–97; Richard Henry Ribb, "José T. Canales and the Texas Rangers: Myth, Identity, and Power in South Texas, 1900–1920," PhD diss., University of Texas, 2001; Lynch and Larralde.
66. On Castañeda, see Félix D. Almaraz Jr., "Carlos Eduardo Castañeda," in *NHOT*, 1:1016–1017; Félix D. Almaraz Jr., *Knight without Armor: Carlos Eduardo Castañeda, 1896–1958* (Austin: University of Texas Press, 1999); Emilio Zamora, *Claiming Rights and Righting Wrongs: Mexican Workers and Job Politics during World War II* (College Station: Texas A&M University Press, 2009); and Marianne M. Bueno, "Intellectually He Was Curious; in Public Action He Was

Cautious and Prudent," in *Latina/os and World War II: Mobility, Agency, and Ideology*, ed. Maggie Rivas-Rodriguez and B. V. Olguín (Austin: University of Texas Press, 2014), 95–112.

67. Sloss-Vento, *Alonso S. Perales*, 55. Castañeda wrote to congratulate her on her article about Perales in *La Verdad*. Carlos E. Castaneda to Mrs. A. S. Vento, September 16, 1954, ASVP.
68. Vento, *Adela Sloss-Vento*, 61.
69. Cynthia E. Orozco, "Regionalism, Politics, and Gender in Southwestern History: The League of United Latin American Citizens' (LULAC) Expansion into New Mexico from Texas, 1929–1945," *Western Historical Quarterly* 29, no. 4 (November 1998): 459–483.
70. Blanton, *George I. Sánchez*; Blanton, "George I. Sánchez, Ideology, and Whiteness"; Blanton, "Citizen Sacrifice"; Carlos Kevin Blanton, "A Legacy of Neglect: George I. Sánchez, Mexican American Education, and the Ideal of Integration, 1940–1970," *Teachers College Record* 114 (June 2012): 1–34.
71. Works about Sánchez include Américo Paredes, ed., *Humanidad: Essays in Honor of Dr. George I. Sánchez* (Los Angeles: Chicano Studies Center, UCLA, 1977); Ricardo Romo, "George I. Sánchez and the Civil Rights Movement, 1940–1960," *La Raza Law Journal* 1 (1986): 342–362; Luisa Durán, "The Life and Legacy of Dr. George Isidore Sánchez" (Albuquerque: New Mexico Association for Bilingual Education, 2011), http://nmabe.net/wp-content/uploads/2011/08/The-Life-and-Legacy-Dr.-Luisa-Duran-web.pdf.
72. Sloss-Vento praises Castañeda in her book, *Alonso S. Perales*, 50.
73. Adela Sloss Vento to Alonso S. Perales, October 3, 1954, ASPP.
74. One such letter reads, "Saludándole a Ud. y a Martita de parte mía y de mi esposo, quedo como siempre, Su amiga y servidora, Adela S. de Vento" (Hello to you and Martita from me and my husband, as always, your friend and servant). Adela Sloss Vento to Alonso S. Perales, November 12, 1947, ASPP.
75. O'Neill, *Opened Letter*, 78.
76. O'Neill, *Opened Letter*, 201.
77. Mrs. A. S. Vento to México-Americanos para Acción Social, February 24, 1970, ASVP.
78. Kabalen de Bichara, "Self-Writing," 252.
79. Kabalen de Bichara, "Expressions of Dissent, 196."
80. Original text: "El reconocimiento de estos líderes méxicoamericanos de sus mismas zonas representa su propia idea nacional." L. Garza, "Jovita González," 92.
81. Sloss-Vento, *Alonso S. Perales*, 6.
82. Sloss-Vento, *Alonso S. Perales*, 7.
83. Sloss-Vento, *Alonso S. Perales*, 11.
84. Sloss-Vento, *Alonso S. Perales*, 58.
85. Sloss-Vento, *Alonso S. Perales*, 67.
86. Sloss-Vento, *Alonso S. Perales*, 62.
87. Adela Sloss-Vento, "Prof. J. Luz Sáenz," typed manuscript, 1966, ASVP.
88. In comparison, the José de la Luz Sáenz Papers contain twenty-seven letters between Saenz and Perales. Box 2, folder 1, JLSP.

89. Vento, *Adela Sloss-Vento*, 53.
90. Adriana Ayala, "Negotiating Race Relations through Activism: Women Activists and Women's Organizing in San Antonio, Texas during the 1920s," PhD diss., University of Texas, Austin, 2005.
91. Mario T. García, "Alonso S. Perales and the Catholic Imaginary: Religion and the Mexican-American Mind," in *In Defense of My People*, ed. Olivas, 162, 168.
92. M. T. García, "Alonso S. Perales and the Catholic Imaginary," 162.
93. In Brandon H. Mila, "Alonso S. Perales and the Creation of the LULAC Spirit," master's thesis, University of North Texas, 2013.
94. Orozco, "Spanish-Speaking PTA."
95. Alonso S. Perales to J. T. Canales, April 8, 1933, https://digital.lib.uh.edu/collection/perales/item/57, accessed June 16, 2018.
96. Adela S. Vento, "Lic. Alonso S. Perales, defensor campeón de la dignidad racial," *La Prensa*, March 28, 1952, ASVP. The letter is reproduced in Sloss-Vento, *Alonso S. Perales*, 30. Sáenz's letter "Spain Honors a Texan" appeared in *La Prensa* three days later. J. Luz Sáenz, "España tributa honores a un texano," *La Prensa*, March 31, 1952, 6, ASVP.
97. A. S. Vento, "Lic. Alonso S. Perales, defensor campeón."
98. Adela Sloss de Vento, "Memorias del fallecimiento del gran defensor," *La Prensa*, May 9, 1960, ASVP.
99. Sloss-Vento, *Alonso S. Perales*, 30–31. The letter was published in *La Prensa* in March 1952, but no specific date is provided. She did not use the original Spanish in her book.
100. Richard A. García, "Alonso S. Perales: The Voice and Visions of a Citizen Intellectual," in *Leaders*, 107.
101. Kabalen de Bichara, "Self-Writing," 254. She also calls Perales Sloss-Vento's mentor in "Expressions of Dissent in the Writings," 201.
102. Orozco, *No Mexicans, Women, or Dogs*; Orozco, "Alonso S. Perales," in *In Defense of My People*.
103. Kabalen de Bichara, "Self-Writing," 254–255.
104. Orozco, "Alonso S. Perales," in *In Defense of My People*, 19.
105. L. Garza, "Jovita González," n.p.
106. Alonso S. Perales to Miss Adela Sloss, June 20, 1931, ASVP.
107. Alonso S. Perales to Señora Adela S. Vento, August 11, 1947, ASPP.
108. Original text: "Yo siempre he admirado su obra, y he dado gracias al Ser Supremo por habernos dado personas como usted que sincera y desinteresadamente se preocupan por el progreso y bienestar de nuestro pueblo." Perales to S. Vento, August 11, 1947.
109. Original text: "La felicito sinceramente por su bella labor en pro de nuestro pueblo. Siempre leyo sus cartas y sus artículos con el mayor interés. ¡Adelante! Me alegra mucho que a Dios gracias, tengamos líderes como usted." Alonso S. Perales to Sra. Adela S. Vento, October 22, 1948, ASVP.
110. Original text: "Que lástima que por no haber más personas como usted que se interesan de veras en solucionar el problema." Alonso S. Perales to Sra. Doña Adela S. de Vento, October 5, 1954, ASVP.

111. Perales to S. de Vento, October 5, 1954.
112. Alonso S. Perales to Mrs. Adela S. Vento, September 16, 1954, ASVP.
113. Adela S. de Vento to Licenciado Alonso S. Perales, December 12, 1951, ASVP.
114. Original text: "Es muy inteligente, activa, entusiasta y sincera y su labor noble y constructiva la ha hecho acreedora al título de excelente líder cívica de nuestro pueblo en este país." Alonso S. Perales, "Arquitectos de nuestros propios destinos," column, June 21, 1953, *La Prensa*, ASVP.
115. Perales, *Are We Good Neighbors?*, 247–249. Sloss-Vento's essay appears in part 4, "Articles and Comments." It originally appeared in the *Valley Morning Star*.
116. Sloss-Vento, *Alonso S. Perales*, 66.
117. Sloss-Vento, *Alonso S. Perales*, ebook, viii.
118. Emilio Zamora, "José de la Luz Sáenz: Experiences and Autobiographical Consciousness," in *Leaders*, ed. Quiroz, 29.
119. Agnes G. Grimm, "Eulalio Velazquez," in *NHOT*, 6:720.
120. Sáenz, *World War I Diary*, 473–476.
121. Grimm, 720.
122. "J. Luz Sáenz Is Dead at 65," unknown newspaper and date, 1953, ASVP.
123. Sáenz to Méndez, 1946, box 1, folder 17, JLSP; Sáenz to O'Shea, 1946, box 2, folder 1, JLSP. On Méndez, see Cynthia E. Orozco, "Consuelo Herrera Méndez," in *NHOT*, 4:618; on O'Shea, see Cynthia E. Orozco, "Maria Elena Zamora O'Shea," in *NHOT*, 4:1176–1177.
124. Original text: "Le envío estos $50.00 y úselos en gastos que tenga que hacer para la misma causa o para o lo que Ud. tenga a bien. . . . Ud. úselo para radiar o para hojas sueltos o para gastos de ponerse en contacto con la demás gente. Ud. sabe mejor que yo lo que se debe hacer." Adela Sloss Vento to J. Luz Sáenz, December 31, 1951, box 2, folder 13, JLSP.
125. José Luz Sáenz to Adela Sloss-Vento, ca. 1952, box 5, folder 18, JLSP.
126. Vento, *Adela Sloss-Vento*, 54.
127. Sloss-Vento, *Alonso S. Perales*, 60; "Great Presentation, J. Luz Sáenz Elementary School," November 20, 1966, program, ASVP.
128. "Portrait Presentation, J. Luz Sáenz Elementary School," Alice Independent School District, November 20, 1966, ASVP.
129. Lynch and Larralde, v.
130. José E. Limón, "El Primer Congreso Mexicanista de 1911: A Precursor to Contemporary Chicanismo," *Aztlán* 5, no. 1–2 (1974): 85–115.
131. Lynch and Larralde, viii, 6.
132. J. T. Canales to Mrs. A. S. Vento, October 24, 1952, ASVP.
133. J. T. Canales to Mr. J. C. Machuca and Mrs. Adela S. Vento, November 23, 1957, ASVP.
134. Lynch and Larralde, 25. Larralde is Canales's nephew.
135. Lynch and Larralde, viii.
136. Lynch and Larralde, 31.
137. Lynch and Larralde, 35.
138. Lynch and Larralde, 81.
139. Lynch and Larralde, 36.

140. Vento, *Adela Sloss-Vento*, 53.
141. Vento, *Adela Sloss-Vento*, 89.
142. Vento, *Adela Sloss-Vento*, 79.
143. Vento, *Adela Sloss-Vento*, 80.
144. Adela Sloss-Vento, manuscript, beginning "In the book 'First Year Annual of Latin Americans,'" ca. 1937, ASVP. The book is by J. Montiel Olvera.
145. Lynch and Larralde, 8.
146. J. T. Canales, "Memoranda sobre la conferencia en San Juan, Texas, diciembre 12, 1943, sobre el tema 'La Revolución Mexicana' by J. T. Canales," ASVP. A similar pamphlet by Canales is titled "Sinopsis de la conferencia del Lic. J. T. Canales en San Juan, Texas, diciembre 12, 1943, sobre el tema 'La Revolución Mexicana,'" ASVP.
147. J. T. Canales to Mrs. Vento, postcard, January 28, 1953, ASVP.
148. Flyer, "Aviso importante," n.d., ASVP. Sloss-Vento and Sáenz are listed as book sales contacts for Edinburg and McAllen.
149. Lynch and Larralde, vi.
150. Lynch and Larralde, 48–49.
151. Lynch and Larralde, 51–52.
152. J. T. Canales to Mrs. Adela S. Vento, April 12, 1954, ASVP.
153. J. T. Canales to Mrs. Adela Sloss Vento, June 1, 1952, ASVP.
154. J. T. Canales to Mrs. A. S. Vento, February 29, 1956, ASVP.
155. Elizabeth Salas, *Soldaderas in the Mexican Military: Myth and History* (Austin: University of Texas Press, 1990), 122.
156. Salas, ix. Salas discusses how Chicana feminists have referred to "La Adelita" on pages 115–117. See also Norma Cantú, "Women, Then and Now: An Analysis of the Adelita Image versus the Chicana Political Writer and Philosopher," in *Chicana Voices: Intersections of Race, Class, and Gender*, ed. Teresa Córdova, Norma Elia Cantú, Gilberto Cárdenas, Juan García, and Christine M. Sierra (Austin: Center for Mexican American Studies, University of Texas, 1986), 8–10.
157. Salas, 121.
158. Original text: "Él ha regalado miles de pesos para templos y escuelas aparte de dar cada año miles de pesos en becas para nuestros jóvenes que no podían asistir a los colegios por falta de dinero. Puede haber otra alma más patriota y generosa? No obstante que nació rico, Dios le ha dado un corazón de oro y una alma grande, generosa llena de patriotismo y de amor por las cosas de Dios y por su próximo." The note is written on an envelope accompanying a photo of Canales viewing a painting at J. T. Canales Elementary School; the photo is in the *McAllen Monitor*(?) of March 22, 1952, ASVP.
159. Adela S. Vento, letter to the editor, *McAllen Evening Monitor*, April 5, 1976, ASVP. For a 1950s homage to Canales, see Gilberto Díaz, "J. T. Canales: Un insigne jurista y un osado defensor de nuestra raza," *Revista Latino-Americana* (Mission, TX) 5, no. 11: 3, 5, ASVP. Canales appears on the magazine's cover.
160. Adela Sloss Vento, letter to the editor, *McAllen Monitor*, September 16, 1976, ASVP. Canales's essay is published in *Primer anuario de los habitantes*

hispano-americanos de Texas/Who's Who in the Latin-American Population of Texas, ed. J. Montiel Olvera (San Antonio: Mexican Chamber of Commerce[?], 1939).

161. Orozco, "Alonso S. Perales," in *In Defense of My People*.
162. Orozco, "Alonso S. Perales," in *In Defense of My People*, 16–17.
163. Orozco, "Alonso S. Perales," in *In Defense of My People*, 11.
164. *LULAC News*, "Special Organizer" and "Se reorganizó el Concilio de Alice, Texas," March 1933, BLAC.
165. Lynch and Larralde, 15.
166. Lynch and Larralde, 20–22.
167. Lynch and Larralde, 21.
168. In Lynch and Larralde, 22n67.

CHAPTER 6: PUBLIC INTELLECTUAL

1. Vento, *Adela Sloss-Vento*, xxi.
2. Conchita Hassell Winner, "Spanish-Language Newspapers," in *NHOT*, 5:4–5.
3. Rosie Mirabal Garza, *El Progreso, 1939–1940: The Work of Rodolfo Zepeda Mirabal and Dora Cervera Mirabal* (Corpus Christi, TX: Printers Unlimited, 2004). On the Hispanic newspaper publisher, editor, and writer Dora Cervera Mirabal, see also Thomas H. Kreneck, "Mirabal, Dora Cervera," *Handbook of Texas Online* (Austin: Texas State Historical Society, 2010), http://www.tshaonline.org/handbook/online/articles/fmi97.
4. Rómulo "Chacho" Munguía, "The Great Mexican Stand-Off: An Outline," unpublished manuscript, p. 33, Rómulo Munguía, box 16, folder 2, BLAC.
5. Sloss-Vento, *Alonso S. Perales*, vii.
6. Original text: "He estado leyendo los periódicos de México como los de aquí tocante a las negociaciones de Braceros." Mrs. A. S. Vento to Lic. Alonso S. Perales, January 19, 1954, ASPP.
7. J. Lee and Lillian J. Stambaugh, *The Lower Rio Grande Valley of Texas* (San Antonio: Naylor, 1954), 303. The authors identify four major English-language newspapers and fifteen weeklies.
8. Munguía, 34.
9. Original text: "tan poco cooperación de los periodicos." Adela S. de Vento to Licenciado Alonso S. Perales, December 12, 1951, ASVP.
10. Adela Sloss-Vento, "Carta para La Verdad," typescript, February 19, 1952, ASVP.
11. In Sloss-Vento, *Alonso S. Perales*, 16.
12. Adela Sloss-Vento, "El eterno dilema de los mojados y de los braceros contratados que solo sirve para prejuicios de los mexicanos y de México," ca. 1947, ASVP.
13. Sloss-Vento, "El eterno dilema."
14. Sloss-Vento, "El eterno dilema."
15. In Alice Fahs, *Out on Assignment: Newspaper Women and the Making of Modern Public Space* (Chapel Hill: University of North Carolina Press, 2011).
16. Kathleen A. Cairns, *Front-Page Women Journalists, 1920–1950* (Lincoln: University of Nebraska Press, 2003), xiii.

17. Fahs, 17.
18. Cairns, 3.
19. Julie A. Golia, "Courting Women, Courting Advertisers: The Women's Page and the Transformation of the American Newspaper, 1895–1935," *Journal of American History* 103, no. 3 (December 2016): 613, 619.
20. Nicolás Kanellos, "Envisioning and Re-Visioning the Nation: Latino Intellectual Traditions," American Latino Theme Study (Washington, DC: National Park Service Advisory Board, 2013), https://home1.nps.gov/heritageinitiatives/latino/latinothemestudy/intellectualtraditions.htm.
21. Eduardo Mendieta, "What Can Latinas/os Learn from Cornel West? The Latino Postcolonial Intellectual in the Age of Exhaustion of Public Space," *Nepantla: Views from the South* 4, no. 2 (2003): 215.
22. M. García, *Mexican Americans*, 231–290.
23. Olivas, "Legal Career of Alonso S. Perales."
24. On Chicana intellectual tradition, see Alma M. García, ed., *Chicana Feminist Thought: The Basic Historical Writings* (New York: Routledge, 1997).
25. On Vásquez, see the book she co-edited focusing on her writing for *El Grito*, *Enriqueta Vásquez and the Chicano Movement: Writings from El Grito del Norte*, ed. Enriqueta Vásquez, Lorena Oropeza, and Dionne Espinoza (Houston: Arte Público, 2006). On Martínez as a public intellectual, see her writing in Elizabeth Martínez, *De Colores Means All of Us: Latina Views for a Multi-Colored Century* (Cambridge, MA: South End, 1999).
26. Marc-Tizoc Gonzales, "Latina/o (Public/Legal) Intellectuals, Social Crises, and Contemporary Social Movements," *Journal of Gender, Social Policy, and the Law* 8, no. 3 (2010): 787–801. On Latino public intellectuals, see also Frank P. Barajas, "Decolonizing the Newspaper: The Historian and the Op-Ed," *Perspectives in History*, February 2015, 38–39.
27. A legislator encouraged her to write, saying, "I sincerely hope it will be possible for you to write the book you have in mind." Rogers Kelley, Texas Senate, to Mrs. Adela S. Vento, June 28, 1941, ASVP.
28. Alonso S. Perales to Mrs. Adela S. Vento, June 18, 1953, ASVP.
29. Sloss-Vento, *Alonso S. Perales*, 50.
30. Christopher Lasch, *The New Radicalism in America, 1880–1963: The Intellectual as a Social Type* (New York: Norton, 1965), i.
31. Edward W. Said, "The Public Role of Writers and Intellectuals," in *The Public Intellectuals*, ed. Helen Small (Oxford, UK: Blackwell, 2001), 31.
32. Barry Gewen, "Who Is a Public Intellectual?," in "ArtsBeat" blog, *New York Times*, June 11, 2008, https://artsbeat.blogs.nytimes.com/2008/06/11/who-is-a-public-intellectual.
33. Harry Frumerman, book review of *Public Intellectuals: A Story of Decline*, in *Library Journal* 126, no. 20 (December 1, 2001): 150.
34. Daniel W. Drezner, "A Different Take on the Female Public Intellectual 'Problem,'" *Foreign Policy*, February 22, 2005.
35. Samuel McCormick, *Letters to Power: Public Advocacy without Public Intellectuals* (University Park: Pennsylvania State University Press, 2011), 1, 2, 18.

36. McCormick, 2.
37. "About Truthout," Truthout, n.d., https://truthout.org/about/, accessed March 3, 2019. Social media require new debates on defining the term "public intellectual," as individuals are more readily referring to themselves as such. One is the *Viva la Feminista* blogger Veronica, who prides herself on getting paid to be a feminist; "Professional Feminist," *Viva la Feminista*, n.d., http://www.vivalafeminista.com/p/professional-feminist.html, accessed September 24, 2016.
38. Gonzales, 801.
39. Ellen Cushman, "Opinion: The Public Intellectual, Service Learning, and Activist Research," *College English* 61, no. 3 (January 1999): 328–336, posted to Service Learning, General, DigitalCommons@UNO,http:/digitalcommons.unomaha.edu/slceslgen/84.
40. Woods, "Mexican Ethnic Leadership," 28.
41. See especially Orozco, "Alonso S. Perales," in *In Defense of My People*; Orozco, "Alonso S. Perales," in *NHOT*; and Orozco, *No Mexicans, Women, or Dogs.*
42. R. García, "Alonso S. Perales," in *Leaders of the Mexican American Generation*, 85–118. None of the contributors overtly addresses him as a public intellectual.
43. Emilio Zamora, "Sáenz, José de la Luz," *Handbook of Texas Online* (Austin: Texas State Historical Society, December 8, 2015), http://www.tshaonline.org/handbook/online/articles/fsa97.
44. Mendieta, note 9.
45. Ronald N. Jacobs and Eleanor Townsley, *The Space of Opinion: Media Intellectuals and the Public Sphere* (Oxford: Oxford University Press, 2011).
46. McCormick, 2.
47. Orozco, notes on Vento tribute to Sloss-Vento, April 30, 1999, CEOP.
48. Sloss-Vento, "El eterno dilema." In 1955 she also mentioned reading *Novedades*; A. S. Vento to Lic. Alonso S. Perales, April 18, 1955, ASVP.
49. Vento, *Adela Sloss-Vento*, 74.
50. On gendered mobility, see Virginia Scharff, *Taking the Wheel: Women and the Coming of the Motor Age* (New York: Free Press, 1991).
51. Antonio Gramsci, *Selections from the Prison Notebooks of Antonio Gramsci*, ed. Quintin Hoare and Geoffrey Nowell (New York: International, 2008), 7.
52. Kabalen de Bichara, "Expressions of Dissent," 203.
53. Jacobs and Townsley, 79.
54. An American of Mexican Descent to Mr. Harry S. Truman, February 15, 1952, ASVP.
55. Arnoldo Vento, conversation with Cynthia E. Orozco, July 2015.
56. Original text: "Yo todo lo hago porque ya sabe que soy de las que sé defender mis derechos y siempre lo he hecho y aún en contra de mi esposo que no quiere que me meta en nada." Adela Sloss-Vento to J. Luz Sáenz, ca. 1951, box 2, folder 13, JLSP.
57. Vento, conversation with Orozco, July 2015.
58. Mrs. P. C. Vento to Joe B. Evins, Atty., May 11, 1966, ASVP. Arnoldo Vento reports that his father started his job at sixty dollars monthly. Vento, *Adela Sloss-Vento*, 42.

59. "A Citizen (Name withheld by request)," letter to the editor, *Harlingen Star*, December 23, 1947, ASVP.
60. Original text: "Es un trabajo que me disgusta por estar atada de los pies y de las manos. No tengo la libertad de la prensa se puede decir. . . . [P]uede publicarlo aunque tal vez me desocupen. Pero qué importa. Buscaré trabajo o trabajaré de otro manera." Adela S. de Vento to Licenciado Alonso S. Perales, December 12, 1951, ASVP.
61. Original text: "estoy atada de los pies y de los manos con este trabajo político. Sino, yo sería la primera de hablar en público." Adela S. Vento to Lic. Alonso S. Perales, December 17, 1951, box 5, folder 8, ASPP.
62. Adela Sloss-Vento to Prof. J. Luz Sáenz, December 31, 1951, box 2, folder 13, JLSP.
63. Adela Sloss-Vento to J. T. Canales, January 29, 1953, ASVP.
64. Original text: "Agradeceré mucho que si da publicidad a esta información no se dé a saber mi nombre ya que tengo un trabajo de política." Sra. A. S. de Vento to Sr. Fidel Velázquez, May 6, 1953, ASVP.
65. Original text: "He vivido sin Libertad de Prensa y me parece una eternidad. Ud. sabe que los trabajos de la asquerosa política la tiene a una sin libertad de Prensa. Solo espero trabajar un poquito más retirarme de aquí. Estoy más enterada que nunca de los problemas del mojado. Aquí se aprende mucho. Me servirá para seguir escribiendo cuando salga de aquí." Adela Sloss-Vento to Lic. Alonso S. Perales, December 13, 1951, ASVP.
66. Adela Sloss-Vento to Bishops Committee for the Spanish-Speaking, June 20, 1953, ASVP.
67. Sloss-Vento, *Alonso S. Perales*, 39.
68. Vento, *Adela Sloss-Vento*, 42.
69. Adela Sloss-Vento to J. T. Canales, January 29, 1953, ASVP.
70. Certificate of Deputation card, January 1, 1953, ASVP.
71. Adela S. Vento to Lic. Alonso S. Perales, December 17, 1951, box 5, folder 8, ASPP.
72. Vento, interview by Orozco, 1991, CEOP.
73. Rodolfo Acuña, "'There Will Be No Change'; Debunking the Illusion," blog post, November 19, 2014, http://rudyacuna.net/there-will-be-no-change-debunking-the-illusion-by-rodolfo-acuna-11-19-14/.
74. Edward Said, "The Public Role of Writers and Intellectuals," in *The Public Intellectual*, ed. Helen Small (Oxford, UK: Blackwell, 2001), 18.
75. Said, "Public Role of Writers and Intellectuals," 31.
76. Kabalen de Bichara, "Self-Writing," 259. I disagree that this was also the life project of Marta Perales, as Kabalen de Bichara suggests.
77. Kabalen de Bichara, "Expressions of Dissent," 196.
78. Adela Sloss-Vento, letter to "The People's Voice," *McAllen Monitor*, February 23, 1969, ASVP.
79. Sloss-Vento, letter to "The People's Voice."
80. Don Salvador Cárdenas, letter to the editor, *Brownsville Herald*, October 9, 1940, ASVP. It is doubtful that someone would refer to himself as "Don," a title of respect.
81. Vento, *Adela Sloss-Vento*, 42.

82. "Latin Americans Loyal," letter to the editor, *Brownsville Herald*, September 22, 1942, ASVP. She penciled on the clipping "Mrs. A. S. Vento."
83. Mrs. A. S. Vento to Mr. Santos de la Paz, February 18, 1952, ASVP.
84. A Latin American Natural born citizen of the United States who will not permit to be classified under any other term but WHITE, "A Latin American Speaks," letter to the editor, *Brownsville Herald*(?), ca. 1943, ASVP.
85. Sloss-Vento, "El eterno dilema."
86. Vento, *Adela Sloss-Vento*, 14–15.
87. Vento, *Adela Sloss-Vento*, 16.
88. Adela Sloss-Vento to Cynthia Orozco, November 3, 1978, ASVP.
89. Dolores Huerta to Cristina Arreola, "Mighty Mujeres," *Latina*, March 2016, 73. On this note I will mention that Arturo Francisco Rosales in his review in the *Western Historical Quarterly* of my book *No Mexicans, Women, or Dogs Allowed* suggests that I did not write chapter 7, a theoretical chapter. This is an example of a man underestimating a woman's intellect.
90. Vento, *Adela Sloss-Vento*, xiv.
91. Stephanie Merrim, "Sor Juana Inés de la Cruz: Mexican Poet and Scholar," *Encyclopedia Britannica*, updated April 10, 2018, https://www.britannica.com/biography/Sor-Juana-Ines-de-la-Cruz.
92. Adela Sloss-Vento, "Mujeres distinguidas de México; Sor Juana Inés de la Cruz," ASVP.
93. In Vento, *Adela Sloss-Vento*, 17.
94. Vento, *Adela Sloss-Vento*, 17.
95. Merrim.
96. Merrim.
97. Vento, *Adela Sloss-Vento*, 82.
98. Fahs, 9.
99. Huerta, 73.

CHAPTER 7: DEMOCRAT IN THE UNITED STATES AND DEMOCRAT FOR MEXICO

1. Mrs. P. C. Vento to Joe B. Evins, Atty., May 11, 1966, ASVP.
2. "Una señorita que defiende a la colonia," *La Prensa*, February 20, 1929, ASVP.
3. Mrs. A. S. Vento to México-Americanos para Acción Social Inc., Rio Grande City, February 24, 1970, ASVP.
4. Nancy Beck Young, "Democratic Party," in *Handbook of Texas Online* (Austin: Texas State Historical Association, 2010), http://www.tshaonline.org/handbook/online/articles/wad01.
5. Young.
6. Pycior, 149.
7. Kabalen de Bichara, "Expressions of Dissent," 203.
8. Márquez, *Democratizing Texas Politics*, 19.
9. US Congress, House Committee on Immigration, Hearings on Western Hemisphere Immigration, 71st Congress, 2nd Session, 1930. In New Mexico throughout the twentieth century there were Hispano state legislators, governors, and congressmen. In California Mexican Americans participated in Franklin Delano

Roosevelt presidential campaigns in the 1930s and the Amigos for Henry Wallace national campaign in the late 1940s. The Latina Lucretia del Valle Grady of Berkeley, California, was a member of the Democratic National Committee in the 1930s. However, not until the election of Edward Roybal to the Los Angeles City Council was there a major breakthrough there. See Burt, *Search for a Civic Voice.* In 1940 Latinos and at least one Latina—Lucretia del Valle—from California, New York, and Florida attended the Democratic National Convention, but none from Texas did. The labor organizer María Moreno, who was born in Texas, may have attended in the 1950s. The film *Adiós Amor*, about Moreno, was directed and produced by Laurie Coyle and premiered in January 2018.

10. Gutiérrez, Meléndez, and Noyola, 13.
11. See Cynthia E. Orozco, "Beyond Machismo, la Familia, and Ladies Auxiliaries: A Historiography of Mexican-Origin Women's Participation in Voluntary Associations and Politics in the U.S., 1870–1990," in *Perspectives in Mexican American Studies* 5 (Tucson: Mexican American Studies and Research Center, University of Arizona, 1995): 1–34.
12. Gabriela Gonzalez, *Redeeming La Raza: Transborder Modernity, Race, Respectability, and Rights* (Oxford: Oxford University Press, 2018), 26; Gabriela Gonzalez, "The Ideological Origins of a Transnational Advocate for La Raza," in *Texas Women, Their Histories, Their Lives*, ed. Elizabeth Hayes Turner, Stephanie Cole, and Rebecca Sharpless (Athens: University of Georgia Press, 2015): 225–248; Young.
13. Gilberto J. Quezada, *Border Boss: Manuel B. Bravo and Zapata County* (College Station: Texas A&M University Press, 2001), 24.
14. Gutiérrez, Meléndez, and Noyola, 13, 23, 25.
15. Gutiérrez, Meléndez, and Noyola, 149. See also Thomas H. Kreneck, "Dr. Clotilde P. Garcia, Physician, Activist, and First Lady of Genealogy," Mary and Jeff Bell Library, Texas A&M University, Corpus Christi, https://library.tamucc.edu.
16. Pycior, 149.
17. Gutiérrez, Meléndez, and Noyola, 23.
18. Pycior, 95.
19. Pycior, 95.
20. In Pycior, 95.
21. David Montejano, *Quixote's Soldiers: A Local History of the Chicano Movement, 1966–1981* (Austin: University of Texas Press, 2010), 153.
22. J. T. Canales to Mrs. A. S. Vento, October 24, 1952, ASVP.
23. Adela Sloss Vento to Albert Peña Jr., PASSO President, April 16, 1964, ASVP.
24. Pycior, 95.
25. Rosie Castro, in the author's notes on women's luncheon, Chicano Movement 20th Anniversary Reunion, San Antonio, 1989, CEOP.
26. Montejano, 152.
27. Gutiérrez, Meléndez, and Noyola, xi; "Latino Elected Officials in Texas 1974–2003," Texas Politics Project (Austin: University of Texas, n.d.), https://texaspolitics.utexas.edu/archive/html/vce/features/0503_04/latinos.html. Also see Sharon Navarro, *Latina Legislator: Leticia Van de Putte and the Road to Leadership* (College Station: Texas A&M University Press, 2008).

28. Adela Sloss-Vento, "The Problems of Many Texas Towns," ASVP. The essay was originally in Spanish in *El Heraldo* in Corpus Christi on September 16, 1943, and published in English the same year in the *Corpus Christi Caller*.
29. Adela Sloss-Vento, in Vento, *Adela Sloss-Vento*, 226.
30. Adela Sloss-Vento, in Vento, *Adela Sloss-Vento*, 228.
31. Adela Sloss-Vento to Clarence La Roche, April 14, 1945, in L. Garza, "Jovita González," 47–48.
32. Mrs. A. S. Vento, "Christians Must Practice Christianity to Stop Communism, Valley Woman Says," *McAllen Monitor*, November 18, 1947, ASVP.
33. Mrs. A. S. Vento to Judge Alonso S. Perales, October 13, 1944, ASPP.
34. Adela Sloss Vento to Mrs. Maurice Brown, State President of the League of Women Voters, December 22, 1963, ASVP. Brown's first name is listed at "Curtis Maurice Brown, Sr.," Find a Grave, https://www.findagrave.com/memorial/134374541/curtis-maurice-brown.
35. Sloss Vento to Brown, December 22, 1963.
36. Mrs. Adela Sloss Vento to Hon. Lyndon B. Johnson, Vice President Elect, November 16, 1960, ASVP.
37. Sloss Vento to Johnson, November 16, 1960.
38. Una México-Americana to Telesistema Del Norte, Monterrey, June 19, 1972, ASVP.
39. Original text: "Gracias a la justicia y humanidad del Presidente Roosevelt, la raza negra ha gozado de un privilegio que no se le había concedido. Este privilegio ha sido que el negro ha gozado de un privilegió que no se le había concedido. Este privilegio ha sido que el negro votará en las elecciones primarias." Sra. Adela S. Vento, letter to the editor, *La Prensa*, October 19, 1944, ASVP.
40. Lupe S. Salinas, "Legally White, Socially Brown: Alonso S. Perales and His Crusade for Justice for La Raza," *In Defense of My People*, ed. Olivas, 75–96.
41. On African Americans in the Valley, see Alberto Rodríguez, "The Making of the Modern Lower Rio Grande Valley."
42. Sanford N. Greenberg, "White Primary," in *Handbook of Texas Online* (Austin: Texas State Historical Association, 2010, modified November 3, 2015), http://www.tshaonline.org/handbook/online/articles/wdw01.
43. Unsigned, to Mr. George Esqueda, October 21, 1947, ASVP.
44. Mrs. P. C. Vento to Mr. Joe B. Evins, May 11, 1966, ASVP.
45. "Citizens' Political Club Organized," *McAllen Monitor*(?), ca. mid-1940s, ASVP.
46. Adela Sloss-Vento, "Un club político que trabaja por la organización de política bien dirigida y por el mejoramiento del pueblo latinoamericano," undated manuscript, ca. mid-1940s, ASVP.
47. "Citizens' Political Club Organized."
48. Nasser Momayez, "Hispanic Representation, Empowerment, and Participation in Texas Politics," *Latino Studies Journal* 11, no. 2 (Spring 2000): 6.
49. Cynthia E. Orozco, "Eleuterio Escobar Jr.," in *NHOT*, 2:889–890.
50. Sloss-Vento, "Un club político."
51. Sloss-Vento, "Un club político."
52. Adela Sloss-Vento, in Vento, *Adela Sloss-Vento*, 137. This letter appeared in *La Prensa* on October 19, 1944.

53. Mrs. A. S. Vento to Judge Alonso S. Perales, October 13, 1944, box 5, folder 8, ASPP. Perales was not a judge; she confused him momentarily with Judge J. T. Canales.
54. Original text: "Sólo el Sr. Kazen fue el único que tuvo el valor civil de hablar de la discriminación y de nuestros problemas. . . . Ni Ellis, ni Celaya ni Bentsen hablaron nada respecto a nuestras problemas. . . . Nosotros prometimos ayudar a Ellis y le vamos a ayudar, pero después de las primarias si el Sr. Kazen se queda es por él que nos vamos a ir." Adela Sloss Vento to J. Luz Sáenz, January 15, 1948, box 2, folder 13, JLSP.
55. Vento, "Adela Sloss Vento, 1901–1998," in Sloss-Vento, *Alonso S. Perales*, ebook.
56. Ozzie G. Simmons, *Anglo Americans and Mexican Americans in South Texas: A Study in Dominant-Subordinate Group Relations* (New York: Arno, 1974), 315–324. This was the dissertation Simmons wrote in 1952.
57. Quezada, 103.
58. Philip A. Kazen to Mrs. Adela S. Vento, August 31, 1948, ASVP.
59. Adela Sloss-Vento, "El problema del mojado y la deshonestidad de parte de empleados que corren cantinas y otros centros de vicios," manuscript, January 27, 1953, ASVP.
60. Adela Sloss-Vento, "Prólogo," ASVP.
61. Original text: "Me da mucho gusto estar aquí con ustedes. Y es un honor para mí poder hablarles sobre los derechos de todo mexicano como ciudadano americano. No hace mucho que nuestros antepasados lucharon por los derechos humanos de [*sic*] todo ciudadano. Ahora nos enfrentamos con otro enemigo, que no nos deja desarrollar, que nos discrimina en las escuelas públicas, que ha llegado a abusar con sus tropas de bandidos americanos, que nos tiene abajo con sus sueldos miserables, que se protege con el sistema corrupto, que se defiende con abogados chuecos y que se esconde detrás de los vendidos mexicanos con sus cantinas, prostitutas y jugadas." Arnoldo Carlos Vento, *La cueva de Naltzatlán* (Mexico City: Fondo de Cultura Económica, 1986), 38–39.
62. William D. Hassett, Secretary to the President, to My dear Mrs. Vento, March 29, 1948, ASVP.
63. American of Mexican descent to Truman, ASVP.
64. A. S. Vento to Eisenhower, February 13, 1954, ASVP.
65. A. S. Vento to Eisenhower, February 13, 1954.
66. Mrs. A. S. Vento to Mr. Alonso S. Perales, February 13, 1954, box 5, folder 8, ASPP.
67. Mrs. A. S. Vento to Lic. Alonso S. Perales, July 25, 1952, box 5, folder 8, ASPP.
68. A. S. Vento to Perales, July 25, 1952.
69. Unsigned (Adela Sloss-Vento) to Alonso S. Perales, March 9, 1953, box 5, folder 8, ASPP.
70. Original text: "Los políticos de la Legislatura de Texas siguen recibiendo millares de votos latinamericanos de todas partes de Texas, pero nosotros no despertamos y no nos unimos." In Perales, "Arquitectos de nuestros propios destinos," June 21, 1953, ASVP.
71. Adela Sloss Vento to Alonso S. Perales, October 3, 1954, box 5, folder 8, ASPP.

72. Alonso S. Perales to Sra. Dona Adela S. de Vento, October 5, 1954, ASVP; J. T. Canales to Mrs. A. S. Vento, December 8, 1959, ASVP.
73. Luis Alvarado to Mr. and Mrs. Pedro Vento, June 11, 1958, ASVP.
74. She sent Senator Edward Kennedy a note of condolence when his brother Robert Kennedy was assassinated; Edward Kennedy responded. Senator Edward Kennedy to Mrs. Adela Sloss Vento, card, October 1, 1968, ASVP.
75. Orozco, "Viva Kennedy."
76. I. García, *Viva Kennedy*, 88–89, 100.
77. Young.
78. I. García, *Viva Kennedy*, 50.
79. Sloss Vento to Brown, December 22, 1963.
80. Mrs. Adela S. Vento, "A Tribute to Our Beloved President John F. Kennedy," *McAllen Monitor*, November 11, 1973, ASVP.
81. Sen. Edward M. Kennedy photo, second Senate term announcement, *Edinburg Daily Review*, June 12, 1970, ASVP.
82. Mrs. P. C. Vento to Joe Evins, May 11, 1966, ASVP.
83. Vento to Evins, May 11, 1966.
84. Adela S. Vento to Hon. Lyndon B. Johnson, Vice President Elect, November 16, 1960, ASVP.
85. A. S. Vento to Johnson, November 16, 1960.
86. Ralph A. Dungan, Special Assistant to the President, to Mrs. Adela S. Vento, March 4, 1964, ASVP.
87. Adela Sloss-Vento to Honorable President Jimmy Carter, March 27, 1977, ASVP.
88. Kabalen de Bichara, "Expressions of Dissent," 201.
89. Flores, *Grounds for Dreaming*.
90. Jimmy Patino, *Raza Si, Migra No: Chicano Movement Struggles for Immigrant Rights in San Diego* (Chapel Hill: University of North Carolina Press, 2017).
91. L. Garza, "La concepcion," 27.
92. Mrs. Adela Sloss-Vento to *McAllen Evening Monitor*, ca. 1978(?), ASVP. This is a request to publish a letter to the editor about the Senate race.
93. Mrs. Adela Sloss-Vento to *McAllen Evening Monitor*, October 23, 1978, ASVP. This is a request to publish a letter to the editor.
94. Márquez, 71.
95. Yolanda Alaniz and Megan Cornish, *Viva La Raza: A History of Chicano History and Resistance* (Seattle: Red Letter Press, 2008), 231.
96. Rosie Castro, interview by Alexa García-Ditta, *Texas Observer*, December 18, 2015, https://www.texasobserver.org/interview-rosie-castro.
97. Juventino Alvarado to Mrs. A. S. Vento, May 29, 1972, ASVP.
98. Martha Cotera to Cynthia Orozco, email, January 2, 2018; Rosie Castro to Cynthia Orozco, email, January 10, 2018. Martha P. Cotera, *Diosa y Hembra: The History and Heritage of Chicanas in the U.S.* (Austin: Information Systems Development, 1976).
99. Original text: "Yo también quiero felicitar a todos los de la raza unida por su interés y unión en favor del Adelanto y de la completa solución de los problemas

México-Americanos." Mrs. Adela S. Vento to Mr. Juventino Alvarado, May 30, 1972, ASVP.

100. Adela Sloss-Vento to México-Americanos para Acción Social Inc., February 24, 1970, ASVP.

101. Governor Ann Richards to Mrs. Adela Sloss Vento, September 24, 1992, ASVP. I searched through nine boxes of the Governor Ann Richards collection at the Briscoe Center for American History at the University of Texas to locate Sloss-Vento's letter to Governor Richards in that archive but was unsuccessful.

102. Vento, *Adela Sloss-Vento,* 72.

103. Original text: "Le sugeriría que estamos perdidos en estos lugares, a menos de que México tome medidas enérgicas para que los miles de hombres y mujeres que hay en el Valle se estén dentro del territorio Mexicano." Adela Sloss Vento to Alonso S. Perales, November 12, 1947, box 5, folder 8, ASPP.

104. Original text: "Al paso que vamos verás que un día de este pasará México a manos de los Anglo-americanos y les suceda lo que nos ha sucedido a nosotros de Texas." Adela Sloss Vento to Lic. Alonso S. Perales, December 18, 1947, box 5, folder 8, ASPP.

105. Luis Duplán, Consulate of Mexico, Austin, to Sra. Adela S. de Vento, October 22, 1943, ASVP.

106. Sra. Adela Sloss de Vento to Professor Jorge del Río, late 1940s, ASVP.

107. Original text: "una carta bien explicada sugiriéndole al Presidente Alemán que no envíe braceros a Tejas, la envié ayer de Reynosa." S. Vento to Perales, December 18, 1947, ASPP.

108. Sra. Adela S. de Vento to Sr. Adolfo Ruíz Cortines, Presidente de México, June 8, 1953, ASVP.

109. "Carta de la señora Adela Sloss de Vento al Sr. Ruíz Cortínez [*sic*] Presidente de Mexico," *Revista Latino-Americano* 17, no. 20 (1953): 25, ASVP.

110. S. de Vento to Ruíz Cortines, June 8, 1953, ASVP.

111. Sra. A. S. Vento to Fidel Velázquez, Secretaria General, Confederación de Obreros Mexicanos, May 6, 1953, ASVP.

112. Original text: "Si el Sr. Presidente de México así como su departamento, hicieron por solucionar el problema de recoger los miles de Espaldas mojados para beneficio del desarrollo económico de México, harán también un gran beneficio a los México-Americanos en la frontera." A. S. Vento to Velázquez, May 6, 1953.

113. A. S. Vento to Velázquez, May 6, 1953.

114. Pérez, 33.

115. Alexa Ura, "Women Still Underrepresented in Legislative Races," *Texas Tribune*, April 4, 2017, https://www.texastribune.org/2016/01/04/campaign-filings-reflect-underrepresentation-women.

116. Emma Hinchliffe, "Texas Has Never Elected a Latina to Congress," *Austin American-Statesman*, March 7, 2016; "More Women than Men: State Legislatures Could Shift for the First Time," *New York Times*, July 3, 2018.

117. Zavaleta, "Women as Political Pioneers," 1. For a national perspective, see Sharon A. Navarro, Samantha L. Hernandez, and Leslie A. Navarro, eds., *Latinas in*

American Politics: Changing and Embracing Political Tradition (Lanham, MD: Lexington, 2016).

118. Roberto Calderon, "Ya Era Tiempo: First Two Chicanas/Latinas on Their Way to Congress for Texas," email to the listserv National Association for Chicana and Chicano Studies, NACCS-Tejas-bounces@lists.naccsonline.org, March 9, 2018. Calderon expanded his thoughts from Abby Livingston and Julian Aguilar, "Texas Poised to Send Its First Two Latinas to Congress," *Texas Tribune*, March 6, 2018.

CONCLUSION

1. Maylei Blackwell, *¡Chicana Power! Contested Histories of Feminism in the Chicano Movement* (Austin: University of Texas Press, 2011), 25.
2. Aarón Sánchez, "Our Children Must Not Suffer . . . Another No-Action Generation: The Limitations of Liberalism in Mexican-American Generation," *Journal of South Texas* 26, no. 2 (Fall 2013): 20. Sánchez says LULAC had a "conservative culture of citizenship promoted by Mexican-Americanism." The historian Zaragosa Vargas has called LULAC "sheepish." Zaragosa Vargas, *Labor Rights Are Civil Rights* (Princeton, NJ: Princeton University Press, 2005), 138.
3. Nils Hammaren and Thomas Johansson, "Homosociality: In between Power and Intimacy," *Sage Open*, January 10, 2014, http://journals.sagepub.com/doi/abs/10.1177/2158244013518057.
4. Sloss-Vento, "El eterno dilema."
5. P. J. Pierce, *"Let Me Tell You What I've Learned": Texas Wisewomen Speak* (Austin: University of Texas Press, 2002).
6. Gutiérrez, Meléndez, and Noyola, *Chicanas in Charge.*
7. Cantú, "Women, Then and Now."
8. Her documents reveal two occasions when she used "white trash." She compares braceras and white women in prison in a letter to Héctor García on December 17, 1951. In Vento, *Adela Sloss-Vento*, 151.
9. Original text: "Tú eres muy inteligente y sé que un día de estos, podrás escribir un gran libro." Adela Sloss-Vento to Miss Cynthia Orozco, January 7, 1970, CEOP.
10. I too am a public intellectual. I wrote my first letter to the editor in 1975, more than forty years ago, in Cuero, Texas. I have written more than a hundred articles, opinion pieces, and letters to the editor scattered across Texas, California, and New Mexico newspapers, many before the age of the internet. Like Sloss-Vento and Perales, I have written about civil rights, immigration, labor, and women; unlike them, I also have written about football, the Lincoln County war, and England's appreciation of Martin Luther King Jr.

BIBLIOGRAPHY

ARCHIVES

Benson Latin American Collection, General Libraries, University of Texas, Austin (BLAC)

Castañeda, Carlos E., Papers (CECP)

Dickerson Montemayor, Alice, Papers (ADMP)

Escobar, Eleuterio, Papers (EEEP)

LULAC News, December 1931–December 1965

Munguia, Romulo, Papers (RMP)

Sáenz, José de la Luz, Collection (JLSC)

Sánchez, George I., Papers (GISP)

Weeks, Oliver Douglas, Papers (ODWP)

Briscoe Center for American History, University of Texas, Austin (BC)

LULAC News, August 1931–May 1933

Richards, Ann W., Papers (ARP)

Callero, Cleofas Papers, C. L. Sonnichsen Special Collections Department, University of Texas, El Paso

Canales, J. T., Estate, Collection, James C. Jernigan Library, South Texas Archives, Texas A&M University, Kingsville (JTCEC)

Orozco, Cynthia E., Papers, Ruidoso, New Mexico (CEOP)

Perales, Alonso S., Papers, Special Collections, M. D. Anderson Library, University of Houston (ASPP)

Sloss-Vento, Adela, Papers, personal archive of Arnoldo C. Vento, Austin (ASVP)

Taylor, Paul Schuster, Collection, Bancroft Library, University of California, Berkeley (PSTC)

SECONDARY SOURCES

Abernathy, Francis E. "James Frank Dobie." In *New Handbook of Texas*, edited by Tyler, Barnett, and Barkley, 2:662–663.

Acuña, Rodolfo. "'There Will Be No Change': Debunking the Illusion." Blog post, November 19, 2014, http://rudyacuna.net/there-will-be-no-change-debunking-the-myth-by-rodolfo-acuna-11-19-14.

Advance News Journal. "LULAC to Honor Adela Sloss Vento." March 24, 1999.
Alaniz, Yolanda, and Megan Cornish. *Viva La Raza: A History of Chicano History and Resistance*. Seattle: Red Letter Press, 2008.
Allsup, Carl. "Dr. Héctor Pérez García: Giant of the Twentieth Century." In *Leaders of the Mexican American Generation: Biographical Essays*, edited by Anthony Quíroz, 191–208. Colorado Springs: University Press of Colorado, 2015.
———. *The American G.I. Forum: Origins and Evolution*. Center for Mexican American Studies Monograph 6. Austin: Center for Mexican American Studies, University of Texas, 1982.
———. "American G.I. Forum of Texas." In *New Handbook of Texas*, edited by Tyler, Barnett, and Barkley, 1:147–148.
Almaraz, Félix D., Jr. "Carlos Eduardo Castañeda." In *New Handbook of Texas*, edited by Tyler, Barnett, and Barkley, 1:1016–1017.
———. *Knight without Armor: Carlos Eduardo Castañeda, 1896–1958*. College Station: Texas A&M University Press, 1999.
Anders, Evan. *Boss Rule in South Texas: The Progressive Era*. Austin: University of Texas Press, 1982.
———. "José Tomás Canales." In *New Handbook of Texas*, edited by Tyler, Barnett, and Barkley, 1:953–954.
Anderson, Benedict. *Imagined Communities: Reflections on the Origin and Spread of Nationalism*. London: Verso, 1983.
Anzaldúa, Gloria. *Borderlands/La Frontera: The New Mestiza*. San Francisco: Aunt Lute, 1987.
Ayala, Adriana. "Negotiating Race Relations through Activism: Women Activists and Women's Organizations in San Antonio, Texas during the 1920s." PhD diss., University of Texas, Austin, 2005.
Baker Jones, Nancy, and Ruthe Winegarten. *Capitol Women: Texas Female Legislators, 1923–1999*. Austin: University of Texas Press, 2000.
Barajas, Frank P. "Decolonizing the Newspaper: The Historian and the Op-Ed." *Perspectives in History*, February 2015, 38–39.
Blackwell, Maylei. *¡Chicana Power! Contested Histories of Feminism in the Chicano Movement*. Austin: University of Texas Press, 2011.
Blanton, Carlos K. "A Legacy of Neglect: George I. Sánchez, Mexican American Education, and the Ideal of Integration, 1940–1970." *Teachers College Record* 114 (June 2012): 1–34.
———. "The Citizenship Sacrifice: Mexican Americans, the Saunders-Leonard Report, and the Politics of Immigration, 1951–1952." *Western Historical Quarterly* 40, no. 3 (Autumn 2009): 299–320.
———. *George I. Sánchez: The Long Struggle for Integration*. New Haven, CT: Yale University Press, 2015.
———. "George I. Sánchez, Ideology, and Whiteness in the Making of the Mexican American Civil Rights Movement, 1930–1960." *Journal of Southern History* 72, no. 3 (August 2006): 569–604.
Boswell, Angela. "From Farm to Future: Women's Journey through Twentieth-Century Texas." *Twentieth-Century Texas: A Social and Cultural History*, edited

by John W. Storey and Mary L. Kelley. Denton: University of North Texas Press, 2008, 105–134.

Bowman, Timothy Paul. *Blood Oranges: Colonialism and Agriculture in the South Texas Borderlands.* College Station: Texas A&M University Press, 2016.

———. "Negotiating Conquest: Internal Colonialism and Shared Histories in the South Texas Borderlands." *Western Historical Quarterly* 46, no. 3 (Autumn 2015): 335–353.

———. "What About Texas? The Forgotten Cause of Antonio Orendain and the Rio Grande Valley Farm Workers, 1966–1982." Master's thesis, University of Texas, Arlington, 2005.

Briegel, Kay. "Alianza Hispano-Americana and Some Mexican-American Civil Rights Cases in the 1950s." In *The Mexican-Americans: An Awakened Minority*," edited by Manuel P. Servín, 174–187. Beverly Hills, CA: Glencoe, 1970.

Brownsville Herald. "'Latinos' Traits Pamphlet Blasted," March 11, 1952. https://texashistory.unt.edu/ark:/67531/metapth250234/.

Bueno, Marianne M. "Intellectually He Was Curious; in Public Action He Was Cautious and Prudent." In *Latina/os and World War II: Mobility, Agency, and Ideology*, edited by Maggie Rivas-Rodriguez and B. V. Olguín, 95–112. Austin: University of Texas Press, 2014.

Buitrón, Richard A., Jr. *The Quest for Tejano Identity in San Antonio, 1913–2000.* New York: Routledge, 2004.

Burt, Kenneth C. *The Search for a Civic Voice: California Latino Politics.* Claremont, CA: Regina, 2007.

Cairns, Kathleen. *Front-Page Women Journalists, 1920–1950.* Lincoln: University of Nebraska Press, 2007.

Caldwell, Laura. "Baker, Anderson Yancey." In *Handbook of Texas Online.* Austin: Texas State Historical Association, 2010. Modified October 24, 2018. https://tshaonline.org/handbook/online/articles/fba19.

Canales, J. T. *Bits of Texas History in the Melting Pot.* Parts 1 and 2. San Antonio: Artes Gráficas, 1950 and 1957.

———. *Character Builders and Leaders of Men.* San Antonio: Artes Gráficas, 1959.

———. *Ethics in the Profession of Law.* San Antonio: Artes Gráficas, 1953.

———. *Juan N. Cortina: Bandit or Patriot?* San Antonio: Artes Gráficas, 1951.

———. *La Guerra de Tejas.* Brownsville: J. T. Canales, 1959.

———. *The Tragic Quadrangle.* San Antonio: Artes Gráficas, 1958.

Cantú, Norma Elia. "Women, Then and Now: An Analysis of the Adelita Image versus the Chicana Political Writer and Philosopher." In *Chicana Voices: Intersections of Race, Class, and Gender*, edited by Teresa Cordova, Norma Elia Cantú, Gilberto Cárdenas, Juan García, and Christine M. Sierra, 8–10. Austin: Center for Mexican American Studies, University of Texas, 1986.

Carlsen, Audrey, and Denise Lu. "More Women than Men: State Legislatures Could Shift for the First Time." *New York Times*, July 3, 2018.

Carrigan, William D., and Clive Webb. *Forgotten Dead: Mob Violence against Mexicans in the United States, 1848–1928.* Oxford: Oxford University Press, 2013.

Castañeda, Carlos E. *Our Catholic Heritage in Texas, 1519–1936.* 7 vols. Austin: Von Boeckmann-Jones, 1936–1958.

Castro, Rosie. Interview by Alexa García-Ditta. *Texas Observer*, December 18, 2015. https://www.texasobserver.org/interview-rosie-castro.

Clinchy, Everett Ross. *Equality of Opportunity: Latin Americans in Texas*. New York: Arno, 1974.

Cohen, Deborah. *Braceros: Migrant Citizens and Transnational Subjects in the Postwar United States and Mexico*. Chapel Hill: University of North Carolina Press, 2011.

Cotera, María. "Jovita González Mireles: A Sense of History and Homeland." In *Latina Legacies: Identity, Biography, and Community*, edited by Vicki L. Ruiz and Virginia Sanchez-Korrol, 158–174. New York: Oxford University Press, 2005.

Cotera, Martha P. *Diosa y Hembra: The History and Heritage of Chicanas in the U.S.* Austin: Information Systems Development, 1976.

Cushman, Ellen. "Opinion: The Public Intellectual, Service Learning, and Activist Research." *College English* 61, no. 3 (January 1999): 328–336. Posted to Service Learning, General, DigitalCommons@UNO, http:/digitalcommons.unomaha.edu/slceslgen/84.

Dallas Times Herald Magazine. "Prosecution and Preserves." April 26, 1964.

Dickerson Montemayor, Alice. Videotaped interview by Norma Cantú with questions by Cynthia Orozco, Laredo, January 26, 1981, CEOP.

"Display in White Library Honors Former Local Activist." *Del Mar College Campus News*, October 5, 2007.

Drezner, Daniel W. "A Different Take on the Female Public Intellectual 'Problem.'" *Foreign Policy*, February 22, 2005.

Durán, Luisa. "The Life and Legacy of Dr. George Isidore Sánchez: A Belated Tribute." Albuquerque: New Mexico Association for Bilingual Education, 2011. http://nmabe.net/wp-content/uploads/2011/08/The-Life-and-Legacy-Dr.-Luisa-Duran-web.pdf.

Fahs, Alice. *Out on Assignment: Newspaper Women and the Making of Modern Public Space*. Chapel Hill: University of North Carolina Press, 2011.

Flores, Lori A. *Grounds for Dreaming: Mexican Americans, Mexican Immigrants, and the California Farmworker Movement*. New Haven, CT: Yale University Press, 2016.

Frumerman, Harry. Book review of *Public Intellectuals: A Story of Decline*. *Library Journal* 126, no. 20 (December 1, 2001): 150.

Galarza, Ernesto. *Merchants of Labor, the Mexican Bracero Story: An Account of the Managed Migration of Mexican Farm Workers in California 1942–1960*. San Jose, CA: Rosicrucian Press, 1964.

García, Alma M., ed. *Chicana Feminist Thought: The Basic Historical Writings*. New York: Routledge, 1997.

García, Ignacio M. *Chicanismo: The Forging of a Militant Ethos among Mexican Americans*. Tucson: University of Arizona Press, 1997.

———. *Héctor P. García: In Relentless Pursuit of Justice*. Houston: Arte Público, 2002.

———. *United We Win: The Rise and Fall of La Raza Unida Party*. Tucson: University of Arizona Press, 1989.

———. *Viva Kennedy: Mexican Americans in Search of Camelot*. College Station: Texas A&M University Press, 2000.

García, Juan Ramón. *Operation Wetback: The Mass Deportation of Mexican Undocumented Workers in 1954*. Westport, CT: Greenwood, 1980.

García, Mario T. "Alonso S. Perales and the Catholic Imaginary: Religion and the Mexican-American Mind." In *In Defense of My People*, edited by Olivas, 241–263.

———. *The Chicano Movement: Perspectives from the Twenty-First Century*. New York: Routledge, 2014.

———. *Mexican Americans: Leadership, Ideology, and Identity, 1930–1960*. New Haven, CT: Yale University Press, 1989.

García, Richard A. "Alonso S. Perales: The Voice and Visions of a Citizen Intellectual." In *Leaders of the Mexican American Generation: Biographical Essays*, edited by Anthony Quíroz, 85–118. Boulder: University Press of Colorado, 2015.

———. *Rise of the Mexican American Middle Class: San Antonio, 1929–1941*. College Station: Texas A&M University Press, 1991.

García, Sonia R., Valerie Martinez-Ebers, Irasema Coronado, Sharon A. Navarro, and Patricia M. Jaramillo. *Políticas: Latina Public Officials in Texas*. Austin: University of Texas Press, 2008.

Garza, Alicia A. "San Juan." In *New Handbook of Texas*, edited by Tyler, Barnett, and Barkley, 5:863.

Garza, Edward. "LULAC: The League of United Latin American Citizens." Master's thesis, Southwest Texas State Teachers College, 1951.

Garza, Laura Patricia. "La concepción de la identidad fronteriza en Jovita González y Adela Sloss de Vento." In *Yet More Studies in Rio Grande Valley History*, edited by Milo Kearney, 19–59. Brownsville: University of Texas, Brownsville, 2015.

———. "Jovita González, Adela Vento y Consuelo Aldape de Vega Hidalgo: Precursoras del pensamiento fronterizo." PhD diss., University of Houston, 2012.

Gewen, Barry. "Who Is a Public Intellectual?" *New York Times*, June 11, 2008.

Gillette, Michael L. "The Rise of the NAACP in Texas." In *The African American Experience in Texas: An Anthology*, edited by Bruce A. Glasrud and James M. Smallwood, 258–278. Lubbock: Texas Tech University Press, 2007.

Goldstone, Dwonna. *Integrating the Forty Acres: The Fifty-Year Struggle for Racial Equality at the University of Texas*. Athens: University of Georgia Press, 2012.

Golia, Julie A. "Courting Women, Courting Advertisers: The Woman's Page and the Transformation of the American Newspaper, 1895–1935." *Journal of American History* 103, no. 3 (December 2016): 606–628.

Gómez-Quiñones, Juan. *Chicano Politics: Reality and Promise, 1940–1990*. Albuquerque: University of New Mexico Press, 1990.

Gómez-Quiñones, Juan, and Irene Vásquez. *Making Aztlán: Ideology and Culture of the Chicana and Chicano Movement, 1966–1977*. Albuquerque: University of New Mexico Press, 2014.

Gonzales, Marc-Tizoc. "Latina/o (Public/Legal) Intellectuals, Social Crises, and Contemporary Social Movements." *Journal of Gender, Social Policy, and the Law* 18, no. 3 (2010): 787–801.

González, Gabriela. "Carolina Munguía and Emma Tenayuca: The Politics of Benevolence and Radical Reform." *Frontiers: A Journal of Women Studies* 24, nos. 2–3 (2003): 200–229.

——. "Jovita Idar." In *Latinas in the United States: A Historical Encyclopedia*, edited by Vicki L. Ruiz and Virginia Sánchez-Korrol, 2:336–337. Bloomington: Indiana University Press, 2006.

——. "Jovita Idar: The Ideological Origins of a Transnational Advocate for La Raza." In *Texas Women: Their Histories, Their Lives*, edited by Elizabeth Hayes Turner, Stephanie Cole, and Rebecca Sharpless, 225–248. Athens: University of Georgia Press, 2015.

——. *Redeeming La Raza: Transborder Modernity, Race, Respectability, and Rights*. Oxford: Oxford University Press, 2018.

González, Isabel. *Step-Children of a Nation: The Status of Mexican-Americans*. New York: American Committee for Protection of Foreign Born, 1947.

Gramsci, Antonio. *Selections from the Prison Notebooks of Antonio Gramsci*. Edited by Quintin Hoare and Geoffrey Nowell. New York: International, 2008.

Green, George N. "Good Neighbor Commission." In *New Handbook of Texas*, edited by Tyler, Barnett, and Barkley, 3:240.

Greenberg, Sanford N. "White Primary." In *Handbook of Texas Online*. Austin: Texas State Historical Association, 2010. Modified November 23, 2015. http://www.tshaonline.org/handbook/online/articles/wdw01.

Grimm, Agnes G. "Eulalio Velazquez." In *New Handbook of Texas*, edited by Tyler, Barnett, and Barkley, 6:720.

Griswold del Castillo, Richard. *World War II and Mexican American Civil Rights*. Austin: University of Texas Press, 2008.

Gritter, Matthew. *Mexican Inclusion: The Origins of Anti-Discrimination Policy in Texas and the Southwest*. College Station: Texas A&M University Press, 2012.

Grytz, Gerhard. "German Immigrants in the Lower Rio Grande Valley, 1850–1920: A Demographic Overview." In *Studies in the Rio Grande Valley*, edited by Milo Kearney, Anthony Knopp, and Antonio Zavaleta, 6:145–165. Brownsville: University of Texas at Brownsville and Texas Southmost College, 2015.

Guglielmo, Thomas A. "Fighting for Caucasian Rights: Mexicans, Mexican Americans, and the Transnational Struggle for Civil Rights in World War II Texas." *Journal of American History* 92, no. 4 (March 2006): 1212–1237.

Gutiérrez, David G. *Walls and Mirrors: Mexican Americans, Mexican Immigrants, and the Politics of Ethnicity*. Berkeley: University of California Press, 1995.

Gutiérrez, José Ángel. "Experiences of Chicana County Judges in Texas Politics." *Frontiers* 20, no. 1 (1999): 181–191.

——. *The Making of Civil Rights Leader José Ángel Gutiérrez*. Houston: Arte Público, 2005.

Gutiérrez, José Ángel, and Rebecca E. Deen. "Chicanas in Texas Politics." JSRI Occasional Paper no. 66. East Lansing, MI: Julian Samora Research Institute, Michigan State University, 2000.

Gutiérrez, José Ángel, Michelle Meléndez, and Sonia Adriana Noyola. *Chicanas in Charge: Texas Women in the Public Arena*. Lanham, MD: Altamira, 2007.

Gutierrez-Mier, John. "The Hispanic Brotherhood." *San Antonio Express-News*, April 19, 1989.

Hammaren, Niles, and Thomas Johansson. "Homosociality in between Power and Intimacy." *Sage Open*, January 10, 2014. https://journals.sagepub.com/doi/full/10.1177/2158244013518057.

Hassell Winner, Conchita. "Spanish-Language Newspapers." In *New Handbook of Texas*, edited by Tyler, Barnett, and Barkley, 5:4–5.

Hernández, José Ámaro. *Mutual Aid for Survival: The Case of the Mexican American.* Malabar, FL: Robert E. Krieger, 1983.

Hernández, Kristian. "Remembering the 1966 Rio Grande City Melon Strike." *McAllen Monitor*, May 9, 2016.

Hernández, María L. de. *México y los cuatro poderes que dirigen al pueblo.* San Antonio: Artes Gráficas, 1945.

Hernández, Sonia. "Morality and Gender in Reynosa in the 1920s and 1930s." In *Additional Stories in Rio Grande Valley History*, edited by Milo Kearney, 349–362. Brownsville: University of Texas at Brownsville, 2008.

——. *Working Women into the Borderlands.* College Station: Texas A&M University Press, 2014.

Hinchliffe, Emma. "Texas Has Never Elected a Latina to Congress." *Austin American-Statesman*, March 7, 2016.

Hine, Darlene Clark. "The Elusive Ballot: The Black Struggle against the Texas Democratic White Primary, 1932–1945." In *The African American Experience in Texas: An Anthology*, edited by Bruce A. Glasrud and James M. Smallwood, 279–301. Lubbock: Texas Tech University Press, 2007.

Hoffman, Abraham. *Unwanted Mexican Americans in the Great Depression: Repatriation Pressures, 1929–1939.* Tucson: University of Arizona Press, 1974.

Hondagneu-Sotel, Pierette. *Gendered Transitions: Mexican Experiences of Immigration.* Berkeley: University of California Press, 1994.

Houston, Ramona Alaníz. "African Americans, Mexican Americans, and Anglo-Americans and the Desegregation of Texas, 1946–1957." PhD diss., University of Texas, Austin, 2000.

Huerta, Dolores, to Cristina Arreola. "Mighty Mujeres." *Latina*, March 2016, 73.

Jacobs, Ronald A., and Eleanor Townsley. *The Space of Opinion: Media Intellectuals and the Public Sphere.* Oxford: Oxford University Press, 2011.

Jeffrey, Britney. "Rangel, Irma Lerma." *Handbook of Texas Online.* Austin: Texas State Historical Association, 2010. Modified June 20, 2016. http://www.tshaonline.org/handbook/online/articles/fra85.

Johnson, Benjamin H. "The Cosmic Race in Texas: Racial Fusion, White Supremacy, and Civil Rights Politics." *Journal of American History* 98, no. 2 (September 2011): 404–419.

Jones, Nancy Baker, and Tiffany J. González. "Irma Rangel." Transcript with audio. Austin: Women in Texas History, 1997. https://www.womenintexashistory.org.

Jones, Nancy Baker, and Ruthe Winegarten. *Capitol Women: Texas Female Legislators, 1923–1999.* Austin: University of Texas Press, 2000.

Kabalen de Bichara, Donna M. "Expressions of Dissent in the Writing of Adela Sloss Vento." In *Recovering the U.S. Hispanic Literary Heritage*, vol. 9, edited by

Donna M. Kabalen de Bichara and Blanca Guadalupe López de Mariscal, 191–207. Houston: Arte Público, 2014.

———. "Self-Writing and Collective Representation: The Literary Enunciation of Historical Reality and Cultural Values." In *In Defense of My People*, edited by Olivas, 241–263.

Kanellos, Nicolás. "Envisioning and Re-Visioning the Nation: Latino Intellectual Traditions." American Latino Theme Study. Washington, DC: National Park Service Advisory Board, 2013. https://home1.nps.gov/heritageinitiatives/latino/latinothemestudy/intellectualtraditions.htm.

Kaplowitz, Craig A. *LULAC, Mexican Americans, and National Policy*. College Station: Texas A&M University Press, 2005.

Kells, Michelle Hall. *Hector P. García: Everyday Rhetoric and Mexican American Civil Rights*. Carbondale: Southern Illinois University Press, 2006.

Kibbe, Pauline. *Latin Americans in Texas*. Albuquerque: University of New Mexico Press, 1947.

Koestler, Fred L. "Operation Wetback." In *New Handbook of Texas*, edited by Tyler, Barnett, and Barkley, 4:1157–1158.

Kohout, Martin Donell. "Cadena, Carlos Cristian." *Handbook of Texas Online*. Austin: Texas State Historical Association, 2010. http://www.tshaonline.org/handbook/online/articles/fcaas.

Kreneck, Thomas H. "Dora Cervera Mirabal." *Handbook of Texas Online*. Austin: Texas State Historical Association, 2010. http://www.tshaonline.org/handbook/online/articles/fmi97.

———. "Dr. Clotilde P. Garcia: Physician, Activist, and First Lady of Genealogy." *Spanish American Genealogical Journal* 1 (1997): 1–10.

———. "The Letter from Chapultepec." *Houston Review* 3, no. 2 (Summer 1981): 268–271.

———. "Mr. LULAC: The Fabulous Life of John J. Herrera." In *Leaders of the Mexican American Generation: Biographical Essays*, edited by Anthony Quíroz, 229–252. Boulder: University Press of Colorado, 2015.

Krochmal, Max. *Blue Texas: The Making of a Multiracial Democratic Coalition in the Civil Rights Era*. Chapel Hill: University of North Carolina Press, 2016.

Larralde, Carlos. "El Congreso in San Diego: An Endeavor for Civil Rights." *Journal of San Diego History* 50, nos. 1–2 (Winter–Spring 2004): 17–29.

———. "Josefina Fierro de Bright and the Sleepy Lagoon Case." *Journal of San Diego History* 92, no. 2 (Summer 2010): 117–160.

Larralde, Carlos, and Richard Griswold del Castillo. "Luisa Moreno and the Beginning of the Mexican American Civil Rights Movement." *Journal of San Diego History* 43, no. 3 (Summer 1997): 158–175.

Lasch, Christopher. *The New Radicalism in America, 1880–1963: The Intellectual as a Social Type*. New York: Norton, 1965.

League of United Latin American Citizens (LULAC), Texas. *LULAC: Fifty Years of Serving Hispanics, Golden Anniversary, 1929–1979*. Corpus Christi: Texas State LULAC, 1979. http://www.azarchivesonline.org/xtf/view?docId=ead/asu/lulac.xml;query=phoenix.

Ledesma, Irene. "Unlikely Strikers: Mexican-American Women in Strike Activity in Texas, 1919–1974." PhD diss., Ohio State University, 1992.

Legislative Reference Library of Texas (LRL). "Barbara Jordan." Austin: LRL, n.d. https://lrl.texas.gov/legeLeaders/members/memberDisplay.cfm?memberID=708. Accessed March 24, 2019.

Lipman-Bluman, Jean. "Toward a Homosocial Theory of Sex Roles: An Explanation of the Sex Segregation of Social Institutions." *Signs* 1, no. 3, part 1 (Spring 1976): 15–31.

Limón, José E. *Américo Paredes: Culture and Critique*. Austin: University of Texas Press, 2013.

———. "El Primer Congreso Mexicanista de 1911: A Precursor to Contemporary Chicanismo." *Aztlán* 5, nos. 1–2 (1974): 85–115.

———. "The Folk Performance of Chicano and the Cultural Limits of Political Ideology." In *And Other Neighborly Names: Social Process and Cultural Image in Texas Folklore*, edited by Richard Bauman and Roger D. Abrahams, 197–205. Austin: University of Texas Press, 1981.

Livingston, Abby, and Julian Aguilar. "Texas Poised to Send Its First Two Latinas to Congress." *Texas Tribune*, March 6, 2018.

Loza, Mireya. *Defiant Braceros: How Migrant Workers Fought for Racial, Sexual, and Political Freedom*. Chapel Hill: University of North Carolina Press, 2016.

Luna Lawhn, Juanita. "Maria Luisa Garza." In *Double Crossings/Entre Cruzamientos*, edited by Mario Martin Flores and Carlos von Son, 83–96. Ediciones Nuevo Espacio, 2001.

———. "Victorian Attitudes Affecting the Mexican Women Writing in *La Prensa* during the Early 1900s and the Chicana of the 1980s." In *Missions in Conflict: Essays on U.S. Mexican Relations and Chicano Culture*, edited by Renate von Bardeleben, Dietrich Briesemesiter, and Juan Bruce Novoa, 65–74. Tubingen, Germany: Gunter Narr Verlad, 1986.

Lynch, Michael, and Carlos Larralde. *Judge J. T. Canales, Latino Civil Rights Leader: An Intimate Portrait*. London: Lambert Academic, 2015.

Maril, Robert Lee. *Poorest of Americans: Mexican Americans of the Lower Rio Grande*. Notre Dame, IN: University of Notre Dame Press, 1989.

Márquez, Benjamin. *Democratizing Texas Politics: Race, Identity, and Mexican American Empowerment, 1945–2002*. Austin: University of Texas Press, 2014.

———. *LULAC: The Evolution of a Mexican American Political Organization*. Austin: University of Texas Press, 1993.

Martínez, Elizabeth. *De Colores Means All of Us: Latina Views for a Multi-Colored Century*. Cambridge, MA: South End, 1999.

McAllen Monitor. "LULAC Fund-Raiser to Honor Sloss-Vento." April 25, 1999.

———. "LULAC to Hold Scholarship Fund-Raiser." February 28, 1999.

———. "LULAC to Honor the Late Adela Sloss Vento." March 24, 1999.

McCormick, Samuel. *Letters to Power: Public Advocacy without Public Intellectuals*. University Park: Pennsylvania State University Press, 2011.

Medellin, Stace. "RIP: Judge Albert Peña-Chicano Activist and Leader." Associated Press. Posted in Dos Centavos blog, July 9, 2006. https://doscentavos.net/2006/07/09/rip-judge-albert-pena-chicano-activist-leader.

Meier, Matt, and Margo Gutiérrez, eds. *Encyclopedia of the Mexican American Civil Rights Movement.* Westport, CT: Greenwood, 2000.

Mendieta, Eduardo. "What Can Latinas/os Learn from Cornel West? The Latino Postcolonial Intellectual in the Age of Exhaustion of Public Space." *Nepantla: Views from the South* 4, no. 2 (2003): 213–233.

Merrim, Stephanie. "Sor Juana Inés de la Cruz: Mexican Poet and Scholar." *Encyclopedia Britannica*, updated April 10, 2018. https://www.britannica.com/biography/Sor-Juana-Ines-de-la-Cruz.

Mila, Brandon H. "Hermanos de Raza: Alonso S. Perales and the Creation of the LULAC Spirit." Master's thesis, University of North Texas, 2013.

Mirabal Garza, Rosie. *El Progreso, 1939–1940: The Work of Rodolfo Zepeda Mirabal and Dora Cervera Mirabal.* Corpus Christi, TX: Printers Unlimited, 2004.

Momayezi, Nasser. "Hispanic Representation, Empowerment, and Participation in Texas Politics." *Latino Studies Journal* 11, no. 2 (Spring 2000): 3–25.

Montejano, David. *Anglos and Mexicans in the Making of Texas, 1836–1896.* Austin: University of Texas Press, 1987.

——. *Quixote's Soldiers: A Local History of the Chicana/o Movement, 1966–1981.* Austin: University of Texas Press, 2011.

Montiel Olvera, J., ed. *Primero anuario de los habitantes Hispano-Americano de Texas: First Year Book of the Latin-American Population of Texas.* San Antonio: Mexican Chamber of Commerce(?), 1939.

Morales, Dionicio. *A Life in Two Cultures: An Autobiography.* Houston: Arte Público, 1997.

Mouton, Norma Adelfa. "Changing Voices: Approaching Modernity from Mexican to Mexican American to Chicano in the Epistolary Archives of Alonso S. Perales." In *In Defense of My People*, edited by Olivas, 221–240.

Muñoz, Carlos. *Youth, Identity, and Power: The Chicano Movement.* London: Verso, 1989.

Muñoz, Ernestina, Alisandra Mancera, Alma Fajardo, Mayra García, and Adriana Alatorre. "El Paso Women Gained Power in LULAC." *Borderlands* 25 (2006–2007): 7.

Muñoz Martínez, Monica. *The Injustice Never Leaves You: Anti-Mexican Violence in Texas.* Cambridge, MA: Harvard University Press, 2018.

Najera, Jennifer R. *The Borderlands of Race: Mexican Segregation in a South Texas Town.* Austin: University of Texas Press, 2015.

Navarro, Sharon A. *Latina Legislator: Leticia Van de Putte and the Road to Leadership.* College Station: Texas A&M University Press, 2008.

Navarro, Sharon A., Samantha L. Hernández, and Leslie A. Navarro, eds. *Latinas in American Politics: Changing and Embracing Political Tradition.* Lanham, MD: Lexington Books, 2016.

Nelson-Cisneros, Victor. "UCAPAWA Organizing in Texas, 1930–1950." *Aztlán* 9 (Spring–Fall 1978): 145–161.

Nuestro. "Women, LULAC Collide." April 1984, 9.

Offen, Karen. "Defining Feminism: A Comparative Historical Approach." *Signs* 14, no. 1 (Autumn 1988): 119–157.

Olguín, Benjamín. "Sangre Mexicana/Corazon Americano: Identity, Ambiguity, and Critique in Mexican American War Narratives." *Journal of American Literary History* 14, no. 1 (Winter 2002): 83–114.

Olivas, Michael A. *Colored Men and Hombres Aquí: Hernández v. Texas and the Emergence of Mexican American Lawyering*. Houston: Arte Público, 2006.

——, ed. *In Defense of My People: Alonso S. Perales and the Development of Mexican-American Public Intellectuals*. Houston: Arte Público, 2012.

——. "The Legal Career of Alonso S. Perales." In *In Defense of My People*, edited by Olivas, 315–343.

Omi, Michael, and Howard Winant. *Racial Formation in the United States: From the 1960s to the 1980s*. New York: Routledge and Kegan Paul, 1987.

O'Neill, Lindsay. *The Opened Letter: Networking in the Early British World*. Philadelphia: University of Pennsylvania, 2015.

Oreleck, Annelise. *Rethinking American Women's Activism*. New York: Routledge, 2015.

Orozco, Aurora E. "Mexican Blood Runs through My Veins." In *Speaking Chicana: Voice, Power, and Identity*, edited by D. Leticia Galindo and Maria Dolores Gonzales, 106–120. Tempe: University of Arizona Press, 1999.

Orozco, Cynthia E. "Adela Sloss-Vento: Mexican American Woman, Civil Rights Activist, Feminist, Author, and Public Intellectual in South Texas, 1927–1990." Paper presented at Organization of American Historians, San Francisco, April 2013.

——. "Alice Dickerson Montemayor: Feminism and Mexican American Politics in the 1930s." In *Writing the Range: Race, Class, and Culture in the Women's West*, edited by Elizabeth Jameson and Susan Armitage, 434–456. Norman: University of Oklahoma Press, 1997.

——. "Alice Dickerson Montemayor's Feminist Challenge to LULAC in the 1930s." *Intercultural Development Research Association Newsletter* (San Antonio), March 1996, 11–14.

——. "Alonso S. Perales and His Struggle for the Civil Rights of La Raza through the League of United Latin American Citizens (LULAC) in Texas in the 1930s: Incansable Soldado del Civismo Pro-Raza." In *In Defense of My People*, edited by Olivas, 3–28.

——. "The Americanization of Mexicans." Unpublished paper. Ca. 1980.

——. "Beyond Machismo, la Familia, and Ladies Auxiliaries: A Historiography of Mexican-Origin Women's Participation in Voluntary Associations and Politics in the U.S., 1870–1990." *Perspectives in Mexican American Studies* 5 (1995): 1–34.

——. "Conflict between Mexican Americans and Mexicans at the Harlingen Convention of 1927: The Genesis of LULAC." Senior honors thesis, University of Texas, Austin, 1980.

——. "50th Anniversary of LULAC." Interview by Armando Gutiérrez. *Onda Latina*, January 25, 1979. Longhorn Radio, University of Texas. http://www.laits.utexas.edu/onda_latina/program?sernum=000524526&term.

——. "Folk Usage of 'Chicano' in Cuero, Texas." Unpublished paper. 1979.

——. "League of United Latin American Citizens." In *The Reader's Companion to U.S. Women's History*, edited by Wilma Mankiller, Gwendolyn Mink, Marysa

Navarro, Barbara Smith, and Gloria Steinem, 378. Boston: Houghton Mifflin, 1998.

———. *No Mexicans, Women, or Dogs Allowed: The Rise of the Mexican American Civil Rights Movement*. Austin: University of Texas Press, 2009.

———. "Pioneer Woman of Mexican Civil Rights." *Corpus Christi Caller*, November 14, 2017.

———. "Regionalism, Politics, and Gender in Southwestern History: The League of United Latin American Citizens (LULAC) Expansion into New Mexico from Texas, 1929–1945." *Western Historical Quarterly* 29, no. 4 (November 1998): 459–483.

———. "Valley's Role in Foundation of LULAC." *McAllen Monitor*, August 26, 2011.

———. Various entries in *Latinas in the United States: A Historical Encyclopedia*, 3 vols., edited by Vicki L. Ruiz and Virginia Sánchez Korrol, s.vv. "Hernández, María Latigo"; "League of United Latin-American Citizens"; "Montemayor, Alice Dickerson"; "Orozco, Aurora Estrada"; and "Sloss-Vento, Adela." Bloomington: Indiana University Press, 2006.

———. Various entries in *New Handbook of Texas*, edited by Tyler, Barnett, and Barkley, s.vv. "Adela Sloss-Vento" (with Jazmin León); "Alice Dickerson Montemayor"; "Alicia Guadalupe Elizondo de Lozano"; "Alonso S. Perales"; "Bernardo F. Garza"; "Carolina Munguía"; "*Del Rio v. Salvatierra*"; "Gustavo Garcia"; "Harlingen Convention"; "Hidalgo County Rebellion"; "Jovita González" (with Teresa Acosta); "Ladies LULAC"; "League of United Latin American Citizens"; "Manuel C. Gonzales"; "María L. Hernández"; "Mexican American Women"; "Order of Knights of America"; "Order of Sons of America"; "Pauline Rochester Kibbe"; "Spanish-Speaking PTA"; "Viva Kennedy–Viva Johnson Clubs." Austin: Texas State Historical Association, 1996.

Padilla, Gloria. "LULAC Here Bars Women." *Corpus Christi Caller-Times*, February 19, 1984.

Palomo Acosta, Teresa. "American G.I. Forum Ladies Auxiliary." In *New Handbook of Texas*, edited by Tyler, Barnett, and Barkley, 1:148.

———. "Cruz Azul Mexicana." In *New Handbook of Texas*, edited by Tyler, Barnett, and Barkley 2:429–430.

———. "Political Association of Spanish-Speaking Persons." In *New Handbook of Texas*, edited by Tyler, Barnett, and Barkley, 5:256.

———. "Texas Farm Workers Union." In *New Handbook of Texas*, edited by Tyler, Barnett, and Barkley, 6:329.

Palomo Acosta, Teresa, and Ruthe Winegarten. *Las Tejanas: 300 Years of History*. Austin: University of Texas Press, 2003.

Paredes, Américo, ed. *Humanidad: Essays in Honor of Dr. George I. Sánchez*. Los Angeles: Chicano Studies Center, University of California, 1977.

———. *With His Pistol in His Hand*. Austin: University of Texas Press, 1958.

Patino, Jimmy. *Raza Si, Migra No: Chicano Movement Struggles for Immigrant Rights in San Diego*. Chapel Hill: University of North Carolina Press, 2017.

Perales, Alonso S. *Are We Good Neighbors?* San Antonio: Artes Gráficas, 1948.

———. *En defensa de mi raza*. 2 vols. San Antonio: Artes Gráficas, 1937.

——. *El México Americano y la política del sur de Texas: Comentarios.* Pamphlet. San Antonio: Artes Gráficas, 1931. Translation of and commentary on Oliver Douglas Weeks, "The Texas-Mexican and the Politics of South Texas," *American Political Science Review* 24 (August 1930): 606–627.

Pérez, Emma. *The Decolonial Imaginary: Writing Chicanas into History.* Bloomington: Indiana University Press, 1999.

Pérez Davis, Araceli. "Marta Pérez de Perales." *El Mesteño*, October 2000, 16–17.

Pierce, P. J. *Texas Wisewomen Speak: "Let Me Tell You What I've Learned."* Austin: University of Texas Press, 2002.

Posner, Richard A. *Public Intellectuals: A Study of Decline.* Cambridge, MA: Harvard University Press, 2003.

Pycior, Julie Leininger. *Democratic Renewal and the Mutual Aid Legacy of US Mexicans.* College Station: Texas A&M University Press, 2014.

——. *LBJ and Mexican Americans: The Paradox of Power.* Austin: University of Texas Press, 1997.

——. "Tejanas Navigating the 1920s." In *Tejano Epic: Essays in Honor of Felix D. Almaraz, Jr.*, edited by Arnoldo De León, 71–86. Austin: Texas State Historical Association, 2005.

Quezada, J. Gilberto. *Border Boss: Manuel B. Bravo and Zapata County.* College Station: Texas A&M University Press, 2001.

Quiroz, Anthony. "'I Can See No Alternative except to Battle It Out in Court': Gus García and the Spirit of the Mexican American Generation." In *Leaders of the Mexican American Generation: Biographical Essays*, edited by Anthony Quíroz, 209–228. Boulder: University Press of Colorado, 2015.

——, ed. *Leaders of the Mexican American Generation: Biographical Essays.* Colorado Springs: University Press of Colorado, 2015.

Ramos, Henry A. J. *The American G.I. Forum: In Pursuit of the Dream, 1948–1983.* Houston: Arte Público, 1998.

Ribb, Richard Henry. "José T. Canales and the Texas Rangers: Myth, Identity, and Power in South Texas, 1900–1920." PhD diss., University of Texas, Austin, 2001.

Río Writers. *One Hundred Women of the Rio Grande Valley of Texas.* Waco, TX: Eakin, 1983.

Rivas-Rodriguez, Maggie. *Texas Mexican Americans and Postwar Civil Rights.* Austin: University of Texas Press, 2015.

Rivas-Rodriguez, Maggie, and B. V. Olguín, eds. *Latina/os and World War II: Mobility, Agency, and Ideology.* Austin: University of Texas Press, 2014.

Rodríguez, Alberto. "The Making of the Modern Lower Rio Grande Valley: Situating and Reframing Race, Class, and Ethnicity in Urbanizing South Texas, 1928–1965." PhD diss., University of Houston, 2012.

Rodríguez, Marc Simon. *Rethinking the Chicano Movement.* New York: Routledge, 2015.

——. *The Tejano Diaspora, Mexican Americanism, and Ethnic Politics in Texas and Wisconsin.* Chapel Hill: University of North Carolina Press, 2014.

Rodríguez, Rodolfo. "Bilingual Education." *Handbook of Texas Online.* Austin: Texas State Historical Association, 2010. Modified July 5, 2017. http://www.tshaonline.org/handbook/online/articles/khb02.

Rodríguez, Samantha M. "Carving Space for Feminism and Nativists: Texas Chicana Activism during the Chicana/o Movement." *Journal of South Texas* 27, no. 2 (Fall 2014): 38–52.

Romo, Ricardo. "George I. Sánchez and the Civil Rights Movement, 1940–1960." *La Raza Law Journal* 1 (1986): 342–362.

Rosales, F. Arturo. *Chicano! The History of the Mexican American Civil Rights Movement*. Houston: Arte Público, 1997.

——. *Dictionary of Latino Civil Rights History*. Houston: Arte Público, 2007.

——, ed. *Testimonio: A Documentary History of the Mexican American Struggle for Civil Rights*. Houston: Arte Público, 2000.

Rosales, Rodolfo. *The Illusion of Inclusion: The Untold Political Story of San Antonio*. Austin: University of Texas Press, 2000.

Rueda Esquibel, Catriona. *With Her Machete in Her Hand: Reading Chicana Lesbians*. Austin: University of Texas Press, 2006.

Ruiz, Vicki L. "Luisa Moreno and Latina Labor Activism." *Latina Legacies: Identity, Biography, and Community*, edited by Vicki L. Ruiz and Virginia Sánchez Korral, 175–192. New York: Oxford University Press, 2005.

——. "Working for Wages: Mexican Women in the Southwest, 1930–1980." Working Paper no. 19. Tucson: Southwest Institute for Research on Women, 1984.

Sáenz, José de la Luz. *Los méxico-americanos y la gran guerra y su contingente en pro de la democracia, la humanidad y la justicia*. San Antonio: Artes Gráficas, 1933.

Said, Edward W. "The Public Role of Writers and Intellectuals." In *The Public Intellectuals*, edited by Helen Small, 19–39. Oxford, UK: Blackwell, 2001.

Salas, Elizabeth. *Soldaderas in the Mexican Military: Myth and History*. Austin: University of Texas Press, 1990.

Salinas, Lupe S. "Legally White, Socially Brown: Alonso S. Perales and His Crusade for Justice for La Raza." In *In Defense of My People*, edited by Olivas, 75–96.

San Antonio Express. "LULAC Pioneers Due Honor." November 12, 1968.

——. "No Sexism, Sort Of." March 9, 1984.

San Antonio Light. "El Paso Ladies LULAC Council 9 Set to Mark Its Golden Anniversary." February 16, 1984.

Sánchez, Aaron. "'Our Children Must Not Suffer . . . Another No-Action Generation': The Limitations of Liberalism in the Mexican-American Generation." *Journal of South Texas* 26, no. 2 (Fall 2013): 10–28.

Sándoval, Moisés. *Our Legacy: The First Fifty Years*. Washington, DC: LULAC, 1979.

San Miguel, Guadalupe, Jr. *"Let All of Them Take Heed": Mexican Americans and the Campaign for Educational Equality in Texas, 1910–1981*. Austin: University of Texas Press, 2000.

Saunders, Lyle, and Olen E. Leonard. *The Wetback in the Lower Rio Grande Valley of Texas*. Inter-American Education Occasional Papers no. 7. Austin: University of Texas, 1951.

Scharff, Virginia. *Taking the Wheel: Women and the Coming of the Motor Age*. New York: Free Press, 1991.

Schmal, John P. "The Tejano Struggle for Representation." Hispanics in Government. Houston: Houston Institute for Culture, n.d. http://www.houstonculture.org/hispanic/tejano1.html. Accessed May 10, 2014.

Seaholm, Megan. "Texas Federation of Women's Clubs." In *New Handbook of Texas*, edited by Tyler, Barnett, and Barkley, 6:331–332.

Segura, Denise A., and Patricia Zavella, eds. *Women and Migration in the U.S.-Mexico Borderlands: A Reader*. Durham, NC: Duke University Press, 2007.

Shockley, John. *Chicano Revolt in a Texas Town*. Notre Dame, IN: University of Notre Dame Press, 1974.

Sillas, Herman. "Mexican American Lawyers Club." *Somos Primos*, August 2015, http://www.somosprimos.com/sp2015/spsep15/spsep15.htm.

Simmons, Ozzie G. *Anglo-Americans and Mexican Americans in South Texas: A Study in Dominant-Subordinate Group Relations*. New York: Arno, 1974.

Sloss-Vento, Adela. *Alonso S. Perales: His Struggle for the Rights of Mexican Americans*. San Antonio: Artes Gráficas, 1977. Reprint as ebook, edited by Arnoldo C. Vento. Austin: Eagle Feather Research Institute, 2008.

Small, Helen, ed. *The Public Intellectual*. Oxford, UK: Blackwell, 2001.

Sosa Zavaleta, Gabriela. "Women as Political Pioneers in the Rio Grande Valley." In *Yet More Studies in Rio Grande Valley History*, edited by Milo Kearney, 155–168. Brownsville: University of Texas, Brownsville, 2015.

Stambaugh, J. Lee, and Lillian J. *The Lower Rio Grande Valley of Texas*. San Antonio: Naylor, 1954.

Stefano, Onofre di. "*La Prensa* and Its Literary Page." PhD diss., University of California, Los Angeles, 1983.

Storey, John W., and Mary L. Kelley, eds. *Twentieth-Century Texas: A Social and Cultural History*. Denton: University of North Texas Press, 2008.

Taylor, Steve. "Farm Workers Have Transformed the Rio Grande Valley." *Rio Grande Guardian*, July 9, 2013.

Tejano Talks Project. "Adela Sloss Vento." Tejano Talks no. 31. Video, 1:48. Texas A&M University, Kingsville, and Tejano Civil Rights Museum, 2017. https://www.youtube.com/watch?v=ql8wp0LQq0Y.

Toscano González, Laura. "In Loving Memory of Our Friend, Husband, Father, and Grandfather Abel Toscano, Jr., 1926–2005." In *Once upon a Time/Más Antes: Family Stories of the Rio Grande Valley*, edited by Alonzo Cavazos Jr., Ofelia Olsson, and Santos V. Canales, 265–270. Harlingen, TX: Rio Grande Valley Hispanic Genealogical Society, 2014.

Treviño, Roberto. "Prensa y Patria: The Spanish-Language Press and the Biculturalization of the Tejano Middle Class, 1920–1940." *Western Historical Quarterly* (1991): 451–472.

Truthout. "About Truthout." https://truthout.org/about/. N.d. Accessed March 3, 2019.

Turner, Elizabeth Hayes, Stephanie Cole, and Rebecca Sharpless, eds. *Texas Women: Their Histories, Their Lives*. Athens: University of Georgia Press, 2015.

Tyler, Ronnie C., Douglas E. Barnett, and Roy R. Barkley, eds. *New Handbook of Texas*. 6 vols. Austin: Texas State Historical Association, 1996.

Ura, Alexa. "Women Still Underrepresented in Legislative Races." *Texas Tribune*, April 4, 2017. https://www.texastribune.org/2016/01/04/campaign-filings-reflect-underrepresentation-women.

Valencia, Richard R. *Chicano Students and the Courts: The Mexican American Legal Struggle for Educational Equality*. New York: New York University Press, 2008.

Vargas, Zaragosa. *Labor Rights Are Civil Rights: Mexican Workers in Twentieth-Century America*. Princeton, NJ: Princeton University Press, 2005.

———. "Tejana Radical: Emma Tenayuca and the San Antonio Labor Movement during the Great Depression." *Pacific Historical Review* 66, no. 4 (November 1997): 553–580.

Vásquez, Enriqueta, Lorena Oropeza, and Dionne Espinoza, eds. *Enriqueta Vásquez and the Chicano Movement: Writings from El Grito del Norte*. Houston: Arte Público, 2006.

Vento, Arnoldo Carlos. "Adela Sloss-Vento, 1901–1998." Introduction to Adela Sloss-Vento, *Alonso S. Perales: His Struggle for the Rights of Mexican Americans*, reprint as ebook. Austin: Eagle Feather Research Institute, 2008.

———. *Adela Sloss-Vento: Writer, Political Activist, and Civil Rights Pioneer*. Lanham, MD: Hamilton Books, 2017.

———. *La cueva de Nalzatlán*. Mexico City: Fondo de Cultura Económica, 1986.

———. *Mestizo: The History, Culture, and Politics of the Mexican and the Chicano; The Emerging Mestizo-Americans*. Lanham, MD: University Press of America, 1997.

Vigness, David M., and Mark Odintz. "Rio Grande Valley." In *New Handbook of Texas*, edited by Tyler, Barnett, and Barkley, 5:588–589.

Villarreal, Mary Ann. "The Synapses of Struggle: Martha Cotera and Tejana Activism." *Las Obreras: Chicana Politics of Work and Family*, edited by Vickie L. Ruiz, 273–295. Los Angeles: Chicano Studies Research Center, University of California Los Angeles, 2000.

Viva la Feminista. "Professional Feminist." Blog post, n.d. http://www.vivalafeminista.com/p/professional-feminist.html. Accessed September 24, 2016.

Weber, John. *From South Texas to the Nation: The Exploitation of Mexican Labor in the Twentieth Century*. Chapel Hill: University of North Carolina Press, 2015.

Winegarten, Ruthe. *Black Texas Women: 150 Years of Trial and Triumph*. Austin: University of Texas Press, 1995.

Wolfe, Alan. *An Intellectual in Public*. Ann Arbor: University of Michigan Press, 2003.

Women in Texas History (WITH). "Timeline of Texas Women's History." Austin: WITH, n.d. https://www.womenintexashistory.org/learn/timeline. Accessed March 24, 2019.

Woods, Frances Jerome. "Mexican Ethnic Leadership in San Antonio, Texas. Phd diss., Catholic University, Washington, DC, 1949.

Yarsinke, Amy Waters. *All for One and One for All: A Celebration of 75 Years of the League of Latin American Citizens (LULAC)*. Virginia Beach, VA: Donning, 2004.

Young, Elliot. "Deconstructing La Raza: Identifying the Gente Decente of Laredo, 1904–1994." *Southwestern Historical Quarterly* 98 (October 1994): 227–259.

Young, Nancy Beck. "Democratic Party." In *Handbook of Texas Online*. Austin: Texas State Historical Association, 2010. http://www.tshaonline.org/handbook/online/articles/wad01.

Zamora, Emilio. *Claiming Rights and Righting Wrongs in Texas: Mexican Workers and Job Politics during World War II*. College Station: Texas A&M University Press, 2009.

——. "Connecting Causes: Alonso S. Perales, Hemispheric Unity, and Mexican Rights in the United States." In *In Defense of My People*, edited by Olivas, 287–313.

——. "Fighting on Two Fronts: José de la Luz Sáenz and the Language of the Mexican American Civil Rights Movement." In *Recovering the U.S. Hispanic Literary Heritage*, vol. 4, edited by José F. Aranda Jr. and Silvio Torres-Saillant, 214–239. Houston: Arte Público, 2002.

——. "José de la Luz Sáenz." *El Mesteño*, April 2000, 4–5.

——. *The World of the Mexican Worker in Texas*. College Station: Texas A&M University Press, 1993.

——, ed. *The World War I Diary of José de la Luz Sáenz*. College Station: Texas A&M University Press, 2014.

INDEX

Numerals in italics indicate an illustration.

CPSIA information can be obtained
at www.ICGtesting.com
Printed in the USA
LVHW042343160422
716243LV00002B/24

9 781477 319871